THE CATHOLIC UNIVERSITY OF AMERICA
CANON LAW STUDIES
NO. 236

The False Denunciation of an Innocent Confessor

A COMMENTARY WITH HISTORICAL NOTES ON THE MANNER OF MAKING JUDICIAL DENUNCIATIONS

BY

REV. HERBERT LINENBERGER, C.PP.S., J.C.L.
Priest of the Society of the Most Precious Blood

A DISSERTATION

Submitted to the Faculty of the School of Canon Law of the Catholic University of America in Partial Fulfillment of the Requirements for the Degree of Doctor of Canon Law

THE CATHOLIC UNIVERSITY OF AMERICA PRESS
WASHINGTON, D.C.
1949

IMPRIMI POTEST:

SERAPHIN W. OBERHAUSER, C.PP.S.,
Superior Provincialis.

Daytonii, die 6 *iunii,* 1948.

NIHIL OBSTAT:

HUBERTUS LUDOVICUS MOTRY, S.T.D., J.C.D.
Censor Deputatus

Washingtonii, D.C., die 8 *iunii,* 1948.

IMPRIMATUR:

✠ PATRICIUS A. O'BOYLE, D.D.,
Archiepiscopus Washingtoniensis

Washingtonii, die 11 *iunii,* 1948.

Printed in the United States of America
by
THE MESSENGER PRESS
Carthagena, Ohio

TABLE OF CONTENTS

CHAPTER III

CHAPTER IV

FOREWORD

That no person is presumed to be evil unless proved to be such is an axiom of law universally recognized. Even though a criminal accusation is made, the accused person is considered innocent before the law until the legal evidence demonstrates his guilt. Civil as well as ecclesiastical society has outlined a detailed criminal procedure to accord legitimate protection to every innocent person who has been maliciously calumniated.

Since a confessor is bound by the seal of confession and when accused of malfeasance has no defense at his command, the Church is most wary in accepting criminal accusations against him. The Holy See, conscious of the words of Proverbs: "A good name is better than riches; the detractor is the abomination of men." (xxii: 1; xxiv: 9) has wisely shielded her priests against calumnious accusations with protective legislation, and enacted penalties against their calumniators. Though the legislation which invokes specific penalties against calumnious denunciators who accuse innocent confessors of the delict of solicitation is only two hundred years old, the distilled legal wisdom and jurisprudence of nearly two thousand years is manifested in that legislation.

Because of his thorough training in asceticism and of his approval by the Church when given faculties to hear confessions, the confessor is favored with the presumption that he is a worthy and a trusted servant of the Church. Accordingly, then, when accusations of misconduct are brought against him, his good name and reputation are such as to mark the accusations as at least questionable, if not also suspicious or even calumnious. *Si tum mulier denuncians, tum confessarius sint famae integrae, praevalere debet fama confessarii. Stante pari qualitate, praevalet confessarius foeminae poenitenti.*[1]

1. Ioseph Pennacchi († 1898), *Commentaria in Constitutionem "Apostolicae Sedis"* (2 vols ., Romae, 1883), II, 201 (hereafter cited *Commentaria*).

All pre-Code Instructions on criminal processes issued by the Holy Office contained the caution that local Ordinaries were never to institute a criminal trial until they had thoroughly inquired whether the persons bringing the accusations could be trusted, and whether they appeared with honorable motives, or were motivated by vindictiveness. With no impartial witnesses to summon in the trial, and inasmuch as the penitent who denounced his confessor was himself the only witness, the local Ordinaries were to follow most exactly the norms for procedure which had been sent to them for the conduct of trials regarding solicitation.

A short history regarding the Church's legislative pronouncements against solicitation and her laws which stressed the obligation of denouncing guilty confessors precedes in this treatise the actual discussion of false denunciations. This conspectus was considered necessary for a proper orientation of the reader to the subject, since a study of the Church's laws on the denunciation of an innocent confessor with reference to the delict of solicitation is but a corollary of the study of her laws on the crime of solicitation itself, and of the corresponding obligation of the denunciation of guilty confessors.

The writer is indebted to the Society of the Most Precious Blood and to its provincial superior, the Very Reverend Joseph M. Marling, C.PP.S., S.T.L., Ph.D., for the opportunity to pursue a course of graduate study in Canon Law. He likewise expresses gratitude to the members of the Faculty of the School of Canon Law of The Catholic University of America for their aid and encouragement.

CHAPTER I

THE CRIME OF SOLICITATION

ARTICLE 1. A HISTORICAL SUMMARY OF THE LEGISLATION ON THE CRIME OF SOLICITATION

The earliest legislation on the crime of solicitation is found in the Council of Trier held on March 1, 1227. This council deprived of office and excommunicated any confessor who solicited a penitent during confession.[1] There are no traces of any similar action taken by other synods or councils. On April 16, 1561, Pius IV (1559-1565) in his Constitution *"Cum sit nuper"* directed an order to the Archbishop of Seville, the Inquisitor General of Spain, and commanded him to proceed against all priests who allured women penitents to sins of impurity (*ad actus inhonestos*) while hearing their confessions. A diligent search was to be made to discover the guilty clerics, a process instituted to convict them, and if found guilty, a heavy penalty was to be inflicted upon them.[2] This constitution, containing the first Pontifical legislation on the crime of solicitation, was directed only to Spain. It did not demand that the solicited penitents denounce their confessors. Paul V (1605-1621) on September 16, 1608 in his Constitution *"Dilecte Fili"* extended the law of his predecessor to Portugal.[3] Ubaldus Giraldi (1692-1775) related that since the crime of solicitation to sins of the flesh (*ad*

1. "...Caveant sibi sacerdotes sub privatione honoris sui, ne sollicitent aliquam personam in confessione, quod et verbis fieri prohibemus; contrarium facientes excommunicamus." — J. Mansi (1692-1769), *Sacrorum Conciliorum Nova et Amplissima Collectio* (53 vols., in 60, Parisiis, 1901-1927), XXIII, col. 33, n. viii; Carl Joseph Hefele (1809-1893) in his *Conciliengeschichte* (5. ed., 9 vols., Freiburg im Breisgau, 1886), V, 951, translated the *aliquam personam* with the words *eine Frauensperson,* a misleading translation.
2. Cf. *Codicis Iuris Canonici Fontes, cura Emi Petri Card Gasparri editi* (9 vols., Romae [postea Civitate Vaticana]: Typis Polyglottis Vaticanis, 1923-1939. [Vols. VII-IX ed. cura et studio Emi Iustiniani Card Seredi]), n. 102 (hereafter cited *Fontes.*)
3. This constitution is not incorporated in the *Fontes,* nor is it contained in the *Bullarum Diplomatum et Privilegiorum Sanctorum Romanorum*

turpia) in the sacrament of penance placed the confessor under the suspicion of heresy, the inquisitors ordered that he was to be denounced in the manner, *eo pari modo,* prescribed in the denunciation of heretics.[4] The same author, together with Del Bene (1623-1673)[5] and Rota († ca. 1890)[6] referred to the Constitutions "*Cum sit nuper*" of Pius IV (1559-1565) issued on April 16, 1561, "*In nomine Domini*" of Clement VIII (1592-1605) issued on December 3, 1592, and "*Dilecte Fili*" of Paul V (1605-1621) issued on September 16, 1608, stating that all of these constitutions encouraged the inquisitors to proceed against confessors who were guilty of the crime of solicitation.[7]

On November 29, 1612, Paul V specified that the solicitation of men (*masculos sollicitatos*) as well as of women penitents was thereafter to be comprised under the crime of solicitation.[8] On July 10, 1614, the same pope ordered that the crime of solicitation was to embrace not only the seduction to sins of impurity committed while the confessor was engaged in administering the sacrament of penance, but also those provocations to sins against the sixth commandment that took place in the confessional, even

Pontificum Taurinensis Editio (24 vols. et 2 Appendices, Augustae Taurinorum-Neapoli, 1857-1885). (hereafter cited *Bullarum.*) Cf. Salmanticenses, *Cursus Theologiae Moralis* (6 vols. in 4, Venetiis, 1714-1728), V, tract. 21, c. 4, punct. 3, nota 3; Anonymous, "Commentaire sur la Constitution *'Apostolicae Sedis'* de Pie IX: Excommunications non reservees," — *Nouvelle Revue Theologique* (Tournai, 1869), XII (1880), 12, nota 2; (hereafter cited *NRT*); Felix Potestas († 1702), *Examen Ecclesiasticum* (2 vols., Venetiis, 1722), II, Pars III, n. 482 (hereafter cited *Examen*).

4. *Expositio Iuris Pontificii* (2 vols., Romae, 1829), II, Pars I, lib. V tit. VII, *De Haereticis,* Sect. DCCCIX, Appendix, p. 630 (hereafter cited *Expositio*).
5. *De Officio Sanctae Inquisitionis circa Haeresim* (2 vols., Lugduni, 1666), II, Pars II, Dubitatio CCXXXVII, Sect. I, p. 550, nn. 2, 8; *ibidem,* Dub. CCXXXVII, Sect. II, nn. 9, 13, 14, and Sect. XX, n. 1 (hereafter cited *De Officio*).
6. *Enchiridion Confessarii et Iudicis Ecclesiastici* (Augustae Taurinorum: Marietti, 1884), n. 197 (hereafter cited *Enchiridion*).
7. None of these constitutions is in the *Fontes,* or in *Bullarum.* Cf. Giraldi, *Expositio,* II, 630.
8. Cf. Giraldi, *op. cit.,* II, 641, n. 1.

though no confessions were heard at that time.[9] Pope Gregory XV (1622-1623) in his Constitution *"Universi,"* issued on August 30, 1622, not only confirmed the laws of his predecessors, but even extended them. Whereas Pius IV had restricted his instruction to Spain, and Paul V had limited his decrees to Portugal, Gregory XV directed that his constitution become law throughout the entire world.[10] He also introduced the law that all confessors were to admonish their penitents, men as well as women, who were solicited by other confessors, to denounce the latter.[11] Heretofore this obligation had been imposed upon the penitents by the inquisitors only, and not by papal law.[12] In the event that any of the penitents refused to denounce their confessors they were under no penalty. On the other hand, a penalty was threatened against confessors who failed to give this admonition to their penitents before granting them absolution.[13] In a detailed manner Pope Gregory XV set forth the elements that were thereafter to be acknowleged as constituting the crime of solicitation:

> 4. . . decernimus et declaramus, quod omnes et singuli sacerdotes. . . qui personas, quaecumque illae sint, ad inhonesta, sive inter se, sive cum aliis quomodolibet perpetranda, in actu sacramentalis confessionis, sive antea, vel post immediate, seu occasione, vel praetextu confessionis huiusmodi etiam ipsa confessione non sequuta, sive extra occasionem confessionis in confessionario, aut in loco quocumque, ubi confessiones sacramentales audiuntur, seu ad confessionem audiendam electo, simulantes ibidem confessiones audire, sollicitare, vel provocare tentaverint, aut cum eis illicitos, et inhonestos sermones, sive tractatus habuerint, in officio Sanctae Inquisitionis severissime. . . puniantur. . .[14]

9. ". . . In generali Congregatione S. Rom. et univ. Inquisitionis coram SS. Paulo Papa V facta relatione quod multi confessarii tractant cum mulieribus in confessionali extra occasionem confessionis de rebus inhonestis: Sanctissimus decrevit, ut contra huiusmodi Confessarios procedatur in S. Officio." — Pennacchi, *Commentaria,* II, 186; Cf. also Giraldi, *Expositio,* II, 641.
10. *Fontes,* n. 201.
11. *Loc. cit.*
12. Cf. Giraldi, *Expositio,* II, 630.
13. *Fontes,* n. 201.
14. *Loc. Cit.*

ARTICLE 2. THE OBLIGATION TO DENOUNCE GUILTY CONFESSORS

The same norms that obtained for the denunciation of heretics were to be applied for the denunciation of confessors who were discovered to have solicited their penitents. All denunciations had to be judicial and in writing. If the deposition was made orally, however, it was to be taken down in writing by a notary. The denunciator had to take an oath to confirm what he had revealed. The custom of requesting honorable persons to be present as witnesses was not required any more when Del Bene wrote his study on the Inquisition in 1666.[15] Both Del Bene and Giraldi alluded to the inefficiency of unsigned letters that divulged the delict of solicitation.[16]

Francis Cardinal Albitius (Albizzi [1593-1684]) after citing three decisions of the *Sancta Romana Universalis Inquisitio*[17] which were successively issued on June 28, 1597, February 28, 1598, and April 15, 1612, stated that if ladies of noble birth could not be induced to denounce their confessors, the Sacred Congregation of the Holy Office was to be consulted. If the penitent lived outside the city of Rome, the guidance of the inquisitor or of the bishop could be sought. The latter were under such circumstances permitted to dispense the women from making the deposition and could allow that absolution be granted to them. The dispensation however had to be conditioned on the existence of a just cause. If the just caused ceased, the obligation to denounce the confessor revived. These women were furthermore to be advised never to go to confession to the confessor who had sought to seduce them.[18] From the dates indicated by Cardinal Albitius it is evident that local inquisitors had already introduced the practice of demanding denun-

15. Cf. *De Officio,* II, Pars I, *Dub.* CLXXXIII, p. 577, nn. 5-7; *ibid.,* I, Dub. XVI, p. 52, n. 1; Giraldi, *Expositio,* II, 640.
16. *De Officio,* I, *Dub.* XVI, p. 52, n. 1; *Expositio, loc. cit.*
17. Hereafter referred to as the Sacred Congregation of The Holy Office.
18. *De Inconstantia in Iure Admittenda vel Non,* Pars Prima, *De Inconstantia in Fide* (Amstelodami, 1683), c. 35 — cited by A Ballerini 1805-1881) — D. Palmieri (1829-1909), *Opus Theologicum Morale* (7 vols., Prati, 1889-1893), V, n. 1151. (hereafter cited *Opus Theologicum*); Cf. also Rota, *Enchiridion,* n. 453.

ciations of guilty confessors. Pope Gregory XV made this a universal duty in his Constitution "*Universi,*" in 1622.

Inasmuch as the various inquisitors followed their own norms in the matter of demanding denunciations, there was no uniformity in the *terminus* within which the depositions had to be made. A general decree emanated from the Holy Office on January 3, 1623. It designated a *terminus* of twelve days within which all heretics suspected of the sin of heresy were to be denounced. Since confessors who sought to seduce their penitents to sins of impurity were suspected of heresy, the same regulation was to be observed by penitents who had been solicited. A *latae sententiae* excommunication reserved to the Holy Father or to the Holy Office was imposed for the first time upon all who failed to denounce the delinquent within that time.[19]

On July 25, 1624, the Holy Office sent forth a decree declaring that even though the penitent solicited the confessor, and the confessor succumbed to the seduction, he was nevertheless to be denounced. In the event however that the confessor became guilty of solicitation and his penitent consented to the proposed sin, the element of formal complicity was to be no excuse for the penitent to refrain from bringing the report to the inquisitors. No obligation rested upon the penitent to divulge the co-operation, nor was the inquisitor or the bishop to propose leading questions which would induce the denouncer to reveal the fact of a given consent on his or her part. If that fact should have been inadvertently or spontaneously revealed, it was to be struck from the records.[20]

19. Cf. Del Bene, *De Officio,* II, *Dub.* CCXXXVII, Sect. XIII, p. 587, n. 2; *ibid.,* Sect. XIII, p. 589, n. 4; L. Ferraris († ca. 1673), *Prompta Bibliotheca Canonica Iuridica Moralis Theologica necnon Ascetica Polemica Rubriscistica Historica,* (9 vols., Editio a Bucceroni curata, Romae, 1885-1899, II, Art. V, col. 1010, n. 49, ad vv. *confessarius quoad eas quae concernunt sollicitationem* [hereafter cited *Prompta Bibliotheca*]) mentioned that the Spanish Inquisitors had set a terminus of six or seven days for the making of the denunciation.
20. Cf. Giraldi, *Expositio,* II, 641, n. II; *ibid.,* II, n. XV. The *Fontes* (n. 900, 6°, in footnote 2.) credit this declaration to Pope Urban VIII, under date of April 17, 1624; cf. also Rota, *Enchiridion,* n. 352; Del Bene, *De Officio,* II, Pars II, *Dub.* CCXXXVII, Sect. XVIII, p. 604, n. 5.

A notable departure from this established precedent for the making and receiving of denunciations occurred in the concession of the Holy Office on September 27, 1624. Since ladies of noble rank were awed at the prospect of appearing before the inquisitors, the Congregation granted them the privilege to summon a notary, properly delegated by the inquisitors, to receive their depositions at home. In such cases the women were placed under oath, their denunciations were put into writing, and the copy was forwarded to the bishop or to the inquisitors.[21] Additional instructions were included by the Holy Office to cover the cases in which the solicited persons demurred even after they were given such extraordinary concessions. If the penitents could not be persuaded to make their denunciations even at their homes, the case was to be referred to the Holy See. In the meantime absolution could not be imparted.[22]

Identical instructions were mailed on the very same day to Frederick Cardinal Borromeo of Milan.[23] These instructions were repeated by the same tribunal on January 24, 1667, and on July 7, 1725. The decree issued on July 7, 1725, commanded that the notary be a priest who had faculties for the hearing of confessions.[24]

An important decree relative to the manner and the time for the making of depositions appeared on March 10, 1677. The Holy Office ruled:

1. Not only the solicited penitents themselves, but likewise all other persons who knew of the delict of solicitation were to declare this fact to the inquisitors;
2. they were bound to do this within one month, and that under the penalty of a *latae sententiae* excommunication;
3. anonymous denunciations were of no value.[25]

21. These documents and formularies of the Holy Office are to be found mentioned in Giraldi, *Expositio,* II, 642, nn. XV, XVII, XVIII.
22. Cf. Giraldi, *loc. cit.*
23. Cf. Aemilius Berardi (1856-1916), *De Sollicitatione* (Faventiae, 1886), n. 143. Frederick Borromeo was a nephew of St. Charles Borromeo (1538-1584). He lived from 1564-1631. He became a cardinal in 1587, and Archbishop of Milan in 1595.
24. Cited by Giraldi, *Expositio,* II, 643. Giraldi (*op. cit.*, II, 643, nn. XVII, XVIII) also has formulas for the receiving of the denunciations in such an extraordinary manner.
25. Cf. Ferraris, *Prompta Bibliotheca,* III, 122, ad vv. *denunciatio quoad delicta spectantia ad S. Officium,* n. 1.

Between the years of the appearance of the Constitution *"Universi"* of Gregory XV in 1622 and the issuance of the decree of March 10, 1677, sixteen *dubia iuris* concerning the delict of solicitation were authoritatively solved and published by the Holy Office. The date of their appearance is February 11, 1661. None of them however has a direct bearing on the manner to be followed in the making of the denunciations.[26]

ARTICLE 3. THE CONSTITUTION *"Sacramentum Poenitentiae"*

The most drastic action to curb the vice of solicitation in the sacrament of penance and to enforce the obligation to denounce confessors guilty of such crimes was taken by Pope Benedict XIV (1740-1758) on June 1, 1741, in his Constitution *"Sacramentum Poenitentiae."* Not only were the laws of the previous pontiffs incorporated and confirmed, but also all the interpretations and decisions issued by the Holy Office on February 11, 1661, as well as two propositions condemned by Pope Alexander VI (1655-1667) relative to the delict of solicitation, were accepted and confirmed in this new law.[27] The legislation of that Constitution is in force today, for not only do canons 904 and 2368, § 2, refer to it by name, but it is also appended as Document V in the Code. The revised and amplified law on solicitation reads:

> 1. . . . Motu proprio, et e certa scientia, ac matura deliberatione Nostra, praefatas litteras huiusmodi, ac omnia, et singula de-

26. They can all be found in Giraldi, *Expositio,* II, 631-632; also in Ballerini-Palmieri, *Opus Theologicum,* V, 583 in footnote (a). None of these decisions are incorporated in the *Fontes.* They are however canonized through a specific reference in the Constitution *"Sacramentum Poenitentiae"* of Benedict XIV, and in so far as the latter Constitution appears in the Code as document V, the decrees are still in force today. An important collection of responses of the Holy Office (46 in number) can be found in "Collectio Resolutionum Responsorumque S. Officii. Sollicitantes," — *Analecta Ecclesiastica* (Romae, 1893-1911), IV, (1896), 361-364, nn. 1151-1197.
27. The condemned propositions can be found in *Fontes,* n. 734, nn. 6, 7, and in Henr. Denzinger, et Clem. Bannwart, et Ioan. Umberg, *Enchiridion Symbolorum, Definitionum et Declarationum de Rebus Fidei et Morum* (21.-23. ed., Friburgi Brisgoviae: Herder, 1937), nn. 1106-1107.

> creta praedicta ad illarum interpretationem et declarationem emanata, Apostolica auctoritate tenore praesentium approbamus et confirmamus, illisque omnibus et singulis inviolabilis Apostolicae firmitatis robur adiicimus; atque etiam, quatenus opus sit, denuo, committimus et mandamus omnibus haereticae pravitatis Inquisitoribus, et locorum Ordinariis omnium regnorum, provinciarum, civitatum, dominiorum, et locorum universi Orbis Christiani, in suis respective dioecesibus, ut diligenter, omnique humano respectu postposito, inquirant, et procedant contra omnes, et singulos sacerdotes tam saeculares, quam regulares quomodolibet exemptos, ac Sedi Apostolicae immediate subiectos, quorumcumque Ordinum, Institutorum, Societatum, et Congregationum, et cuiuscumque dignitatis, et praeeminentiae, aut quovis privilegio, et indulto munitos, quae aliquem poenitentem, quaecumque persona illa sit, vel in actu sacramentalis confessionis vel ante, vel immediate post confessionem, vel occasione, aut praetextu confessionis, vel etiam extra occasionem confessionis in confessionali, sive in alio loco ad confessiones audiendas destinato, aut electo, cum simulatione audiendi ibidem confessionem, ad inhonesta, et turpia sollicitare, vel provocare, sive verbis, sive signis, sive nutibus, sive tactu, sive per scripturam, aut tunc aut post legendam, tentaverint, aut cum eis illicitos, et inhonestos sermones, vel tractatus temerario ausu habuerint; et quos in aliquo ex huiusmodi nefariis excessibus culpabiles repererint, in eos pro criminum qualitate et circumstantiis, severe animadvertant, per condignas poenas, iuxta memoratam Gregorii Praedecessoris Nostri constitutionem quam hic de verbo ad verbum pro inserta haberi volumus: dantes etiam, si opus sit, et rursus concedentes facultatem, ne delictum tam enorme, et Ecclesiae Dei iniuriosum, remaneat, ob probationum defectum, impunitum, iam alias in praefata constitutione tributam, procedendi cum testibus etiam singularibus, dummodo praesumptiones, indicia et alia adminicula concurrant.[28]

In the second paragraph of this constitution Benedict XIV restated the obligation of confessors to admonish their penitents, if they were solicited, to denounce their guilty confessors to the inquisitors or to the local Ordinaries. The confessors were, moreover, to withhold absolution until the denunciation was made, or at least a

28. *Codex Iuris Canonici Pii X Pontificis Maximi iussu digestus Benedicti Papae XV auctoritate promulgatus* (Westminster, Maryland: The Newman Bookshop, 1942), Document V.

serious promise was elicited from their penitents that they would fulfill this duty as soon as they were able (*cum primum poterunt*).[29]

The Constitution made no mention whatever of the decree of March 10, 1677, which had imposed a *latae sententiae* excommunication upon all who failed within one month to denounce those confessors whom they knew to have committed the crime of solicitation. Without naming any authors to support his assertion, Giraldi stated that all theologians agree on the binding force of that decree. Solicitors were still considered as suspects of heresy, and were therefore to be reported as such.[30] The binding force of the excommunication was taken for granted by the authors, though they were in dispute whether the excommunication was reserved.[31]

Article 4. Judicial Denunciations

A. The Concession To The Vicar Apostolic Of Cochin-China.

In keeping with the traditions set by the Holy Office to simplify the acceptance of denunciations, the Sacred Congregation for the Propagation of the Faith made an extraordinary concession to the Vicar Apostolic of Cochin China on August 26, 1775. The grant simplified the judicial norms both for the receiving of the judicial denunciations and also for the instituting of the judicial processes in the trial of confessors accused of the crime of solicitation. Because of the difficulties of travel to which the deponent would be exposed, the Vicar Apostolic was permitted to delegate another

29. Cf. Document V in the Code.

30. *Expositio,* II, 640.

31. Cf. Alphonsus Liguori St. (1696-1787), *Theologia Moralis* (Editio Stereotypa, 9 vols., Taurini, 1872), lib. VI, n. 693; Giraldi, *Expositio,* II, 627; Ballerini-Palmieri, (*Opus Theologicum,* V, n. 1146) cited Cozza († 1729) who held that the absolution from the excommunication was reserved even after the belated denunciation had been made. Cozza however honored the opposite opinion as probable. Giraldi (*Expositio,* II, 627) cited two decisions of the Holy Office, issued in 1735 and 1758 which lifted the reservation.

priest to accept the denunciation. Whatever form of procedure the Vicar Apostolic considered to be the better adapted for an extra judicially instituted process (*extra iudicii ordinem*) was left to his wise and prudent judgment. [32]

B. The Instruction Of 1866.

In the course of a century after the appearance of the Constitution "*Sacramentum Poenitentiae*" negligence in procedure against guilty confessors occasioned an Instruction by the Holy Office. This Instruction was issued on February 20, 1866[33] This Instruction emphasized the need for keeping the law on procedure, and offered practical help to the local Ordinaries on procedure. Denunciations were no longer to be made to the inquisitors, but directly to the Holy Office or to the local Ordinaries.[34] The decree of March 10, 1677 was only partially incorporated. The Instruction did not allude to any consequent excommunication for the failure to make the denunciations. On the other hand, it referred to the fact that not only the solicited penitent, but also any other person who knew of the crime of solicitation, was subject to a judicial examination, though the latter was not bound to report the guilty confessor as the earlier decree of March 10, 1677 had ordered.[35]

32. Cf. *Collectanea S. Congregationis de Propaganda Fide* (2 vols., Romae: ex Typographia Polyglotta Vaticana, 1907), S. C. de Prop. Fide, instr. (ad Vic. Ap. Cochinchin), 26 aug. 1775, n. 509 (hereafter cited *Collectanea*). Cf also *Fontes,* n. 990, and *Collectanea,* n. 1282.

33. S. C. S. Off., 20 febr. 1866 — *Fontes,* n. 900. A footnote in the Gasparri edition of the Code cites this Instruction under date of February 20, 1866. Cf. footnotes to canons 894, 904, 2368 The *Acta Sancta Sedis* (41 vols., Romae, 1865-1908,) III (1867), 499 [hereafter cited *ASS*]) as well as all pre-Code authors gave the date as February 20, 1867. The year 1867 does appear to be the proper date, for the preamble to the Instruction cites a decree of the Holy Office issued on June 27, 1866, four months later than the indicated date of the Instruction itself if the earlier assigned date of publication were assumed as historically correct.

34. Cf. *Fontes,* n. 990, 1°.

35. Cf. *Fontes,* n. 990, 9°.

Since the directions of numbers six, seven, eight, and fifteen of the 1866 Instruction are of special importance to this study on false denunciations, they shall be quoted in their entirety and from the original.

> 6. Denunciationes anonymae contra sollicitantes ad turpia nullam vim habent: denunciationes enim fieri debent in iudicio, nempe coram Episcopo eiusve delegato cum interventu ecclesiastici viri, qui notarii partes teneat, et cum iuramento, et cum expressione et subscriptione sui nominis; nec sufficit si fiat per apochas vel per litteras sine nomine et cognomine auctoris. Ceterum prohibetur, ne in recipiendis denunciationibus praeter iudicem et notarium, virum utrumque ecclesiasticum, speciali et scripto exarata Episcopi deputatione munitum, testes intersint. Cavendum quoque ne ex denunciantibus quaeratur, num sollicitationi consenserint; et convenientissimum foret, si de huiusmodi consensu, quantumvis sponte manifestato, nihil notetur in tabulis.
>
> 7. Denunciationis onus est personale, et ab ipsa persona sollicitata adimplendum. Verum si gravissimis difficultatibus impediatur, quominus hoc perficere ipsa possit, tunc vel per se, vel per epistolam, vel per aliam personam sibi benevisam suum adeat Ordinarium, vel Sanctam Sedem per sacram Poenitentiariam, vel etiam per hanc supremam Inquisitionem, expositis omnibus circumstantiis, et deinde se gerat iuxta instructionem quam erit acceptura. Si vero necessitas urgeat, se gerat iuxta consilia et monita sui confessarii. Ast si nullo impedimento detenta denunciationem omnino renuat, in hoc casu aliisque supra memoratis, laudandus est confessarius, quo operam suam poenitenti non denegaverit, et vel Ordinarium vel Sanctam Sedem pro opportunis providentiis consuluerit, suppresso tamen poenitentis nomine...
>
> 8. Non infrequenter occurrit casus, ut confessarius aliusve ecclesiasticus vir ab Episcopis (quorum utique haec potestas est) deputetur ad denunciationes recipiendas in re ad sollicitationis crimen spectante absque interventu notarii. Huic instructioni folium adiicitur circa modum, quo hisce in casibus confici denunciatio debet.[36] Qui enim ad hoc gravissimum munus viri maxime ideonei destinantur, de actu denunciationis iudiciaria

36. This formula is not in the *Fontes,* n. 990, where these various directives are given. It can be found in *ASS,* III (1867), 505-506.

ratione assumendo instrui debent, ac moneri, ut statim a recepta denunciatione eam continuo ad ipsum Episcopum, a quo fuerunt deputati, caute transmittant, neque confecti actus exemplum vel vestigium aliquod sibi retineant. Atque in hunc fere modum haud difficulter denunciandi munus adimpletur...

15. Indultum fuit a Pio VI in instructione, de qua antea dictum est, anno 1775 ad Vicarium Apostolicum Cocincinae data, ut cum difficilimum sit in illis tam dissitis ac disparatis regionibus ea omnia adamussim servare, quae in hisce causis servanda sunt; et cum si aliqua ex his omittantur, iustitia non patiatur, ut poenae infligantur adversus reos, de quorum crimine iudiciaria ratione adhuc sufficienter non constat, tunc consultius fortasse esset si extra iudicii ordinem procedatur ad occurrendum tanto malo mediis et modis magis facilibus et expeditis, quos in casibus particularibus Vicarii Apostolici prudentia cum animarum zelo coniuncta suggeret. Iam vero quisque videt hanc indulgentiam pro locis adeo dissitis, ac disparatis factam, neque omnibus esse communem, neque absque Apostolicae Sedis auctoritate iure posse ubivis induci.[37]

C. The Extension Of The Indult Of 1775.

Not many years after the appearance of this Instruction of 1866 the Vicars Apostolic of China asked that the grant made to one of their number in 1775, and alluded to in number fifteen of the 1866 Instruction of the Holy Office, be extended to all China. The Sacred Congregation for the Propagation of the Faith acquiesced readily.

Quo propositis huic S. C. dubiis fieret satis, a Sacra Supremae Inquisitionis Cong. quaesitum fuit: *'An Vicarii Ap. absque speciali facultate possint excipere denunciationes in materia sollicitationis ad turpia, et an, eiusmodi denunciationibus acceptis teneantur eas ad S. Officium deferre.'* Emi PP. Inquisitores Generales, in fer. IV 20 Iunii curr. anni, respondendum censuerunt: *'Supplicandum SSmo pro extensione ad omnes Vicarios App. Instructionis pro Vicario Ap. Cocincinae diei 1 iunii 1775, cum addito quod remittat ad S. Officium, per medium S. C. de Propaganda Fide in epistola clausa, nomina sollicitantium.* Cum autem Summus Pont. Leo XIII in audi-

37. S. C. S. Off., instr. 20 febr. 1866 — *Fontes*, n. 990.

> entia eiusdem feriae ac diei, decretum Emorum PP. approbare dignatus sit, et petitam concedere extensionem, hinc praedictam Instructionem, quae Vicario Ap. Cocincinae data fuit per epistolam diei 26 aug. 1775 ad A. T. mitto, ex qua Instructione eadem A. T. intelliget, qua ratione se gerere debeat si quando, quod Deus avertat, huius casus occurrant.'[38]

D. The Constitution *"Apostolicae Sedis."*

The next official document that had a bearing on judicial denunciations was the Constitution *"Apostolicae Sedis"* of Pius IX, issued on October 12, 1869. It took over one of the elements of the March 10, 1677 decree, and enacted a *latae sententiae* excommunication against all penitents who neglected or culpably omitted to denounce within one month the confessors by whom they were solicited. The excommunication was reserved to no one.[39] Canon 2368 § 2, incorporated this law of the Constitution *"Apostolicae Sedis,"* but introduced one minor change. It inserted the word *scienter.*

> Fidelis vero, qui scienter omiserit eum, a quo sollicitatus fuerit, intra mensem denuntiare contra praescriptum can. 904, incurrit in excommunicationem latae sententiae nemini reservatam, non absolvendus nisi postquam obligationi satisfecerit aut se satisfacturum serio promiserit.

Only the solicited persons were obliged under pain of excommunication to denounce the confessors guilty of solicitation. The authors who wrote after the appearance of this Constitution still maintained that the decree of March 10, 1677, obliged all persons who knew of the crime of solicitation, including the *impuberes,* to denounce such a confessor. That obligation, so they taught, was present from the natural law. They were however under no penalty of excommunication if they failed to reveal the crime.[40]

38. S. C. de Prop. Fide, litt. encycl. 25 iul. 1883 — *Collectanea* n. 1604; *Fontes,* n. 4902.
39. Pius IX, const. *"Apostolicae Sedis,"* 12 oct. 1869, § IV, 4 — *Fontes,* n. 552.
40. Cf. Ballerini-Palmieri, *Opus-Theologicum,* V, n. 1146; Rota, *Enchiridion,* n. 370; Pennacchi, *Commentaria,* II, 161; S. Many, "De Peccato

Sollicitationis," — *Le Canoniste Contemporain* (Paris, 1878-1922), XVIII (1895), 718 (hereafter cited *Le Canoniste*); Berardi, *De Sollicitatione,* n. 190; D. Craisson († 1881), *Manuale Totius Iuris Canonici* (5. ed., 4 vols., Pictavii, 1877), III, n. 3870 (hereafter cited *Manuale*); Iosephus D'Annibale (1815-1892), *Summula Theologiae Moralis* (5. ed., 3 vols., Romae, 1908), III, 300 (hereafter cited *Summula*); F. Santi (1830-1885), *Praelectiones Iuris Canonici iuxta Ordinem Decretalium Gregorii IX* (4. ed., 5 vols. in 3, Emendata et Recentissimis Decretis Accomodata cura Martini Leitner, Ratisbonae: Pustet, 1903-1905), lib. V, tit. 2, n. 4 (hereafter cited *Praelectiones*); Ianuario Bucceroni (1841-1918), *Institutiones Theologiae Moralis secundum Doctrinam S. Thomae et S. Alphonsi* (3. ed., 2 vols., Romae, 1898), II, nn. 1266-1268 (hereafter cited *Institutiones*); Aemilius Berardi, *Theologia Moralis* (5 vols., Faventiae, 1905), V, nn. 599, 649; Ioannes P. Gury (1801-1886) et Antonius Ballerini, *Compendium Theologiae Moralis* (7. ed., 2 vols., Romae, 1882), II, n. 590, ii (hereafter cited *Compendium*); Ignatz Schuech, *Handbuch der Pastoraltheologie* 5. ed., Linz, 1880), p. 694, footnote 4 (hereafter cited *Handbuch*).

CHAPTER II

THE FALSE DENUNCIATION OF AN INNOCENT CONFESSOR OF THE CRIME OF SOLICITATION

ARTICLE 1. PONTIFICAL LEGISLATION

A. In The Constitution *"Sacramentum Poenitentiae."*

The first legislation that strove to protect the reputation of innocent confessors and to penalize persons who attempted to defame them by imputing to them the crime of solicitation was enacted by Benedict XIV in his Constitution *"Sacramentum Poenitentiae."*

> Inasmuch, indeed, as one finds inquitous men, who either through hatred or anger, or motivated by some other unworthy cause, or incited thereto by the wicked persuasion of others, or by their promises, their flattery, or their threats, or instigated by them in any other manner, counting for nought the fearful judgment of God, and despising the authority of the Church, falsely bring an accusation of the crime of solicitation against innocent priests to ecclesiastical judges: therefore, in order that such a wicked audacity and such a detestable crime be restrained by the fear of the enormity of the penalty, any and every person who shall disgrace himself with the perpetration of so exsecrable a crime by impiously calumniating innocent confessors, or shall criminally scheme that this be accomplished by others, let him perpetually be without hope of obtaining absolution from any priest, however privileged and honored with authority and dignities, unless he have come to the end of life, and in any case wherein death impends; this absolution We reserve to Ourselves and to Our Successors as previously indicated.[1]

1. This translation is offered by the writer. The original official text reads as follows: "3. Et quoniam improbi quidem homines reperiuntur, qui vel odio, vel ira, vel alia indigna causa commoti, vel aliorum impiis suasionibus, aut promissis, aut blanditiis, aut minis, aut alio quovis modo incitati, tremendo Dei iudicio posthabito, et Ecclesiae auctoritate contempta, innoxios sacerdotes apud ecclesiasticos iudices falso sollicitationis insimulant: ut igitur tam nefaria audacia, et tam detestabile facinus metu magnitudinis poenae coerceatur, quaecumque

The Holy Office in its Instruction of 1866 briefly summarized this law, but it did not change it.[2]

B. In The Code.

Whereas the Constitution *"Sacramentum Poenitentiae"* enacted but a single penalty for the delict of false denunciation, the Code has introduced two penalties. In canon 894 the present law has retained the reserved sin, with modifications however, which shall be demonstrated in the course of this study. In canon 2363 a *latae sententiae* excommunication reserved *speciali modo* to the Holy See has further been added.

> Canon 894. The only sin which in its nature of a sin is reserved to the Holy See is the false accusation by means of which an innocent priest is accused of the crime of solicitation before ecclesiastical judges.
>
> Canon 2363. If anyone, either in person or through others, falsely denounces a confessor to the superiors as guilty of solicitation, he automatically incurs excommunication reserved in a special manner to the Apostolic See. From this penalty he can in no case be absolved until he has formally retracted the false denunciation and has, in so far as he is able, repaired the damages, if any were occasioned by his crime. Besides he should be subjected to an exacting and protracted penance. The law as here stated effects no modification for the prescription contained in canon 894.[3]

persona, quae exsecrabili huiusmodi flagitio se inquinaverit, vel per se ipsam innocentes confessarios impie calumniando, vel sceleste procurando, ut id ab aliis fiat, a quocumque sacerdote quovis privilegio, auctoritate, et dignitate munito, praeterquam a Nobis, Nostrisque Successoribus, nisi in fine vitae, et excepto mortis articulo, spe absolutionis obtinendae, quam Nobis et Successoribus praedictis reservamus, perpetuo careat." — Document V in the Code.

2. S. C. S. Off., instr. 20 febr. 1866, in the Preamble — *Fontes,* n. 990.
3. Canon 894. Unicum peccatum ratione sui reservatum Sanctae Sedi est falsa delatio, qua sacerdos innocens accusatur de crimine sollicitationis apud iudices ecclesiasticos.

Canon 2363. Si quis per seipsum vel per alios confessarium de sollicitationis crimine apud Superiores falso denuntiaverit, ipso facto incurrit in excommunicationem speciali modo Sedi Apostolicae reservatum a qua nequit ullo in casu absolvi, nisi falsam denuntiationem

Article 2. The Crime of Falsity

Falsity is spoken of in canon law in three different senses: *largissime, large,* and *stricte.*[4] Under the first and general division (*largissime*) is placed everything that is not objectively true. Under it the element of imputability is not considered. Under the second and more specific division (*large*) is included the perversion of the truth as brought about with malice or grave negligence.[5] When the truth is objectively not perverted, even though the delinquent had the evil intention to pervert it, the crime of falsity is not committed. A sin of deception however is committed. The corruption of the truth in conjunction with the intention to deceive the hearer is always present in falsity *large dicta.* Under the third and most specific division (*stricte*) is incorporated the falsity whose concept derives from the proper and commonly accepted definition of falsity. Besides embracing the two elements referred to under *largissime* and *large,* namely, the fraudulent corruption of the truth to deceive the listener, the crime of falsity also contains the notion of causing harm to some person. The harm in some instances may not be immediately present, but is considered to be potentially

formaliter retractaverit, et damna, si qua inde secuta sint, pro viribus reparaverit, imposita insuper gravi ac diuturna poenitentia, firmo praescripto can. 894.

The foregoing translation is furnished by the writer. A substantially identical translation is offered by Stanislaus Woywod (1880-1941), *A Practical Commentary on the Code of Canon Law* (2 vols., New York: Joseph F. Wagner, 1925), I, 439, II, 505 (hereafter cited *Commentary*).

4. Cf. Franciscus Schmalzgrueber (1663-1735), *Ius Ecclesiasticum Universum* (5 vols. in 12, Romae, 1843-1845), lib. V, tit. 20, n. 2 (hereafter cited *Ius Ecclesiasticum*).
5. "... requiritur enim mala fides..." — Santi, *Praelectiones,* lib V, Appendix, p. 232, n. III, 1°; Cf also Franciscus X. Wernz († 1913) - Petrus Vidal, *Ius Canonicum ad Codicis Normam Exactum* (7 tomes in 8 vols., Vol. VII, *Ius Poenale Ecclesiasticum,* 1937, Romae: Apud Aedes Universitatis Gregorianae, 1923-1938), VII, n. 500 (hereafter cited *Ius Canonicum*); Heribert Jone, *Gesetzbuch des kanonischen Rechtes* (3 vols., Paderborn: Ferdinand Schoeningh, 1939-1940, Vol. II, *Sachenrecht,* Vol. III, *Prozess-und Strafrecht*), II, 126, c (hereafter cited *Gesetzbuch*).

present.[6] Sole († 1921) in his definition adds the element of advantage to oneself as an alternative for the harm that might befall another.[7] The potential harm is classified as the equivalent of the actual harm. Cerato does not include this third element of harm (*damnum, damnosum*) in his definition of false denunciation, though he implies at least its potential presence, for in his monograph *De Delicto Sollicitationis* he speaks of the obligation of making restitution for the damage unjustly caused by the calumny.[8] The crime of falsity therefore presupposes the presence of these three elements:

1. the truth must be changed or perverted;
2. the perversion must result from malice;
3. the corruption of the truth must be harmful, actually or potentially.[9]

6. Schmalzgrueber, *Ius Ecclesiasticum,* lib. V, tit. 20, n. 4; Cf also Anacletus Reiffenstuel (1642-1703,) *Ius Canonicum Universum* (7 vols., Parisiis, 1864-1870), lib. V, tit. 20, n. 1 (hereafter cited *Ius Canonicum*); Stephanus Sipos, *Enchiridion Iuris Canonici ad Usum Scholarum et Privatum* (3. ed., Pecs: ex Typographia "Haladas R. T.", 1936), p. 1012 (hereafter cited *Enchiridion*); Franciscus X. Wernz, *Ius Decretalium ad Usum Praelectionum in Scholis Textus Canonici sive Iuris Decretalium* (2. ed., 6 vols., Romae-Prati, 1906-1913), VI, 423 (hereafter cited *Ius Decretalium*); Michael Lega (1860-1935), *Praelectiones in Textum Iuris Canonici, De Iudiciis Ecclesiasticis* (4 vols., Romae: Typis Vaticanis, Vol. I, 1896, Vol. II, 1898, Vol. III, 1899, Vol. IV, 1901), III, n. 446 (hereafter cited *De Iudiciis Ecclesiasticis*).
7. *Praelectiones in Lib. V Codicis Iuris Canonici, De Delictis et Poenis* (Romae: Pustet, 1920), p. 338 (hereafter cited *De Delictis et Poenis*).
8. "...Duo importat, a) ut crimen sollicitationis non existat; b) ut denuntiantes sciant, confessarium esse innocentem ab hoc crimine." — Prosdocimus Cerato, *Censurae Vigentes Ipso Facto a Codice Iuris Canonici Excerptae* (2. ed., Patavii: Typis Seminarii, 1921), n. 79, e (hereafter cited *Censurae Vigentes*); "...retractanda sit falsa denuntiatio etiamsi denuntiatus iam perierit,..." — *De Delicto Sollicitationis* (Patavii: Typis Seminarii, 1922), n. 136 (hereafter cited *De Delicto*); Cf. also Berardi, *De Sollicitatione,* nn. 354-356.
9. "Tria requiruntur, mendacium, dolus, damnum... mendacium damnosum deliberatum." — D. M. Pruemmer (1866-1931), *Manuale Iuris Canonici in Usum Clericorum Praesertim Eorum Qui ad Instituta*

Some canonists prefer the terms of moral theology, material and formal falsity, in their description of false denunciations. Though the terms are not perfectly synonymous nor interchangeable with *largissime* and *large* their use will not be misleading. Material falsity is present when the truth is objectively corrupted, but the deponent is in good faith, since he thinks the declaration to be true; formal falsity occurs when the truth is knowingly and wilfully distorted.[10] A false denunciation of the crime of solicitation then, is one that is based on untruth, is done with ill will, and is actually injurious or at least potentially so.

If a factual solicitation occurred in the confessional, or in the circumstances in which, as specified in the law, a crime of solicitation can take place, but the denunciator nevertheless acts with a bad faith as deriving from an erroneous conviction, the delict of the false denunciation as contemplated in law is not committed. The objective truth was not distorted.[11] The crime of false denunciation is absent, too, if the deponent indeed perverts the truth, but in consequence of ignorance or of error. The element of good faith is a factor that will excuse from the sin, and consequently from the crime and its penal sanctions.[12]

Religiosa Pertinent (3. ed., Freiburgi Brisgoviae, 1922), n. 599, 1° (hereafter cited *Manuale Iuris Canonici*); Cf. also Schuech, *Handbuch,* p. 685.

10. Cf. Cerato, *Censurae Vigentes,* n. 79, h. 1; Cerato, *De Delicto,* n. 132, 4°; B. H. Merkelbach, *Summa Theologiae Moralis ad Mentem D. Thomae et ad Normam Iuris Novi* (3. ed., 3 vols., Parisiis: Desclee, De Brouwer, 1938-1939), III, n. 643, C, 2 (hereafter cited *Summa*).
11. "Si crimen adsit vere consummatum, non datur locus censurae etsi denuntians putaverit crimen non esse consummatum, et ex odio, ex vindicta, ex alienis suasionibus denuntiaverit..." — Cerato, *Censurae Vigentes,* n. 79, e; *ibid.,* n. 79, h. 2, c; *Cerato, De Delicto,* n. 132, 4°; Berardi, *De Sollicitatione,* n. 349.
12. Canon 2242, § 2. Censura punitur tantummodo delictum externum, *grave,* consummatum, cum contumacia coniunctum; (Italics inserted); Cf. also Wernz-Vidal, *Iüs Canonicum,* VII, n. 500; Joseph Hollweck 1854-1926), *Die kirchlichen Strafgesetzen* (Mainz, 1899), p. 280; Cerato, *De Delicto,* n. 132, 4°; Cerato, *Censurae Vigentes,* n. 79, 2; Schuech, *Handbuch,* p. 685; Eduard Eichmann, *Das Strafrecht des Codex Iuris Canonici* (Paderborn, 1920), p. 196 (hereafter cited *Das*

The report of a non-existent solicitation as having occurred under the circumstances specified by the Constitution "*Sacramentum Poenitentiae*" constitutes the crime of a false denunciation. The necessary requirements for the constitution of the crime of solicitation are reduced to these four:

1. the solicitation must deal with a sin against the sixth commandment of God;
2. it must be a grave sin;
3. it must be committed in a sacramental confession, or at least have a proximate relation to the sacrament of penance;
4. it must be certain that the sin of solicitation was committed.[13]

Article 3. The Crime of Solicitation

A. Sins Of Impurity.

No confessor can be accused of the crime of solicitation unless a sin *in re turpi* has been committed by him in any of the modes

Strafrecht); Berardi, *De Sollicitatione,* n. 349; Guidus Cocchi, *Commentarium in Codicem Iuris Canonici* (8 vols. in 5, Taurinorum Augustae: Marietti, 1922-1930. Vol. VIII, *De Delictis et Poenis,* 3. ed., 1938), VIII, n. 223 (hereafter cited *De Delictis et Poenis*); Ioannes Chelodi, *Ius Poenale et Ordo Procedendi in Iudiciis Criminalibus iuxta Codicem Iuris Canonici* (Tridenti: Libr. Edit. Tridentum, 1925 [1920]), n. 88 (hereafter cited *Ius Poenale*).

13. Cf. Constitution "*Sacramentum Poenitentiae,*" §§ 2, 3 — Document V in the Code; Felix Cappello, *Tractatus Canonico-moralis de Sacramentis* (3 vols. in 6, Vol. II, *De Poenitentia,* 3. ed., 1938, Romae: Marietti, 1932-1939), nn. 667-670 (hereafter cited *De Poenitentia*); Heribert Jone, *Moral Theology,* Englished and Adapted to the Code and Customs of the United States of America by Urban Adelman (Westminster, Maryland: The Newman Bookshop, 1945), nn. 592-595; Matthaeus Conte a Coronata, *Institutiones Iuris Canonici ad Usum Utriusque Cleri et Scholarum* (5 vols., Taurini [Italia]: Marietti, 1928-1936, Vols, I-II, 2. ed., 1939, Vols. III-V, 1933-1936), IV, 525-554 (hereafter cited *Institutiones*); F. Claeys Bouuaert - G. Simenon, *Manuale Iuris Canonici* (3 vols., Vols. I, III, 3. ed., 1931, Vol. II, *De Sacramentis,* 2. ed., 1935, Liege: Dessain), II, n. 149, 1-3 (hereafter cited *Manuale*); H. Noldin (1838-1922) - A. Schmitt, *Summa Theologiae Moralis iuxta Codicem Iuris Canonici* (20. ed., 3 vols., Vol. III, *De Sacramentis,* Oeniponte: Fel. Rauch, Pustet, 1930), *De Sacramentis,* n. 375 (hereafter cited *De Sacramentis*).

outlined by the Constitution "*Sacramentum Poenitentiae.*"[14] Whenever the confessor carries on a sinful impure conversation with his penitent; presents evil literature to be read by him either in the confessional or later;[15] makes impure signs, executes lewd gestures, or perpetrates indecent touches in the presence of his penitent; arranges for an appointment to commit sins of the flesh at some later time; uses the penitent to serve as an intermediary agent to sin with a third party, the crime of solicitation is committed.[16]

Not only by positive forthright actions can the sin of solicitation take place, but also by innuendo. Thus a confessor would have to be denounced when he indirectly suggests that sins against the sixth commandment are not reprehensible; when he confirms the sinful impure habits of his penitent by implying that for reasons of health these habits may be tolerated;[17] when he leaves the impres-

14. "... procedant contra... sacerdotes... qui aliquem poenitentem ad inhonesta et turpia sollicitare, vel provocare, sive verbis, sive signis, sive nutibus, sive tactu, sive per scripturam, aut tunc aut post legendam, tentaverint, aut cum eis, illicitos, et inhonestos sermones, vel tractatus temerario ausu habuerint;..." — Document V in the Code.
15. "1°. An sit denuntiandus confessarius, qui dat poenitenti chartam in confessione, postea legendam in qua ad venerem sollicitabat. Domini qualificatores censuerunt, esse denuntiandum et negativam opinionem non esse probabilem." S. C. S. Off. decr. 11 febr. 1661 — Ballerini-Palmieri, *Opus Theologicum,* V, 583, footnote (a).
16. Cf. Claeys Bouuaert-Simenon, *Manuale,* II, n. 149; Coronata, *Institutiones,* IV, 541, and footnote 3; Thomas A. Iorio, *Compendium Theologiae Moralis iuxta methodum Ioannis Petri Gury ad normam Codicis Iuris Canonici redactum a Raphaele Tummolo* (5. ed., quam recognovit emendavit et auxit, Thomas A. Iorio, 2 vols., Neapoli: M. D'Auria, 1934-1935), II, n. 576, *Quaer.* 1°, b 3), (hereafter cited *Compendium*).
17. "Tibullus excipiens confessiones mulierum, quarum viri saepe abesse solent, et quae non facile se continent, docet et suadet easdem mulieres non peccare in sequentibus casibus: 1. Si desiderando proprium virum absentem, patiantur commotionem sensualem seu pollutionem. 2. Si desiderant hanc eandem pollutionem in se experiri ex ardenti amore viri absentis. 3. Si pollutionem in se excitent tactibus secum habitis, dummodo hos actus referant ad virum absentem. S. Poenitentiaria dilecto in Christo... scribenti subiungit iam bis hac super re ab hoc sacro Tribunali responsum fuisse, et actus huiusmodi esse graviter illicitos, et confessarium eos probantem esse denuntiandum." — Responsum S. C. Poenit., 2 sept. 1904 — Quoted by Vig. Dalpiaz, "De

sion that onanism is not forbidden,[18] or that the penitent may live an adulterous life with another.[19]

It is evident that no crime of solicitation is committed by a confessor who requests his penitent to commit sins against the remaining commandments of God.[20] This is true even if the sins are analogous, or even if they are more grevious, as sins of blasphemy or perjury.[21] The conclusion then follows that no person can make a false denunciation of the crime of solicitation when any other sin except the one against the virtue of purity is falsely denounced. The penalties of the law would consequently not be in force either.

abusu matrimonii et crimine sollicitationis" — *Apollinaris* (Romae, 1928-), VI (1933), 247. Cf. also Cappello, *De Poenitentia,* n. 655, 3, and n. 657, 7; Coronata, *Institutiones,* IV, 530, 540.

18. Cf. Jone, *Moral Theology,* n. 592, 1; Coronata, *Institutiones,* IV, 531; Claeys Bouuaert-Simenon, *Manuale,* II, n. 149.

19. Cf. Eduardus Genicot, *Institutiones Theologiae Moralis* (14. ed., Quam Recognovit I. Salsmans, 2 vols., BuenosAires-Dedebec: Edicione Desclee, De Brouwer, 1939), II, n. 395, I, B (hereafter cited *Institutiones*); Rota *Enchiridion,* nn. 255, 305, 369; Jone, *Moral Theology,* n. 592; Cappello, *op. cit.,* nn. 655, 3, 657, 7; Coronata, *op. cit.,* IV, 530, 540.

20. An exception must be made for the ninth commandment because of its close relationship with the sixth, because sins of thought and desire against the virtue of purity can be mortal sins. Ordinarily no solicitation is involved when the confessor indirectly occasions such thoughts and desires in his penitent. If he however informs his penitent that there is nothing sinful in entertaining them, the crime of solicitation is had. Cf. Aloysius De Smet, *De Absolutione Complicis et Sollicitatione* (2. ed., Brugis: Beyaert, 1921), p. 39 (hereafter cited *De Absolutione*); Cerato, *De Delicto,* n. 37; Coronata, *Institutiones,* IV, 531.

21. "11. An confessarius, qui sollicitat poenitentem ad actus illicitos extra actus venereos, sit denuntiandus? Censuerunt opinionem negativam esse probabilem." — S. C. S. Off., decr. 11 febr. 1661 — Ballerini-Palmieri, *Opus Theologicum,* V, 583, footnote (a). Cf. also Berardi, *De Sollicitatione,* nn. 359, 252, 349; Rota, *Enchiridion,* n. 104, 6°; Santi, *Praelectiones,* lib. V, Appendix, p. 232, n. III, 1°; Cappello, *De Poenitentia,* n. 606, 4; Many, "De Peccato Sollicitationis" — *Le Canoniste,* XVIII (1895), 720, 1°; St. Alphonsus, *Theologia Moralis,* lib. VI, n. 684; Coronata, *Institutiones,* IV, 532; Albertus Cipollini, *De Censuris Latae Sententiae iuxta Codicem Iuris Canonici* (Taurini: Marietti, 1925), p. 128 (hereafter cited *De Censuris*).

B. The Sins Must Be Grave.

One of the conditions for incurring a censure is that the violation of the law be a grave transgression.[22] In determining whether the provocation to sins against the sixth commandment of God are grave, authors are guided by a decree of the Holy Office issued on February 11, 1661, which denied probability to the contention that *in rebus venereis* the presence of lightness of matter would excuse the penitent from denouncing his confessor.[23] Canonists interpret this decree strictly and refer the phrase *in rebus venereis* to venereal pleasure only and not sins of curiosity, immodesty, or sensuality.[24] Whenever indifferent acts, or slightly sinful acts are employed by the perverse intention of the confessor as provocative means to solicit, they are to be construed as constituting a grave sin of solicitation.[25]

22. Canon 2242, § 1. Censura punitur tantummodo delictum externum, *grave,* consummatum, cum contumacia coniunctum. (Italics inserted.)
23. "3. An confessarius sollicitando propter parvitatem materiae sit denuntiandus? Cum in rebus venereis non detur parvitas materiae et, si daretur, in re praesenti non daretur, censuerunt esse denuntiandum, et opinionem contrariam non esse probabilem." — Ballerini-Palmieri, *Opus Theologicum,* V, 583, footnote (a).
24. "Tactus, oscula, aspectus, quae licet in actu confessionis fiant ex parte confessarii in partibus minus honestis poenitentis sine ulla praevia sollicitatione seu provocatione ad turpia in genere, et sine ullo signo voluntatis progrediendi etiam ad graviora, sed cum manifesta voluntate in his quiescendi exclusive, materiam delicti non fundunt, etiamsi poenitens consenserit et peccatum confessarii appareat formaliter grave. Si vero haec adhibeantur tamquam medium ad graviora, materiam delicti iam fundunt." — Cerato, *De Delicto,* n. 39; "Sensus obvius decreti hic est: *Cum in rebus venereis;* non in actibus venereae voluptatis; non detur parvitas materiae, cum quaelibet res, vel minima, venerea sit peccatum mortale,..." — Ianuarius Bucceroni, *Commentaria De casibus reservatis, De censuris, De C. Pii IX "Apostolicae Sedis", De C. "Sacramentum Poenitentiae", De Absolutione danda, differenda, deneganda* (5. ed., Romae, 1899), *De C. "Sacramentum Poenitentiae",* n. 22 (hereafter cited *De C. "Sac. Poenit."*); Cf. also Jone, Moral Theology, n. 593, 2; Coronata, *Institutiones,* IV, 531.
25. "... Sollicitatio *ad actus leves* non constituit delictum, sollicitatio *per actus leves* facile delictum constituit, quotiens nempe ex circumstantiis facile deduci potest confessarium per actus leves sollicitare voluisse

Since the crime of solicitation consists in alluring penitents to grave sins of impurity, whenever an innocent confessor is declared to be guilty of such misconduct, that report would constitute the crime of false denunciation and the penalty would be in force.[26] This is true when a phrase or action of the confessor is maliciously distorted and exaggerated and the crime of solicitation attributed to him. The classic example given by Berardi is the practice of extending a sacred image for a reverent kiss before or after a confession. The penitent uses this as an excuse to denounce him of solicitation.[27]

It is conceivable that a hard-hearing penitent can culpably misconstrue the confessor's words and incriminate him by a false accusation. A misapprehension caused by the confessor's indelicate use of expression offensive to refined tastes can readily be exaggerated. In such instances, the confessor, at most guilty only of crudeness in speech, is nevertheless falsely denounced of the crime of solicitation.[28] When the objective intention of the confessor cannot be questioned even though his actions are indiscreet, then to exaggerate these to a degree that the local Ordinary or his

ad graviora." — Coronata, *Institutiones,* IV, 531 (Italics in original); cf. also Cappello, *De Poenitentia,* n. 668, 3, 2°; Jone, *Moral Theology,* n. 593, 2; Cerato, *loc. cit.*

26. Cf. Rota, *Enchiridion,* nn. 104, 5°, 394; Charles Augustine (1872-1943), *A Commentary on the New Code of Canon Law* (8 vols., Vol. IV, *On The Sacraments* [*except Matrimony*] *and Sacramentals,* 3. ed., 1925, Vol. VIII, *Penal Code,* 3. ed., 1931, St. Louis: Herder), IV, 318; VIII, 424 (hereafter cited *Commentary*): Alphonsus De Meester, *Juris Canonici et Juris Canonico-Civilis Compendium* (nova ed., 3 vols. in 4, Brugis: Desclee, 1921-1928), lib. III, Pars II, 268 (hereafter cited *Compendium*); Albertus Blat, *Commentarium Textus Codicis Iuris Canonici* (5 vols. in 6, lib. III, Pars I, *De Sacramentis,* 2. ed., Romae: ex Typographia Pontificia in Instituto Pius IX, 1924; lib. V, *De Delictis et Poenis,* Romae: Collegio Angelico, 1924), lib. V, n. 214, d; lib. III, Pars I, 260 (hereafter cited *Commentarium*); A. Vermeersch-J.Creusen, *Epitomae Iuris Canonici cum Commentariis ad Scholas et ad Usum Privatum* (3. ed., 3 vols., Mechliniae-Romae: Dessain, 1927-1928), III, n. 565 (hereafter cited *Epitome*).
27. *De Sollicitatione,* n. 319.
28. Cf. D'Annibale, *Summula,* III, n. 368, footnote 19; Rota *Enchiridion,* n. 394; Berardi, *op. cit.,* nn. 252, 219, 259.

delegate who receives the denunciation will recognize them as culpable grave sins of solicitation implies that a false denunciation has taken place.

Because of the distinction made in moral theology between the *partes corporis honestae, minus honestae,* and *inhonestae,* or the *partes ex se incitantes, aliqualiter excitantes,* and *ex se non incitantes,*[29] authors generally concede the possibility of a lightness of matter in actions or conversations against modesty and self-restraint, but never *in re turpi, in rebus venereis.*[30] Slight indiscretions against modesty and chastity when placed by the confessor with no intention to seduce the penitent are not sufficient to constitute the crime of solicitation.[31] If, however, such slight acts are placed with a view to the solicitation of the penitent by means of these slight sins, the crime of solicitation is committed and the confessor is to be denounced.[32] Whenever it is evident to the penitent that the imprudent conduct of the confessor could not be construed as solicitation, but he nevertheless accuses him of depraved and libidinous intentions, the crime of false denunciation is present.

29. Cf. Noldin-Schmitt, *Summa* (De Sexto Praecepto, 24. ed., 1931), n. 51, 2°; Cerato, *De Delicto,* n. 39.

30. "Oscula et tactus in partibus honestis vel minus honestis sunt venialia si fiant ex levitate, ioco, curiositate. ... Non est per se mortale proferre turpia quidem sed non graviter obscoena, si fiat breviter, per iocum aut vanum solatium..." — Gury, *Compendium,* I, nn. 413, 420; Cf. also Rota, *Enchiridion,* n. 253; St. Alphonsus, *Theologia Moralis,* lib. VI, n. 683, *prima sententia*; Bucceroni, *De C. "Sac. Poenit.",* n. 22.

31. "... Iterum atque iterum revocamus, tactum etiam in partibus minis honestis, immo et honestis, fieri posse peccatum *formaliter* grave in agente ob ejus affectum vel finem graviter malum et tamen delictum non consummari..." — Cerato, *De Delicto,* nn. 27, 39 (Italics in original).

32. "Si poenitentem *ad actus leves* tantum inducere intendat, delictum sollicitationis denuntiandum non habetur. ... Sedulo notandum, aliud esse sollicitare *ad actus leves,* aliud vero sollicitare *per actus leves;* in hoc secundo casu peccatum potest esse grave, atque proinde haberi potest verum delictum sollicitationis." — Cappello, *De Poenitentia,* n. 668, 3, 3°, 4° (Italics in original); Cf. also Coronata, *Institutiones,* IV, 530, 531; De Smet, *De Absolutione,* n. 67; Noldin-Schmitt, *De Sacramentis,* n. 374.

When a confessor in all simplicity and innocence offers a picture of himself, presents a gift to his penitent, lightly touches the penitent (*tactus leviter inhonestus*),[33] presses the penitent's hands or pinches his cheeks (*digitos intorqueret, vel leviter genas vellicaret*),[34] gives a roguish wink of the eye (*ictu oculi signum malitiosum*),[35] or gives the penitent a light kiss after confession,[36] and the penitent, though having no moral certitude of the confessor's depraved designs, in indignation exaggerates these slightly suspicious acts and accuses the confessor of solicitation, the elements of a false denunciation are had, and the crime is complete for the incurring of the penalties.[37]

Rota recorded the instance of a devout confessor who was accustomed reverently to kiss a crucifix held in his hand while he heard confessions. The sound of the kiss became audible to his penitents, and this led to his downfall. *Haec initia dolorum pro incauto confessario!* A lightminded *devotula* told her companions that her confessor threw her a kiss (*narrat sociis compluribus confessarium sibi misisse oscula in confessione*). These companions in turn averred that he had shown them the same signs of affection. Denunciations were made. These led to his suspension. His priestly work was ruined, and his spirit so broken that he had no peace thereafter.[38]

Berardi recorded the following instances: A confessor at the conclusion of every confession said "va' in pace," go in peace. One of his penitents accused him of the crime of solicitation by quoting him as saying "da un bacio." Another confessor used the expletive, "Oh bella!" at the slightest disturbance. Its frequent

33. Noldin-Schmitt, *De Sacramentis,* n. 274, b.
34. Berardi, *De Sollicitatione,* n. 24.
35. Berardi, *loc. cit.*
36. Cf. Dominicus Pruemmer, *Manuale Theologiae Moralis secundum Principia S. Thomae Aquinatis* (2. et 3. ed., 3 vols., Friburgi Brisgoviae: Herder, 1923), III, n. 461 (hereafter cited, *Manuale Theologiae Moralis*); cf. also Gury, *Compendium,* I, n. 420.
37. Rota, *Enchiridion,* nn. 253, 254, 395; Berardi, *De Sollicitatione,* nn. 23, 252, 359; St. Alphonsus, *Theologia Moralis,* lib. VI, nn. 683, 703.
38. *Enchiridion,* n. 394; Cf. also Berardi, *De Sollicitatione,* n. 319.

use in the confessional led to false denunciations of the crime of solicitation.[39]

C. Solicitation In Relation To The Sacrament Of Penance.

1. The Soliciting Agent.

The third element needed in the constitution of the delict of solicitation is the relationship of sins of impurity to the sacrament of penance. No crime of solicitation is understood by the law when a priest resorts to the sin of solicitation in administering other sacraments or sacramentals.[40] Nor is the crime of solicitation present when a priest commits sins of impurity with another, but apart from exercising his ministry as confessor, or disassociated from those circumstances that are closely related to the sacrament of penance.[41] If a person falsely attributes the sin of solicitation to a priest while the latter was administering a sacrament other than penance, no delict of false denunciation could result. The false denunciation of the crime of solicitation as it obtains in law was not

39. "... Alter ad modum intercalaris saepissime dicere solebat: oh bella! oh bella! et illum quoque muliercula, quasi de pulchritudine illam laudaverit, accusavit. Sors fuit quod Episcopo illum advocanti eique dicenti sollicitationis accusationem adversum eum latam fuisse, statim respondit oh bella! nec desinebat dicere: oh bella! oh bella! Unde Episcopus illico rem intellexit, et risum continere nequivit." — *De Sollicitatione,* n. 319.

40. "10. An confessarius incidat in poenas constitutionis Apostolicae contra sollicitantes, si sollicitet mulierem in aliis sacramentis, scilicet baptismi, matrimonii, et sit denuntiandus et denuntiatus possit ab Inquisitoribus puniri. Quoad utrumque articulum censuerunt opinionem negativam esse probabilem." — S. C. S. Off., decr. 11 febr. 1661 — Ballerini-Palmieri, *Opus Theologicum,* V, 583, footnote (a); Cf. also Cappello, *De Poenitentia,* n. 670, 4; St. Alphonsus, *Theologia Moralis,* lib. VI, n. 684; Coronata, *Institutiones,* IV, 541; Michael Benger, *Pastoraltheologie* (3 vols., Regensburg, 1863), III, 434, n. 1.

41. C. Ioannes Ferreres, *Casus Conscientiae* (2 vols., Barcinone: Eugenius Subirana, 1926), II, 369, *Casus,* XXXII; Iorio, *Compendium,* II, n. 582 bis, *Resolves* 2°; Raffaele Salucci, *Il Diritto Penale secondo il Codice di Diritto Canonico* (2 vols. in 1, Subiaco: Tipographia del Monasteri, 1926-1930), II, n. 312 (hereafter cited *Il Diritto Penale*); Cipollini, *De Censuris,* p. 127; Rota *Enchiridion,* n. 394.

the crime that was denounced. It is equally apparent that whenever a priest is falsely denounced of complicity *in re turpi qua sacerdos* and not *qua confessarius* the delict of false denunciation cannot be present.[42]

Not only priests who are possessed of faculties to hear confessions are capable of committing the crime of solicitation if they are in the circumstances outlined by the Constitution *"Sacramentum Poenitentiae,"* but also priests without jurisdiction can commit this crime if they place themselves in the same circumstances.[43]

If a deacon, a subdeacon, a minor cleric, or a lay person should simulate the office of confessor and solicit while acting as an imposter, the crime of solicitation could not be committed.[44] There is no ecclesiastical law that imposes an obligation on the so-called penitent to denounce these imposters. An interpreter, even though he be a priest, who solicits the confessor's penitent, is not comprehended in the law and need not be denounced with a view to escaping the censure of excommunication.[45] Since the factual crime

42. Cf. Pruemmer, *Manuale Theologiae Moralis,* III, n. 468, 2; Rota, *Enchiridion,* n. 104, 6°; Jone, *Gesetzbuch,* II, 126, a); Cappello, *De Poenitentia,* n. 670, 4; Sole, *De Delictis et Poenis,* n. 416, 2°; Cerato, *Censurae Vigentes,* n. 79, c.

43. "5. An sacerdos carens iurisdictione, si sollicitat in confessione poenitentem, sit denuntiandus? Censuerunt [qualificatores] esse denuntiandum et opinionem negativum non esse probabilem." — S.C.S. Off., decr., 11 febr. 1661 — Ballerini-Palmieri, *Opus Theologicum,* V, 583, footnote (a); Cf. also Const. *"Sacramentum Poenitentiae,"* § 2, Document V in the Code.

44. Cf. Cappello, *De Poenitentia,* n. 690, 4°; Rota, *Enchiridion,* nn. 255, 334; Coronata, *Institutiones,* IV, 564; *ibid.,* IV, 540; D'Annibale, *Summula,* III, n. 365; Ballerini-Palmieri, *Opus Theologicum,* V. n. 1091, 3.

45. "6. An interpres, si sollicitat in confessione poenitentem, est denunciandus? Censuerunt opinionem negativam non carere probabilitate; habita scilicet ratione solius Bullae Pontificiae, non iuris naturae." — S. C.S. Off., decr. 11, febr. — Ballerini-Palmieri, *Opus Theologicum,* V. 583, footnote, (a); Cf also Antonius Arregui, *Summarium Theologiae Moralis ad Recentem Codicem Iuris Canonici Accomodatum* (11. ed., Bilbao: El Mensajero Del Corazon de Jesus, 1930), n. 653, b (hereafter cited *Summarium*); Coronata, *Institutiones,* IV, 565; *ibid.,* IV, 540; Cappello, *De Poenitentia,* n. 690, 4.

of solicitation is not comprehended in the law when a deacon, a subdeacon, a minor cleric, a lay person, or an interpreter is guilty of solicitation in a feigned confession, the false denunciation of any of these persons will not constitute the crime of false denunciation. No penalties will be incurred if such a false denunciation is attempted.[45a]

2. The Circumstances In Which Solicitation Can Occur.

a. During A Sacramental Confession.

The crime of solicitation is not considered as committed unless the grave sin of impurity is committed during the administering of the sacrament of penance or in situations which have a close connection with confession. The very first circumstance referred to in the Constitution "*Sacramentum Poenitentiae*" is that which associates the impure act with sacramental confession itself (*in actu sacramentalis confessionis*).[46] This phrase has been universally interpreted as pointing to the time elapsed between the initial blessing imparted by the confessor and the final blessing in the absolution, exclusive of the prayer, *Passio*.[47] The condition denoted by the phrase *in actu sacramentalis confessionis* is fulfilled even if the absolution was refused or deferred, as long as the penitent began the act of confession with the intention to seek forgiveness.[48]

b. Immediately Before Or Immediately After A Confession.

The provocation to sins of impurity will constitute the crime of solicitation if it occurs immediately before or immediately after a sacramental confession. The adverb "immediately," though used only once in the Constitution "*Sacramentum Poenitentiae,*" and though not directly connected with the word *ante,* has nevertheless been accepted to modify the word "*ante*" as well as the word "*post.*"

45a. Rota, *Enchiridion,* n. 104, 3°.
46. Document V, § 2, in the Code.
47. Cf. Rota, *Enchiridion,* n. 268; Berardi, *De Sollicitatione,* (2. ed., 1897), nn. 101-102; Coronata, *Institutiones,* IV, 541.
48. Cf. Cerato, *De Delicto,* n. 41; Berardi, *op. cit., loc. cit.;* Cappello, *De Poenitentia,* n. 672; De Smet, *De Absolutione,* n. 72; Iorio, *Compendium,* II, n. 576, *Quaer.* 1°, b.

Since a penal law is considered, a strict interpretation is given to the phrase, "*vel ante vel immediate post confessionem.*"[49] If the confessor was engaged in other activities between the confession and the eventual provocation to sins against the sixth commandment, or vice versa, the crime of solicitation is in the law not considered as present under such divergent circumstances.[50]

If a confessor continues to hear three or four additional confessions after having heard the confession of penitent *A*, the element associated with the phrase *immediate post confessionem* will no longer be verified when he solicits *A*. In such an instance the crime of solicitation cannot result, provided that the solicitation does not take place in a confessional. The crime of solicitation is not contemplated in the law when the confessor, after hearing penitent *A's* confession, proceeds immediately to solicit *B*, but not under the circumstances delineated in the Constitution "*Sacramentum Poenitentiae.*" The phrase, *post confessionem,* refers to a sacramental confession which in the case as contemplated here is associated only with *A*, but not with *B*.[51]

Granted that no provocation to sins of the flesh occurred, if either penitent *A* or penitent *B* falsely reports that the confessor was guilty of solicitation under the conditions just discussed, the delict of false denunciation is not committed.

c. On The Occasion Of A Confession.

The third circumstance in which the sin of solicitation becomes a crime of solicitation is that which contemplates the occasion of a confession (*occasione confessionis*). This presupposes that the penitent has a serious intention to confess and to receive sacramental absolution, seeks a confessor who consents to hear the confession

49. Canon 19. Leges quae poenam statuunt, . . . strictae subsunt interpretationi.

50. Cf. Berardi, *De Sollicitatione,* (2. ed., 1897), nn. 103, 104; Cerato, *De Delicto,* n. 43; St. Alphonsus, *Theologia Moralis,* lib. VI, n. 677; Rota, *Enchiridion,* n. 279; Cappello, *De Poenitentia,* n. 674, 4°; Coronata, *Institutiones,* IV, 542; Iorio, *Compendium,* II, n. 575, *Quaer.* 1°, b); Jone, *Moral Theology,* n. 594, 3, b.

51. Cf. Cappello, *De Poenitentia,* n. 688; Coronata, *Institutiones,* IV, 544; Rota, *Enchiridion,* n. 285; Iorio, *Compendium,* II, n. 582, *Quaer.* 2°.

and proceeds to a confessional, but instead of administering the sacrament of penance commences to solicit the prospective penitent before the confession is begun.[52]

The crime of solicitation is not perpetrated if the penitent makes arrangements at some earlier time to go to confession at a specified hour later on and then is solicited on the occasion when this appointment is made for the subsequent confession.[53] The confessor cannot be stigmatized with the crime of solicitation who did not consent to hear the confession when the penitent requested that it be heard presently, but seduced the prospective penitent to sinful actions.[54] The reason alleged by Ballerini (1805-1881) — Palmieri (1829-1909) is that the solicitation did not take place *occasione confessionis*, but *occasione petitionis confessionis*.[55] The latter element is not comprised in the law as constituting a crime of solicitation. If the request is made in a confessional and the provocation occurs there, the crime of solicitation is present because one of the other phrases of the Constitution *"Sacramentum Poenitentiae,"* namely the phrase *"in confessionali,"* specifies the action as an act of solicitation for the reason that it occurred in the confessional.[56]

The crime of solicitation is not verified when a person requests

52. Coronata, *Institutiones,* IV, 543, 544; Cerato, *De Delicto,* n. 45; Cappello, *De Poenitentia,* n. 679, 6°; Noldin-Schmitt, *De Sacramentis,* n. 376, 3; Ioannes Ferreres, *Compendium Theologiae Moralis* (14. ed., 2 vols., Barcinone: Eugenius Subirana, 1928), II, n. 698 (hereafter cited *Compendium*).
53. "4. An confessarius qui foeminam in confessionario dicentem, se velle in crastinum confiteri, sollicitat et a confessione dissuadet, sit denuntiandus? Responsum: Si sollicitatio fiat extra locum confessionis et absque praetextu confessionis censuerunt [qualificatores] negativam opinionem esse probabilem: secus si in confessionario, seu in loco confessionis." — S. C. S. Off. decr. 11 febr. 1661 — Ballerini-Palmieri, *Opus Theologicum,* V, 583, footnote (a); cf. also Jone, *Moral Theology,* n. 594, c); Coronata, *Institutiones,* IV, 545; Noldin-Schmitt, *De Sacramentis,* n. 376, 3.
54. Cf. Coronata, *op. cit.,* IV, 545.
55. *Opus Theologicum,* V, n. 1098. Noldin-Schmitt (*De Sacramentis,* n. 376, 3, a) do not agree to this doctrine. They consider such a provocation to sin to be a true crime of solicitation.
56. Document V, § 1, in the Code; S. C. S. Off., decr., 11 febr. 1661 n. 4.

a priest to hear another penitent's confession and in connection with his request the confessor uses the occasion to sin with the person who makes the appointment.[57] The circumstance connoted by the phrase "*occasione confessionis*" in the latter instance stands in relation to a different penitent, and not to the person who makes the arrangements for the confession. As is evident, if the crime of solicitation in the cases considered is falsely attributed to an innocent confessor, the delict of false denunciation could not be committed nor could the penalties be incurred.

d. On The Pretext Of Hearing Confession.

The sin of solicitation becomes a crime of solicitation when it takes place under the pretext of hearing confessions, *praetextu confessionis.*[58] Under the circumstance connoted by the phrase "*occasione confessionis*" there was postulated a sacramental confession as requested by the penitent. After expressing willingness to proceed with the confession, the confessor solicited instead. Under the circumstance associable with the phrase "*praetextu confessionis*" the invitation to hear confession is suggested by the confessor with the view that he can disguise the subsequent provocation to sin under the pretense that he is hearing a confession.[59] It presupposes a deception perpetrated by the confessor who allures the penitent into believing that the confessor will hear the penitent's confession. Other bystanders, too, may be deceived in so far as they are led to believe that a confession is in progress. The circumstance inherent in the phrase "*praetextu confessionis*" is not only verified when a confessor invites the penitent to the confessional, but also when he asks the members of a family to leave the sick room in order that, as he piously alleges, he may hear the sick person's

57. Cappello, *De Poenitentia,* n. 680, 8°, d.
58. Const. "*Sacramentum Poenitentiae,*" § 1, Document V, in the Code.
59. "Dicitur *occasione confessionis,* quando confessarius vel poenitens incitat ad confessionem veram; *praetextu,* vero quando ad confessionem fictam." — St. Alphonsus, *Theologia Moralis,* lib. VI, n. 678 (Italics in original); Cf. also Ballerini-Palmieri, *Opus Theologicum,* V, n. 1096; Iorio, *Compendium,* II, n. 576, *Quaer.* 1, b, 4); Coronata, *Institutiones,* IV, 546; Cerato, *De Delicto,* n. 46; Cappello, *De Poenitentia,* n. 681, 1°.

confession, but proceeds to solicit the penitent after they have departed.[60]

e. In A Confessional.

The last circumstance in which the crime of solicitation can occur is

1. in a confessional;
2. in a place permanently designated for confessions;
3. in a place temporarily chosen for confessions.

A sacramental confession however must be simulated in any one of these three places before the solicitation can be designated a crime.[61]

Canons 908 and 910 give the regulations concerning the location, structure, and necessity of confessionals. The specially constructed confessionals are the ones alluded to by the phrase *in confessionali.* Other places permanently destined for hearing confessions are the special rooms set aside for the confessions of penitents that are hard of hearing, the sacristies, parlors of religious institutes, and various other places designated for hearing the confessions of convalescents, invalids, or prisoners.[62]

The phrase *"in alio loco ad confessiones audiendas electo"* refers to the place temporarily assigned for confessions on the occasion of a great concourse of people who assemble on a pilgrimage, for a mission, or for a similar gathering. In such emergencies any suitable place may be destined for confession. The open road and field may be used.[63]

Before the crime of solicitation can be said to be complete in any of these places permanently or temporarily designated for the

60. Jone, *Moral Theology,* n. 595, d); Ballerini-Palmieri, *Opus Theologicum,* V, n. 1102, 3°; Cappello, *De Poenitentia,* n. 681, 4°; Berardi, *De Sollicitatione,* (2. ed., 1897), n. 149.
61. Const. *"Sacramentum Poenitentiae,"* § 1, — Document V in the Code. "Requiritur *duplex* conditio *simul,* scil. circumstantia loci, et simulata confessio." — Cappello, *De Poenitentia,* n. 683, 5, 1°; Noldin-Schmitt, *De Sacramentis,* n. 375, 5.
62. Berardi, *De Sollicitatione,* (2. ed., 1897), n. 155; Cerato, *De Delicto,* n. 47.
63. Jone, *Moral Theology,* n. 595, e; Cerato, *De Delicto,* n. 47; Coronata, *Institutiones,* IV, 550; Noldin-Schmitt, *De Sacramentis,* n. 375, 5.

hearing of confessions the external signs of simulating a confession must be in evidence.[64] The simulation must be definitely established, especially when a private room or a sacristy is used for the hearing of confessions. Any positive act which leaves the impression that a confession is in progress is sufficient. Among these signs are the blessing of the priest, the kneeling posture of the penitent, the bowed head of the priest, and so on.[65] If there is no manifest simulation of a sacramental confession, even though the penitent reports calumniously that the crime of solicitation occurred, the delict of false denunciation is not committed. The element of simulation must go hand in hand with the provocation to the sins of impurity before the crime of solicitation is understood.

Before canons 894 or 2363 become juridically operative the crime of false denunciation as it is comprehended in the law must be fully realized. If a *sin* of solicitation is falsely reported, but not as having been committed under any of the five circumstances that have a close connection with confession, the calumny would constitute simply a *sin* of false denunciation, but not also the *crime* of false denunciation. The guilt or innocence of the confessor on previous occasions is not to be considered when false denunciations are reported.

If a confessor had committed the crime of solicitation as contemplated in the Constitution *"Sacramentum Poenitentiae"* the penitent will be expected to denounce him in consequence of the prescriptions of canon 904 and in order to escape the threat of excommunication enacted in canon 2368, § 2. The penitent, upon learning of this obligation, is to approach the local Ordinary or his delegate, and make a judicial report of the crime of solicitation.

64. "15. An sit denuntiandus confessarius, qui sedens in confessionario, sollicitat mulierem stantem ante confessionarium, non simulando confessionem? Censuerunt, opinionem negativam non carere probabilitate." — S. C. S. Off., decr. 11 febr. 1661 — Ballerini-Palmieri, *Opus Theologicum,* V, 683, footnote (a).

65. Iorio, *Compendium,* II, n. 576, *Quaer.* 1, b) 5; Coronata, *Institutiones,* IV, 553; Ferreres, *Compendium,* II, n. 701; Ballerini-Palmieri, *Opus Theologicum,* V, n. 1108; Cappello, *De Poenitentia,* nn. 685, 7°, 683, 5, 1°.

If however the penitent vouches that the crime occurred twice, knowing that the confessor was innocent on one of the two occasions, the penitent is indeed fulfilling the obligation mentioned in canons 904 and 2368, § 2, but he is at the same time violating either canon 894 or canon 2363 by denouncing a false crime. Though the confessor is guilty before the law in one instance, he is innocent in the other. The false denunciation is complete according to the meaning of either canon 894 or of canon 2363, and the respective penalties will be in force.[66]

Whenever a doubt of law exists whether an action of the confessor is comprehended in the law against solicitation, and the penitent, basing his accusation on that action, falsely denounces him of solicitation, the norm of canon 2219, namely, *in poenis benignior est interpretatio facienda,* is to prevail. In effect, then, the informer is held excused from the penalty consequent upon any act of false denunciation. It is a mooted question whether the priest is guilty of solicitation if he allures a penitent to sins of sex outside of confession after he has learned of the penitent's proclivities for these sins through the hearing of his or her confession. The extrinsic weight of authority todays favors the milder view, namely, that such an act of misconduct is not to be regarded as an act of solicitation which stands penalized in the law.[67]

66. Jone, *Gesetzbuch,* II, 126, b) ; Santi, *Praelectiones,* lib. V, Appendix, p. 232, III, 1°; Hubert Louis Motry, *Diocesan Faculties According to the Code of Canon Law,* The Catholic University of America Canon Law Studies, n. 16 (Washington, D.C.: The Catholic University of America, 1922), p. 110 (hereafter cited *Diocesan Faculties*) ; Cappello, *De Poenitentia,* n. 607, 6°; Many, "De Peccato Sollicitationis," — *Le Canoniste,* XVIII (1895), 720, 2°; Cerato, *Censurae Vigentes,* n. 79, h, 2, c; Blat, *Commentarium,* lib. III, Pars I, 260.
67. This opinion is defended by Vermeersch-Creusen (*Epitome,* II, n. 190), Jone (*Moral Theology,* n. 594, c), Cappello (*De Poenitentia,* n. 675, 3), Cerato (*De Delicto,* n. 76), Arregui (*Summarium,* n. 652, B, 2, c), Augustine (*Commentary,* IV, 318), Noldin-Schmitt (*De Sacramentis,* n. 376, 3, b), Augustinus Lehmkuhl (1834-1918) (*Theologia Moralis* [11. ed., 2 vols., Freiburg im Breisgau: Herder, 1910], II, n. 975) and others. Coronata (*Institutiones,* IV, 544 footnote 5) cites many pre-Code authors who defended the opposite view. St. Alphonsus (*Theologia Moralis,* lib. VI, n. 678, *dubitatio* 2) cites many

In the event that a penitent falsely denounces a confessor as having made use of confessional knowledge to seduce him or her to a sin *in re turpi,* there exists a doubt of law whether the crime of solicitation was reported. The milder opinion will prevail and the penitent will stand free of all penalties. The same solution holds in all other doubts of law regarding the existence of the crime of solicitation.

Article 4. The Total False Denunciation

Whenever a priest, when he acted as a confessor or *de facto* was in one of the circumstances in which a crime of solicitation is possible, is falsely reported as guilty of solicitation, the informer commits the crime of false denunciation. This form of denunciation can be called a total false denunciation.[68] This state of affairs is true also when a trivial or an imprudent action or word of the confessor is exaggerated to such a degree that the specifications of the law with reference to what constitutes an act of false denunciation of solicitation become realized in the particular case.[69]

Iorio cites an example wherein a confessor may have given correct advice to his penitent, though it could be readily distorted or misinterpreted and the confessor accused of solicitation. He points to the case in which a penitent who is determined to commit a sin of adultery is dissuaded by his confessor from committing the kind of sin which is branded with the stigma of a double malice *peccatum*

more. Cappello, and Arregui (*locc. citt.*) and D'Annibale (*Summula,* III, n. 367) state that the *praxis* of the Holy Office demands that the confessors who solicit under such circumstances are to be denounced. The reason that the majority of commentators denies such an obligation is based on the fact that no one needs to incriminate himself. The penitent would, by denouncing the confessor, reveal the weakness to which he is prone.

68. Cf. Berardi, *De Sollicitatione,* nn. 349, 359.

69. "Talis [accusatio calumniosa] esse totaliter, . . . si Sacerdos recte se gessisset vel ad summum levem imprudentiam commisisset; et nihilominus denuntiaretur, sive delictum penitus confingendo, sive reticendo contextum sermonis aliasve circumstantias, ex quibus eum innocentem esse vel de levi dumtaxat imprudentia accusari posse dignosceretur." — Berardi, *loc cit.*; Cf. also Rota, *Enchiridion,* n. 104, 5°.

qualificatum and is implored to resort instead, if he must, to a less serious sin against the same commandment. Apart from questioning the wisdom or prudence which prompted such advice, in the light of all the circumstances to be considered in the case one can admit that objectively the confessor's act was not sinful. He did nothing to involve himself in the crime of solicitation. By passing over the reasons that influenced the confessor to suggest the advice as he gave it a spiteful penitent could readily succeed in making a false deposition.[70]

In almost every manual of moral theology which deals with the sin of onanism modern moralists tolerate a wife's material co-operation in her husband's practice of the natural mode of onanism,[71] if there is a moderately grave reason for doing so, *ex causa mediocriter gravi*. Among the reasons that are recognized as moderately grave are the danger of incontinence, the preservation of domestic peace, and the danger of exposing herself or her husband to the sin of adultery.[72] If the circumstances warrant the act whereby the confessor informs his penitent, with caution and discretion of this accepted doctrine, no solicitation could be attributed to him.

Dalpiaz presents the instance of a poorly educated confessor, who advised his penitent that natural onanism was permissable. Such a confessor, though guilty of serious negligence in failing to acquire the necessary knowledge for his proper functioning as a confessor, was not guilty of solicitation. The delict of solicitation was not present for the reason that there was absent that degree of moral imputability which would have sufficed to make the act

70. *Compendium,* II, n. 579, *Quaer.* 6°.
71. "Actus copulae naturali modo inchoatur, sed inordinatio inter vel post actum accedit; ita si vir ante effusionem se retrahit et semen effundit; vel si mulier post actum rite factum lotionibus semen expellit vel destruit. . ." — Noldin-Schmitt, *De Sexto Praecepto,* n. 72.
72. Cf. Josephus Aertnys, *Theologia Moralis iuxta Doctrinam S Alphonsi Mariae de Ligorio* (11. ed., nunc tertio ex integro recognovit C. A. Damen, 2 vols., Taurinorum Augustae: Marietti, 1928), II, n. 896, *Quaer.* 1 (hereafter cited *Theologia Moralis*); Noldin-Schmitt, *op. cit.,* n. 74, 2; Arregui, *Summarium,* n. 815, b; Jone, *Moral Theology,* n. 758, II, 1.

mortally sinful beyond all doubt.[73] The confessor was not motivated by a deliberate will to violate the law. He strove to give counsel, even though it eventuated as an erroneous counsel. Since there was no delictual intent to incite the penitent to sins of the flesh, no crime of solicitation was committed by him. It is clear, however, that the confessor sinned gravely *ex ignorantia graviter culpabili,* and hence he is to be denounced to the local Ordinary, not as guilty of solicitation, but as a priest inadequately prepared to hear confessions.[74]

If the circumstances that occasioned the advice as given by the confessors in the foregoing three instances are not revealed to the judge when the penitents denounce their confessors of the crime of solicitation, then these penitents must be regarded as guilty of making false denunciations. By maliciously ignoring the reasons that led the confessors to act as they did in the advice they gave the informers then must be regarded as wilfully defaming their confessors.

Article 5. The Partial False Denunciation

A. Reporting A Doubtful Crime Of Solicitation As A Certain Crime.

In a partial false denunciation some of the elements that constitute the crime of solicitation are present, but not to the degree that warrants them as sufficient for a rightful denunciation of the confessor.[75] When the conduct of the confessor is such that his motives can indeed be questioned, but nevertheless no certainty can be arrived at, then there is no obligation to denounce him. In such instances the good name of the confessor is in possession. It cannot rightfully be put into jeopardy by means of a report which brands him as guilty of solicitation when it is no more than

73. "De abusu matrimonii et crimine sollicitationis." — *Apollinaris,* VI, (1933), 248; Cf. canon 2202, §§ 1, 3.

74. Cf. canon 887, § 2.

75. ". . . [Accusatio] esset calumniosa *partialiter* si delictum fuisset dubium et nihilominus daretur ut certum: vel si (quamvis Sacerdos certe et graviter deliquisset) exaggerationes superadderentur;" — Berardi, *De Sollicitatione,* n. 349, (Italics in original).

probable that his act may have been of such a nature.[76] Thus, when authors speak of a confessor seeking to seduce a penitent *ad actus leves* against modesty or purity, then the crime of solicitation as contemplated by the law is not perpetrated.[77]

Cappello does aver that it is difficult in many instances to discern whether the confessor resorted to coquettish signs for the sake of seducing his penitent to slight indecencies (*ad actus leves*), or employed them as a means (*per actus leves*) to seduce the penitent to graver sins against purity.[78] Canon 2200 §§ 1, 2, offers some guiding principles. In the commission of an external violation of a law, *dolus,* or the deliberate will to violate the law, is presumed. That norm however is not applicable with absolute aptness when a confessor places lightly sinful acts to tempt his penitent *ad actus leves* against the virtue of purity. By exaggerating the slight indiscretions to make them appear as grave sins, or to say they were resorted to for the sake of seducing the penitent to graver sins (*per actus leves*), or by representing doubtfully sinful indiscretions as certainly sinful actions, the denunciators definitely invite the penalties which the law inflicts upon false denunciators.

B. Falsifying The Circumstances.

When a provocation to sins *ad turpia* has occurred, but not during a sacramental confession or in any of the circumstances in which a crime of solicitation can take place, and yet a person falsely supplies the circumstances in his act of false denunciation, the delict is complete. If a factual sin of misconduct which sought to accomplish a seduction to sins against the sixth commandment of God did occur outside a sacramental confession or outside the circumstances closely related to confession, but the penitent falsely reports that during her last confession her confessor invited her to his home where the sin took place, whereas no such invitation

76. Cerato, *De Delicto,* n. 38; Cappello, *De Poenitentia,* n. 667, 2; Rota, *Enchiridion,* n. 311.
77. Cf. Cerato, *De Delicto,* n. 39; Buoceroni, *De C. "Sac. Poenit.",* n. 22; Coronata, *Institutiones,* IV, 531; Cappello, *De Poenitentia,* n. 668, 3, 2°; Jone, *Moral Theology,* n. 593, 2.
78. *Op. cit.,* n. 668, 3, 3°.

was extended, or it was indeed extended, but for an altogether honorable motive, then the delict of a false denunciation is committed. The circumstantial elements associated with the misconduct are falsified in such instances, though the *sin* of solicitation as such truly existed. Berardi is the only author whom the writer has discovered as recognizing the falsification of the circumstances as a factor which properly constitutes the crime of a false denunciation of the crime of solicitation.[79]

All modern authors who were consulted, except Ferreres, pass over this observation and speak only of the falsification of the sin of impurity. Ferreres refers to the falsification of the circumstances, but denies that that would meet the qualifications in law to constitute the crime of false denunciation. He reasons that, since the priest in such an instance is neither a confessor nor constituted in any of the circumstances postulated by the Constitution *"Sacramentum Poenitentiae"* for the commission of the crime of solicitation, it is impossible for him to commit a crime of factual solicitation. Accordingly then, it is impossible for a calumniator to attribute to such a priest a crime of solicitation.[80]

However, a falsification of the circumstances fulfills the requirement of the law that prohibits the false accusation of the crime of solicitation just as substantially as does the falsifying of the sin of impurity itself. The crime of solicitation consists of two constitutive elements. It embraces not merely the commission of a sin against purity, but its commission must also occur in one of the

79. ". . . [Accusatio] esset calumniosa *partialiter* si . . . delictum sine ulla criminosa relatione ad Sacramentum Poenitentiae commissum fuisset, et nihilominus (quasi Sacerdos verus sollicitator iuxta Apostolicarum Constitutionum clausula extitisset) relatio ista confingeretur. Casus esset, v.g. si Sacerdos extra confessionem poenitentem suam tentasset, eaque denuntiationem faceret dicendo dic et simpliciter, Confessarium in confessione illam ad domum suam (ubi tentata fuit) invitasse, dum revera haec invitatio vel nullo modo locum habuerit, vel evidenter ex alio fine prorsus honesto facta fuerit." — *De Sollicitatione,* n. 349 (Italics in original).

80. Cf. *Casus Conscientiae,* II, Casus XXXII. In that *Casus* Ferreres tries to establish that the word *sacerdos* of canon 894 is synonymous with the word *confessarius* of canon 2363.

five circumstances specified in the Constitution "*Sacramentum Poenitentiae.*" The crime of solicitation is not perpetrated unless these two components are present simultaneously. The deduction of Berardi that the falsification of the circumstances can constitute the delict of false denunciation in equal measure with the falsification of the sin of seduction is in perfect harmony with the definition of false denunciation.

C. Falsifying Both Component Elements.

No author speaks of the possibility of a false denunciation resulting from the calumnious statement that an innocent priest who is in no way exercising the ministry of a confessor, is accused of having been guilty of solicitation in a sacramental confession. In such an instance both the sin of impurity and the circumstances in which it supposedly occurred are fictitious. In reality two falsehoods are told in the accusation. Both of these falsehoods, however, form but one sin, in so far as the two conjointly constitute the crime of false denunciation.

Iorio observes that the word *confessarius* of canon 2363 is to receive a strict interpretation.[81] By that assertion he indirectly implies that the simultaneous falsification of both elements can constitute the delict of false denunciation. The proposition that the transgression mentioned in canon 894, which punishes the false accusation of an innocent priest (*sacerdos*) of the crime of solicitation, differs from the crime of falsely denouncing an innocent confessor (*confessarius*) of the crime is directly based on the supposition that a falsification of the circumstances or also the simultaneous falsification of both component elements will constitute the delict of false denunciation.

It can be stated that a priest (*sacerdos*), whether he possesses or whether he lacks faculties for the hearing of confessions, can become the object of a false denunciation as well as a confessor (*confessarius*). This is possible:

a. if the priest is falsely accused of having sought to seduce a person to commit grave sins of sex, and

81. *Compendium,* II, n. 582 bis, Notanda, I, c.

b. if what is falsely charged is reported as having occurred during a sacramental confession, immediately before or immediately after a confession, on the occasion or the pretext of hearing the confession, or in connection with the simulated hearing of a confession in a confessional, or in any other place assigned for the administration of the sacrament of penance.

The falsehood that extends to both elements postulated for the crime of solicitation perfectly fulfills the concept of a false denunciation. An innocent priest (*sacerdos*) is falsely accused in such an instance of having committed the crime of solicitation.

A crime of false denunciation is in effect:

1. when the act of the attempted seduction to sins of sex is falsified, the while the circumstances associated with the represented act are verified;
2. when the circumstantial factors are falsified, the while the sin of seduction associated with the represented circumstances is factual;
3. when both constitutive elements, the act of provocation to sins of impurity and also the circumstances associating it with the sacrament of penance are falsified.

Oversight of the fact that that falsification of both constitutive elements which are postulated for the delict of solicitation could constitute the delict of false denunciation points perhaps to the reason why only a few commentators have entertained the conjecture that a distinction between canon 894 and canon 2363 is plausible, in so far, namely, that canon 894 contrasts the word priest (*sacerdos*) with the word confessor (*confessarius*) in canon 2363.

In the light of the consideration that the crime of solicitation is perpetrated when there has been an attempt to seduce a penitent to grave sins of impurity in a sacramental confession or in any other of the circumstances outlined by the *clausulae* of the Constitution *"Sacramentum Poenitentiae"* the deduction can be made that a false denunciation exists in each of the following instances:

1. When an act of provocation to sins of impurity is falsely imputed to an innocent confessor (*confessarius*) while he heard a sacramental confession, or while he functioned in any of the circumstances specified in the Constitution "*Sacramentum Poenitentiae.*"
2. When the same sin is falsified and attributed to a priest (*sacerdos*) who has no faculties for imparting a valid absolution, but who nevertheless attempted to hear confession.
3. When slight indiscretions of the confessor (*confessarius*) are exaggerated to make them appear as grave sins *in re turpi.*
4. When a suspicious act of the confessor (*confessarius*) is not recognized as an evident sign of solicitation but is falsely reported as an evident sign.
5. When a sin of impurity actually occurred outside the restricted circumstances necessarily and essentially postulated for the crime of solicitation, but the conditions and circumstances as designated in the *clausulae* are falsified for the sake of bringing the alleged act of attempted seduction within the sphere wherein it is recognized as the crime of solicitation. In this case a priest (*sacerdos*), irrespective of whether he possessed faculties for the hearing of confessions or not, is falsely accused *qua confessarius.*
5. When both the alleged provocation to sins of sex and also the circumstances in which the provocation supposedly took place are falsified. Here again the priest (*sacerdos*) is falsely denounced *qua confessarius.*

CHAPTER III

THE QUESTION OF TWO DISTINCT TRANSGRESSIONS

Article 1. General Observations

An overwhelming number of canonists defends the view that the sin reserved by canon 894 to the Holy See is identical with the crime that is penalized in canon 2363 with a *latae sententiae* excommunication reserved *speciali modo* to the Holy See.[1] By calling it the more common opinion Coronata implicitly admits

1. De Smet, *De Absolutione,* nn. 121, 143; Eichmann, *Das Strafrecht,* p. 196; Coronata, *Institutiones,* IV, 503 and footnote 3; *ibid.,* IV, 574, and footnote 5 (continued from page 573); Wernz-Vidal, *Ius Canonicum,* VII, n. 500; Sipos, *Enchiridion,* n. 246, 4°; Jone *Gesetzbuch,* II, 126, 127; Augustine, *Commentary,* IV, 318, 319; VIII, 424; Cappello, *De Poenitentia,* nn. 604, 2°, 605, 5°, 701, 6°; Felix Cappello, *Tractatus Canonico-moralis de Censuris iuxta Codicem Iuris Canonici* (3. ed., Taurinorum Augustae: Marietti, 1933), n. 291, 2° (hereafter cited *De Censuris*); H. A. Ayrinhac, and P. J. Lydon, *Penal Legislation in the New Code of Canon Law* (revised edition, New York: Benziger, 1936), n. 324, d (hereafter cited *Penal Legislation*); De Meester, *Compendium,* III, Pars II, 268; Chelodi, *Ius Poenale,* n. 88; Cipollini, *De Censuris,* pp. 128, 129; Nicholaus Farrugia, *De Casuum Conscientiae Reservatione iuxta Codicem Iuris Canonici* (2. ed., Augustae Taurinorum-Romae: Marietti, 1922), pp. 14, 15, 55; H. J. Davis, *Moral and Pastoral Theology* (4 vols., London: Sheed and Ward, 1935), III, 406; Sole, *De Delictis et Poenis,* n. 416; Pruemmer, *Manuale Theologiae Moralis,* III, n. 513; Cocchi, *De Delictis et Poenis,* nn. 221, c, 225; Claeys Bouuaert-Simenon, *Manuale,* II, n. 142; Salucci, *Il Diritto Penale,* II, n. 314; Vermeersch-Creusen, *Epitome,* III, n. 565; J. B. Pighi, *Cursus Theologiae Moralis* (4. ed., 4 vols., Veronae: in Via Croce Verde, 1926), III, 217; Genicot-Salsmans, *Institutiones,* II, n. 400; Camillus Colli-Lanzi, *Theologia Moralis Universa,* (3 vols., Taurini-Romae: Marietti, 1927-1928), III, 326; Pie Joseph Mothon, *Institutions Canoniques a l'Usage des Curies Episcopales, du Clerge Paroissial, et des Familles Religieuses* (3 vols., Lille-Bruges: Desclee, 1922-1924), II, nn. 1930, 3039; Joannes Cavigioli, *De Censuris Latae Sententiae Quae in Codice Iuris Canonici Continentur Commentariolum* (Torino: Libreria Editrice Internazionale, 1919), p. 91 (hereafter cited *De Censuris*); J. B. Raus, *Institutiones Canonicae iuxta Novum Codicem Iuris pro Scholis vel ad Usum Privatum synthetice*

that the opposite view has at least some merit.[2] In the face of this great array of authors there are nevertheless some canonists who venture to say that two separate and distinct transgressions, each sanctioned with its own penalty, are involved.[3]

Iorio and Merkelbach state that no one can be constrained to admit that the two canons treat of the same moral evil under

Redactae (2. ed., Lugduni-Parisiis: Typis Emmanuelis Vitte, 1931), pp. 441, 718; Ferreres, *Compendium,* II, nn. 698, *Quaer.* 12, 672, *Quaer.* 5, R. 2; Udalricus Beste, *Introductio in Codicem,* (2. ed., Collegeville, Minn.: St. John Abbey, 1944), p. 961; Edward V. Dargin, *Reserved Cases According to the Code of Canon Law,* The Catholic University of America Canon Law Studies, n. 20 (Washington, D.C.: The Catholic University of America, 1924), p. 28 (hereafter cited *Reserved Cases*); Eduardus Regatillo, *Institutiones Iuris Canonici* (2 vols., Vol. II, *De Rebus, De Processibus, De Delictis et Poenis,* Sal Terrae: Santander, 1942), II, n. 1111 (hereafter cited *Institutiones*); Ludovicus Wouters, *Manuale Theologiae Moralis* (2 vols., Brugis: Beyaert, 1932-1933), II, n. 427 (hereafter cited *Manuale*).

2. *Institutiones,* IV, 503, footnote 3.

3. Motry, *Diocesan Faculties,* p. 112; Cerato, *De Delicto,* n. 129, 3°; Iorio, *Compendium,* II, n. 582 bis, Notanda I, b); Blat *Commentarium,* lib. III, Pars I, 260, lib. V, n. 204, c; Merkelbach, *Summa,* III, n. 643, C, b; n. 594, B; the anonymous writer in "Il Codice di Diritto Canonico: Riassunto e Diluzidationi," — *Il Monitore Ecclesiastico* (Romae, 1876-), XXXI (1919) [4. Series, Vol. I], 149; P. Michel, *Nouveau Code Canonique* (6. ed., Alger: Mission d'Afrique des Peres Blancs, Maison Caree, 1930), nn. 240, 490; Caesar Badii, *Institutiones Iuris Canonici* (3. ed., 2 vols., Vol. II, *De Rebus,* Florentiae: Libreria Editrice, 1921-1922), II, n. 368, d (hereafter cited *Institutiones*); Ad. Tanquerey, *Synopsis Theologiae Moralis et Pastoralis* (11. ed., 3 vols., Vol. I, *De Paenitentia, De Matrimonio et Ordine,* Parisiis-Tornaci: Desclee et Socii, 1930), I, n. 455, 1° and footnote 4 (hereafter cited *Synopsis*); Mario Pistocchi, *I Canoni Penali del Codice Ecclesiastico Esposti e Commentati* (Torino-Romae: Marietti, 1925), p. 211 (hereafter cited *I Canoni Penali*); Johann B. Haring (*Grundzuege des katholischen Kirchenrechts* [2 vols., Graz: Ulrich Mosers Buchhandlung, 1924], II, 993, in footnote 3) credits Hoeller-Mair as defending this view (*Pro Praxi Confessariorum,* n. 41), but he himself does not accept it; Martin Leitner, *Handbuch des katkolischen Kirchenrechts* (4 vols., Vol. IV *Sakramente,* Regensburg: Jos. Koesel and Friedrich Pustet, 1921), IV, 133.

the same aspect.[4] These two authors however disagree regarding the divergent aspects of the two canons. Merkelbach,[5] Motry,[6] Cerato,[7] Leitner,[8] and Tanquerey[9] interpret the word *denuntiaverit* of canon 2363 as pointing to a simple denunciation made to ecclesiastical superiors, whereas they accept the word *accusatur* of canon 894 as implying a judicial denunciation made to ecclesiastical judges. Blat[10] and the anonymous writer in *Il Monitore Ecclesiastico*[11] consider the formal distinction between the two canons to be founded in the observation that the denunciation in canon 894 is brought to ecclesiastical judges who receive the report as judges, while in canon 2363 they receive it as ecclesiastical superiors. Iorio stands alone in defending the view that the distinction is to be found in the deliberate choice of the word *sacerdos* in canon 894 as contrasted with the word *confessarius* in canon 2363.[12]

Article 2. The *FIRMO PRAESCRIPTO CAN.* 894 Argument

The only argument presented by the proponents of the opinion that the crime delineated in canon 2363, namely, that a false denunciation of an innocent confessor is brought to ecclesiastical superiors, is the same as the sin by which an innocent priest is reported to ecclesiastical judges, is the presence of the clause *firmo praescripto can.* 894 at the end of canon 2363. These words can hardly signify anything else, so they maintain, than that the false denunciation of an innocent confessor remains reserved *ratione sui* to the Apostolic See, even though the simultaneously annexed censure has ceased by absolution,[13] was never perhaps incurred because of ignorance, namely, as long as the ignorance was not

4. Cf. *Compendium,* II, n. 582 bis, Notanda I, b); *Summa,* III, nn. 643, C, b, 594, B.
5. *Summa,* III, n. 643, C, b.
6. *Diocesan Faculties,* p. 111,
7. *De Delicto,* n. 129, 1°-6°.
8. *Handbuch des katolischen Kirchenrechts,* IV, 133.
9. *Synopsis,* I, n. 455, footnote 4.
10. *Commentarium,* lib. III, Pars I, 260, and lib. V, n. 204, c.
11. *Loc. cit.*
12. *Compendium,* II, 417, footnote (3).
13. Cf. canon 2346, § 3.

affected, supine or crass,[14] or for some other reason in law was never contracted by the denunciator.[15]

All of the canonists who uphold the majority view, by implication if not by forthright statement, teach that a privileged confessor or an ordinary confessor who invokes the aid of canon 2254, §§ 1, 3 to absolve a penitent from the excommunication of canon 2363 cannot by operation of canon 2246, § 3[16] proceed to absolve the reserved sin. The confessor has to obtain additional faculties to absolve the reserved sin, or determine whether the law enacted in canon 900 or in canon 882 will supply him with the needed jurisdiction.[17] According to these canonists the presence of the phrase *firmo praescripto can.* 894 at the end of canon 2363 implies the reservation of the sin as mentioned in the latter canon not only *ratione censurae,* but also *ratione sui.*

The interpretation thus given to the clause *firmo praescripto can.* 894 can be countered with the contention that the reserved sin is in force only when the sin of canon 894 is committed in accordance with the concept and meaning of the law as specified in that canon. Canon 2363 legislates that if the conditions specified in it as constituting the crime of solicitation are verified, then a penalty of excommunication will *ipso facto* be incurred. The added clause *firmo praescripto can.* 894 indicates that, if perchance the conditions of canon 894 are fulfilled, the reservation of the sin will also be

14. Cf. canon 2229, § 1, § 3, 1°.
15. Canon 2230 excuses the impuberes from *latae sententiae* penalties. Canon 2227, § 2 exempts Cardinals from penal laws. Cf. Ferreres, *Compendium,* II, n. 672, *Quaer.* 5, R. 2; De Meester, *Compendium,* III, Pars, II, 268, g; Sole, *De Delictis et Poenis,* pp. 174, 346; Claeys Bouuaert-Simenon, *Manuale,* II, n. 142.
16. Reservatio censurae impedientis receptionem Sacramentorum importat reservationem peccati cui censura adnexa est; verum si quis a censura excusatur vel ab eadem fuit absolutus, reservatio peccati penitus cessat.
17. Cf. De Smet, *De Absolutione,* n. 143, Nota; Claeys Bouuaert-Simenon, *Manuale,* n. 142; *ibid.,* II, 125, footnote, (1); Aertnys-Damen, *Theologia Moralis,* III, 290, 265, 2°; P. Maroto, "De ignorantia quoad falsam delationem, qua sacerdos innocens accusatur de crimine sollicitationis," — *Apollinaris,* V (1932), 97, 98; Noldin-Schmitt, *De Sacramentis,* n 379, 6; H. Noldin-A. Schoenegger, *De Censuris* (24. ed., Oeniponte: Fel. Rauch: Pustet, 1931), n. 72, XIII.

in force. According to this writer's contention it will be demonstrated that the law in canon 2363 excommunicates a person who falsely incriminates an innocent confessor (*confessarius*) with the crime of solicitation, whereas canon 894, on the other hand, decrees that the false denunciation of an innocent priest (*sacerdos*) will be a sin the absolution of which is reserved to the Holy See.[18] Two distinct transgressions are to be understood, each with its own penalty. Under no conditions are the two penalties to rest upon the denunciator for one and the same transgression. The acceptance of this proposition will lend itself readily to the interpretation of the clause *firmo praescripto can.* 894 as intimated in the opening sentence of this paragraph.

The phrase *firmo praescripto can.* 894 is not to be restricted to merely that portion of the canon which treats of the conditions under which absolution from the excommunication can be granted, but is to be extended to the entire canon. There is no punctuation within the canon to limit the application of the phrase to merely that latter part of the canon. A semicolon within the canon would have broken the continuity of thought and then there would have been reason to believe that the phrase is related solely to that part which treats of absolution and the conditions under which it is to be imparted. According to the rule of interpretation the clause refers to the whole canon unless there is an indication that points to the contrary. *Quod clausula in fine referenda sit ad omnia praecedentia nisi aliqua vel evidens vel saltem probabilis ratio contrarium suadet.*[19]

If the legislator wanted to punish with excomunication the sin of the false accusation of an innocent priest (*sacerdos*) he could not logically place the subject matter of canon 894 under the title on the reservation of sins. He was constrained to insert it in the fifth book of the Code, which is devoted to the consideration of legislating regarding crimes and their penalties. It would have been necessary to change the sin (*peccatum*) by which an innocent priest (*sacerdos*) is falsely accused of the crime of solicitation into a delict (*delictum*) by which an innocent priest (*sacerdos*) is falsely accused.[20] Instead

18. Cf. Iorio, *Compendium,* II, 417, footnote (3).
19. Cf. Motry, *Diocesan Faculties,* p. 112.
20. Cf. Cappello, *De Poenitentia,* n. 507, 4°.

of transforming the sin into a delict with its attached penalty, the legislator retained the pre-Code reservation of the sin for the false accusation of an innocent priest (*sacerdos*) and formulated a new law by attaching a penalty of excommunication to the false denunciation of an innocent confessor (*confessarius*).

If the sanctions enacted in the two canons were not applicable to two *distinct* violations, then one of the laws would seem superfluous.[21] Granted that full knowledge of the excommunication decreed by canon 2363 is had by the person who falsely reports an innocent confessor, his action *ipso facto* places him under the excommunication. That excommunication, reserved in a special manner to the Holy See, would at the same time reserve the sin *ratione censurae* by operation of canon 2246, § 3 and prohibit the absolution of the sin.[22] What practical purpose, then, would be served in reserving the absolution of the sin a second time?

Assumed that ignorance of the censure is present, then as long as the ignorance is not an affected or a crass or supine ignorance, the excommunication enacted in canon 2363 is not incurred. According to the majority view, however, the reservation of the sin spoken of in canon 894 is in effect in consequence of the clause *firmo praescripto can.* 894. The reason they allege for the presence both of the censure and of the reservation of the sin *ratione sui* is to keep the penal law affecting the false denunciation of a priest from being defeated.[23] As long as they follow the more common

21. Cf. Cerato, *De Delicto*, n. 129, adn. 5; Motry, *Diocesan Faculties*, p. 112.
22. Reservatio censurae impedientis receptionem Sacramentorum importat reservationem peccati cui censura adnexa est. Cf. also canon 2250, § 2 which decrees that whenever a censure impedes the reception of the sacraments the censured person cannot be absolved from the sin which caused the censure until the censure has been removed by a prior absolution.
23. Cf. Stanislaus Woywod, "False Accusation of Solicitation," — *The Homiletic and Pastoral Review* (New York, 1900-), XXXVIII (1938), 718 (hereafter cited *HPR*); T. Slater, "False Accusation of Solicitation and the New Code," — *Ecclesiastical Review* (Originally *The American Ecclesiastical Review*, Philadelphia, 1889-1943; Washington, 1944-), LIX (1918), 463 (hereafter cited *ER*).

opinion that, ignorance of the reservation itself does not release the culprit from being affected by the reservation, then their view has merit.

Even though it is the more common teaching today that ignorance of the reservation will not free the violator of the law from the effects of the reservation, there is current a safe and probable opinion that ignorance of the unique reservation specified in canon 894 will free the delinquent from the consequences of the reservation.[24] In following this probable opinion the aim of the legislator would not be realized anyhow even if he attached a dual penalty to the act of falsely accusing a priest of the crime of solicitation. The whole force of the clause *firmo praescripto can.* 894 would then be nullified. If the view that two distinct transgressions are contemplated in the Code is upheld, the value of the phrase could not be explained away.

Another reason leading to the conviction that a distinction in the two canons is contemplated is based on the observation that the reserved sin of canon 894 is governed by the norms that reserve sins *ratione sui,* while the delict of canon 2363 follows the norms that regulate the conditions for the reservation of and absolution from censures.[25] When a penitent is in danger of death any priest can absolve from the sin reserved *ratione sui* and from the reserved censure.[26] In the more urgent cases any confessor can absolve from the excommunication enacted in canon 2363 under the conditions indicated in the latter canon, that is, upon obtaining a formal retractation of the false denunciation, upon reparation of the harm that has come to the innocent confessor, and the imposition of an exacting and protracted penance.[27] When the concession of canon 2254 § 1 is employed, a recourse to the Holy See is prescribed. No recourse is necessary when absolution is granted by virtue of the privilege granted in canon 900 from the papally reserved sin.[28]

24. Cf. Chapter VI, Article IV.
25. Cf. canons 893-900; 2245-2254.
26. Canon 882.
27. Cf. canon 2254, §§ 1, 3, collated with canon 2363.
28. Genicot-Salsmans, *Institutiones,* II, n. 400, IX.

If any of the conditions outlined in canon 900 are present, the reservation of the sin papally reserved *ratione sui* ceases.[29] The confessor, according to the majority opinion which maintains that one transgression is involved but with a twofold juridical consequence, could not proceed with sacramental absolution since canon 2363 is still in force and reserves the sin *ratione censurae.*[30] Since canon 2246, § 3 declares that the censure can be removed only by means of a legitimate absolution, it follows that the sin reserved *ratione censurae* cannot be absolved until the censure is removed, even though the reservation of the sin *ratione sui* ceases in virtue of canon 900.[31]

In order to use the privilege of canon 900 it would be necessary to obtain faculties to absolve from the excommunication imposed by canon 2363, or to use the concessions granted by canon 2254. Granted that canons 894 and 2363 treat of the same transgression and under the same aspects, it would have been necessary for canon 900 to contain the clause "*firmo praescripto can.* 2363," for if the reservation of the sin papally reserved ceases by the law of canon 900, the excommunication of canon 2363 would nevertheless be in force. This was not done. The absence of this clause from canon 900, and from the question to which the Pontifical Commission for the Interpretation of the Code replied, is a strong indication that

29. Cf. *Pontificia Commissio Interpretationis,* 16 nov. 1925, ad VII — *Acta Apostolicae Sedis, Commentarium Officialis* (Romae, 1909-1929, Civitate Vaticana, 1929-) XVII (1925), 583 (hereafter cited *PCI* and *AAS*).

30. Cf. canon 2246, § 3; De Smet, *De Absolutione,* nn. 121, b, 143; Claeys Bouuaert-Simenon, *Manuale,* II, n. 142, 2.

31. Cerato (*Censurae Vigentes,* p. 33), Cappello (*De Censuris,* nn. 106, 107, 147, 465), Aertnys-Damen (*Theologia Moralis,* II, nn. 329, 3°, 997, 1004) and Francis E. Moriarty (*The Extraordinary Absolution from Censures,* The Catholic University of America Canon Law Studies, n. 113 [Washington, D.C.: The Catholic University of America, 1938], p. 78 (hereafter cited *Extraordinary Absolution*) hold that in danger of death the absolution from the sin prior to the absolution from the excommunication would be valid but gravely illicit. By analogy then, a confessor would sin gravely if he would absolve the reserved sin by operation of canon 900 before he employs the emergency faculties of canon 2254.

two distinct juridical sanctions are invoked for two distinct transgressions. The use of the phrase "*firmo praescripto can.* 894" finds a plausible explanation only in the assumption that two separate transgressions are postulated by the lawgiver.[32] It is highly improbable that two juridical sanctions should be utilized for the same transgression, unless some very clear reference to the plurality of such sanctions is made by the legislator. If there were an identity, reference to that fact would have been necessary. It cannot be read into the canons when one studies the evident meaning of the words. Quite the contrary appears to be the case. As an identity in the law is clearly brought out for instance, in canon 2368, § 2, in conjunction with canon 904, so the same clarity is naturally to be looked for in canon 894 in conjunction with canon 2363.[33]

Article 3. "*SACERDOS*" of Canon 894 Contrasted With "*CONFESSARIUS*" of Canon 2363

The first difference to be noted in canons 894 and 2363 is the word *sacerdos* standing in contrast with the word *confessarius*. There are a number of canonists who pass by this distinction and consider the two words to be identical in meaning.[34] Although the two canons speak of the same moral evil, it is doubtful whether they do so under the same aspect.[35] Iorio favors the opinion that the difference in the transgressions in the two canons does not

32. Cf. Motry, *Diocesan Faculties,* p. 112. Cf. also Cerato, *De Delicto,* n. 129, adn. 3, 5; Blat, *Commentarium,* lib. V, n. 204, d); Iorio, *Compendium,* II, n. 582 bis, *Quaer.* 30°, Notanda I; *ibid.,* II, 417, footnote (1).
33. Motry, *loc. cit.*
34. "Cfr. c. 894 ubi sermo est de *sacerdote innocente* et non de confessario. Delictum autem idem esse videtur." — Coronata, *Institutiones,* IV, 504, footnote 7; Augustine, *Commentary,* IV, 319; Dargin, *Reserved Cases,* p. 27; Ferreres, *Casus Conscientiae,* II, 369, *Casus* XXXII; Jone, *Gesetzbuch,* III, 520; Tanquerey (*Synopsis,* I, n. 455, 1°), Cl. Marc, Fr. X. Gesterman, J. B. Raus (*Institutiones Morales Alphonsianae* [18. ed., 2 vols., Lugduni: Vitte, 1927], II, n. 1771, I, 1°) and Eichmann (*Das Strafrecht,* n. 72) speak of the false denunciation of an innocent *confessor* when commenting on canon 894.
35. Cf. Merkelbach, *Summa,* III, n. 594, B; Iorio, *Compendium,* II, n. 582 bis, *Quaer,* 30°, Notanda I, b).

consist in the contrasted terms *falsa delatio apud iudices ecclesiasticos* and *falso denuntiaverit apud Superiores,* as Cerato,[36] Blat,[37] Motry,[38] Merkelbach[39] and the anonymous writer in *Il Monitore Ecclesiastico*[40] hold, but chiefly in the contrast that exists between the words *sacerdos* and *confessarius.*[41] The reservation of the sin which is reserved *ratione sui* is incurred, according to Iorio, by a person who falsely accuses an innocent priest (*sacerdos*), that is, accuses him *qua confessarius* of the crime of solicitation, whereas the excommunication falls upon the penitent who falsely denounces an innocent confessor (*confessarius*) of the same transgression.[42]

To maintain that the word *sacerdos* is formally synonymous with the word *confessarius* is doing violence to the evident meaning of the words. Of all the authors consulted, Iorio is the only one who emphasizes the distinction that exists between the term *confessarius* of canon 2363 and the term *sacerdos* of canon 894. As canon 19 specifies he accepts the word *confessarius* in its strict significance, because a penal law is under consideration.[43] The confessor mentioned in canon 2363 is a priest who possesses faculties for imparting valid absolution and to whom a penitent *de facto* goes to confession.[44] All canonists agree that the word *sacerdos* differs not only materially, that is verbally, but also formally from the word *confessarius.* The Code itself alludes to this

36. *De Delicto,* n. 129, adn. 3; *Censurae Vigentes,* n. 79, adn.
37. *Commentarium,* lib. V, n. 204, c; *ibid.,* III, Pars. I, 260.
38. *Diocesan Faculties,* pp. 111, 112.
39. *Summa,* III, n. 643, C, b.
40. "Il Codice di Diritto Canonico: Riassunto e Dilucidazioni," — XXXI (1919), 149.
41. *Compendium,* II, 417, footnote (1).
42. *Op. cit.,* II, n. 582 bis, *Quaer.* 30°, Notanda I, b), c).
43. Leges quae poenam statuunt, . . . strictae subsunt interpretationi.
44. Vox ergo confessarius sensu proprio et stricto heic sumenda est, **scilicet saltem pro sacerdote qui,** etiam extra periculum mortis, *et valide* confessiones audire queat, etiamsi a quibusdam peccatis, v. gr. reservatis actu absolvere non possit, *et* apud quem persona denuntians *de facto* confessionem instituit vel instituere tentaverit, eamque praecise in qua falso confessarium de sollicitatione denuntiat. . ." — Iorio, *Compendium,* II, n. 582 bis, *Quaer.* 30°, Notanda I, c). (Italics in original.)

distinction in canon 892, where it decrees that in urgent necessity all confessors (*confessarii*) are bound in charity to hear the confession of the faithful; in danger of death all priests (*sacerdotes*) have the same obligation. In canon 882 the law provides faculties to all priests for granting absolution to persons who are in danger of death, although these priests are not approved for confessions. Any validly ordained priest, therefore, can licitly and validly absolve persons who are in danger of death from all sins and censures, provided only that the prescriptions noted in canons 884 and 2252 be properly observed.[45]

A *confessarius*, on the other hand, besides possessing the power of orders must also be endowed with jurisdiction to absolve from sins. Included in the term *confessor* are the Holy Father, Cardinals, Ordinaries, pastors, and those priests who in law are reckoned as the equivalent of pastors;[46] secular and religious priests who are approved by the local Ordinary for the hearing of confessions;[47] for women religious, priests who possess the proper jurisdiction demanded by the Code;[48] for exempt clerical religious, not only those who possess ordinary or delegated jurisdiction in the diocese, but also all competent superiors of such institutes according to the norms of their respective constitutions, as well as any member of the religious or secular clergy who has received delegated jurisdiction from the superiors of these exempt religious institutes;[49] priests who obtain jurisdiction through the operation of canon 209 which supplies jurisdiction in view of a common error or of a positive doubt of law or of fact.[50] Though a confessor does not possess those special faculties which permit him to absolve from reserved

45. Canon 884 treats of the conditions under which absolution can be imparted to an accomplice in a sin *in re turpi.* Canon 2252 indicates that recourse for the mandates is necessary when absolution has been granted from *specialissimo modo* and from *ab homine* reserved censures.
46. Cf. canons 874; 881; 239, § 1, 1°, 2°.
47. Cf. canons 874; 881, § 1.
48. Cf. canons 876; 520; 522; 523.
49. Cf. canons 874; 875, § 1; 518; 519.
50. Cf. Cappello, *De Censuris* (1919 edition), n. 126, 6; Moriarty, *Extraordinary Absolution,* pp. 154, 155.

sins and censures, he is nevertheless considered a confessor provided he has the usually granted faculties.[51]

Though it is apparent that there is a difference between a priest and a confessor, that distinction is not of itself adequate in reference to the crime of solicitation. Further distinctions in the word *confessarius* must be made. A priest who is approved for confessions but who does not exercise his ministry must be classified as a confessor in a wide sense (*improprie dictus*). A priest who possesses jurisdiction for the granting of a valid sacramental absolution and is actually engaged in the hearing of a sacramental confession is termed a confessor in a strict and proper sense (*proprie dictus*). In any discussion regarding the denunciation of an innocent confessor or of an innocent priest, the quality of the office which the confessor exercises, as well as the status of the priest who is denounced, must be given consideration.[52]

Article 4. The Confessor - Penitent Relationship

Relative to the denunciation of an innocent priest or also the denunciation of an innocent confessor the following observation must be kept in mind. According to the Constitution *"Sacramentum Poenitentiae"* all ministers of the sacrament of penance who take sacrilegious advantage of their power while hearing confessions to seek to seduce a penitent into the commission of sins against the virtue of purity are guilty of the crime of solicitation. When the solicitation takes place during a sacramental confession (*in actu sacramentalis confessionis*), the minister is designated a *confessarius proprie dictus*. Between him and the penitent a confessor - penitent relationship is established. It lasts only during the time that elapses in the course of the sacramental confession, and terminates with the absolution. If the solicitation occurs in any of the remaining circumstances postulated in the Constitution, the solicitator is referred to as a *confessarius improprie dictus*. In the circumstance which points to the time *"immediate post confessionem,"* the con-

51. Iorio, *Compendium,* II, n. 582 bis, *Quaer.* 30° Notanda, I, b), 3, c.
52. ". . . Ratio igitur duplicis sanctionis repetenda est ex *qualitate* muneris *utriusque* personae falso denuntiatae." — Iorio, *Compendium,* II, 417, footnote (1). (Italics in original.)

fessor - penitent relationship has ceased; in all of the other postulated circumstances in which the crime of solicitation is possible, the confessor - penitent relationship has never been truly established.

The Constitution "*Sacramentum Poenitentiae*" ordered local Ordinaries to punish

1. confessors *proprie dicti* who solicited their penitents during the course of a sacramental confession (*in actu sacramentalis confessionis*);
2. confessors *improprie dicti* who were denounced as having sought to seduce their penitents in any of the circumstances postulated in the remaining *clausulae* outlined in the Constitution;[53]
3. priests who lacked jurisdiction for the granting of a valid absolution, but who while pretending to function as confessors committed a sin of solicitation in the course of the feigned act of hearing a sacramental confession.[54]

It is evident that there is no confessor - penitent relationship, but rather a priest - lay person relationship, when a confessor *improprie dictus* or priest without faculties who attempts to hear confessions is guilty of the crime of solicitation. Even though a confessor *improprie dictus* possesses faculties for granting a valid sacramental absolution, if he does not exercise that power by hearing the confession there can be no confessor - penitent relationship established between him and his false accuser. Whenever a penitent falsely accuses an innocent confessor *proprie dictus* of the crime of solicitation he becomes guilty of a single falsehood, namely that which prefers the charge of having been solicited to sins of impurity. When a calumniator imputes the crime of solicitation to a confessor *improprie dictus* by falsely stating that he confessed to that priest, the denuncitor is not calumniating an innocent confessor, but an innocent priest. By his false denunciation he places the confessor *improprie dictus* in the role of a confessor

53. Document V, § 1 in the Code.

54. *Loc. cit.;* Cf. also S. C. S. Off., decr., 11 febr. 1661, n. 5 — Ballerini-Palmieri, *Opus Theologicum,* V, 583, footnote (a); S. C. S., instr., 20 febr. 1866, nn. 1, 2 — *Fontes,* n. 990.

proprie dictus. Both of the elements associated with the crime of solicitation were falsely alleged, namely, that of a confession, and the provocation to sins of the flesh.

What is said of a confessor *improprie dictus* can also be applied to a priest who has no faculties to hear confessions when he is falsely accused of the crime of solicitation. In either case the false denunciation implies a double falsehood: one that misrepresents the priest as a confessor, and another that levels the false charge of solicitation against him.

Reduced to an outline, the crime of false denunciation can occur in any of the following ways:

I. The false denunciation of an innocent confessor *proprie dictus*.
  A. A sacramental confession is undertaken;
  B. No solicitation has occurred in that confession;
  C. The penitent maliciously incriminates his confessor as having sought to seduce him or her into committing sins of impurity.

II. The false denunciation of an innocent confessor *improprie dictus*.
  1) A. 1. A sacramental confession has just been completed (*immediate post confessionem*); or
    2. A sacramental confession is about to take place (*immediate ante confessionem*); or
    3. A person has asked the confessor to hear his confession, and the confessor has agreed to do so (*occasione confessionis*); or
    4. The confessor has invited the penitent to go to confession (*praetextu confessionis*); or
    5. a. The confessor is in a confessional (*in confessionali*); or
      b. in a place permanently designated for the hearing of confessions (*in alio loco ad confessiones audiendas destinato*); or
      c. in a place temporarily assigned for the hearing of confessions (*in loco electo ad confessiones audiendas*);

B. While the confessor *improprie dictus* was *de facto* operative in any of the foregoing sets of circumstances, no solicitation took place;

C. The penitent however falsely attributes to him the crime of solicitation.

2) A. No sacramental confession took place;

B. No solicitation took place;

C. The lay person accuses a confessor *improprie dictus* of having

a. heard his or her confession; and

b. of having solicited him or her during that falsely alleged confession.

3) A. The confessor *improprie dictus* was not operative in any of the sets of circumstances postulated in the Constitution for the possible occurrence of the penalized act of solicitation;

B. No solicitation took place;

C. A lay person maliciously denounces that:

a. the confessor *improprie dictus* was operative in one of the aforementioned sets of circumstances, and

b. while thus engaged, perpetrated the sin of solicitation.

4) A. The confessor *improprie dictus* was not actually engaged in the hearing of a confession;

B. An act of provocation to sins of impurity was committed by him, but outside a sacramental confession;

C. The report is maliciously distorted with a view of deceiving the local Ordinary into believing that the solicitation occurred during a sacramental confession.

5) A. The confessor *improprie dictus* was not operative in any of the sets of circumstances postulated in the Constitution;

B. A sin against the sixth commandment of God was committed;

C. The false charge is made that an act of solicitation occurred in one or other set of circumstances outlined in the Constitution.

III. The false denunciation of an innocent priest who did not possess confessional faculties.

The very same sets of circumstances as outlined under II are applicable when a priest who has no jurisdiction for the hearing of confessions is falsely denounced. An exception must be made however for II, 1) A. 1. and 2., since the sets of circumstances there listed (*immediate ante* and *immediate post confessionem*) cannot be realized in a priest who has no faculties for the hearing of a sacramental confession.

Article 5. The Penalty for False Denunciations

A. In Pre-Code Law.

Before the promulgation of the Code a sin reserved personally to the Holy Father was committed by him who:

a. calumniated an innocent confessor *proprie dictus*;
b. falsely accused an innocent confessor *improprie dictus*;
c. falsely denounced a priest who had no jurisdiction for granting valid sacramental absolution.[55]

In issuing its Instruction to the local Ordinaries throughout the world the Holy Office in 1866 briefly summarized the law against solicitation and the penalty for false denunciations, as contained in the Constitution *"Sacramentum Poenitentiae"* of Benedict XIV. It did not introduce any changes.[56] Later documents emanating from the Holy Office and from the *Sacra Poenitentiaria* did nothing more than refer to the Constitution *"Sacramentum Poenitentiae"* and confirm its provisions.[57]

B. Interpretation Of The Law By Pre-Code Authors.

Pre-Code canonists in their commentaries adhered mainly to the wording of the Constitution *"Sacramentum Poenitentiae,"* some of them merely quoting paragraph three of the Constitution, others

55. Cf. Const. *"Sacramentum Poenitentiae,"* §§ 1, 2, 3, Document V in the Code.
56. S. C. S. Off., instr. 20 febr. 1866, Preamble — *Fontes,* n. 990.
57. Cf. S C. S. Off., decr. 27 iun. 1866 — *Fontes,* n. 995; *Collectanea,* n. 1294; S. C. Poenit., decr. 7 nov. 1888, ad 1 — *Fontes,* n. 6347; *Collectanea,* n. 1695; S. C. S. Off., instr. 20 iulii 1890 — *Fontes,* n. 1123.

paraphrasing it.[58] Berardi († 1916) and Many († 1922) gave a little more than a fleeting reference to the crime of false denunciation.[59] Since the reservation of the sin was in force whether a *confessarius proprie dictus,* a *confessarius improprie dictus,* or a priest who possessed no faculties was falsely denounced of the crime of solicitation, most of the pre-Code canonists used the words *sacerdos* and *confessarius* indiscriminately when they spoke of the crime of false denunciation of the crime of solicitation. The context was usually such that, even though they employed the word *sacerdos,* the meaning was that of a *confessarius proprie dictus.*[60]

From the words of the Constitution *"Sacramentum Poenitentiae,"* from the Preamble of the Instruction of the Holy Office of February 20, 1866, and from the jurisprudence developed by the authors up to the promulgation of the Code, the papal reservation was in effect in the following instances:

1. Whenever a confessor *proprie dictus* established a confessor - penitent relationship by exercising his office as a confessor *in actu sacramentalis confessionis* and his penitent falsely accused him of the crime of solicitation.
2. When a person falsely attributed the crime of solicitation to a confessor *improprie dictus* who *de facto* was operative in one of the following circumstances:

   A. immediately before or immediately after a confession;

58. Cf. Lega, *De Iudiciis,* IV, n. 7; Lehmkuhl, *Theologia Moralis,* II, n. 526; Wernz, *Ius Decretalium,* VI, 449; Ballerini-Palmieri, *Opus Theologicum,* V, n. 1155; Hollweck, *Die kirchlichen Strafgesetze,* p. 280; Edmundus Voit, *Theologia Moralis* (2 vols., Augustae Taurinorum, 1833), II, n. 818; A. Konings, *Theologiae Moralis* (7. ed., 3 vols., New York-Cincinnati-Chicago: Benziger Bros., 1889), II, n. 1400, IV; Noldin, *De Sacramentis* (5. ed., 1904), n. 393, 5; Bucceroni, *De C. "Sac. Poenit.",* nn. 59, 60.
59. *De Sollicitatione,* nn. 359, 2°, 349; "De Peccato Sollicitationis," — *Le Canoniste,* XVIII (1895), 720, 1°; Cf. also Rota, *Enchiridion,* n. 104.
60. Cf. Berardi, *De Sollicitatione,* n. 349; *ibid.,* n. 359; Rota, *Enchiridion,* nn. 104, 5°, 394, 253, 254, 395; Schuech, *Handbuch,* p. 685; D'Annibale, *Summula,* III, nn. 366, 368, footnote 19; Bucceroni, *De C. "Sac. Poenit.",* nn. 59, 60; Hollweck, *Die kirchlichen Strafgesetze,* p. 280; Santi, *Praelectiones,* lib. V, Appendix, p. 232, III, 1°.

B. on the occasion of requesting that a confession be heard, but no confession followed;

C. under the pretext of hearing a confession, no confession resulting;

D. while

a. simulating the administration of the sacrament of penance;

b. in a place permanently designated for the hearing of confessions; or

c. in a place temporarily chosen for the hearing of confessions.

3. When a person falsely denounced a confessor *improprie dictus* of hearing a sacramental confession and of having committed an act of solicitation during that falsely alleged confession.

4. When a person calumniated a confessor *improprie dictus,* though not operative in any of the circumstances postulated in the Constitution, of actually having operated in those circumstances and of having sought to seduce the penitent to sins of impurity.

5. When a denunciator was induced to commit sins against the virtue of purity apart from any occasion associated with confession, but in reporting that sin, charged that it was committed in connection with the reception of the sacrament of penance, or in such circumstances which had a proximate relation to the sacrament of penance.

6. When an innocent priest, not having any faculties for the hearing of confessions was falsely reported as being guilty of solicitation in any of the circumstances outlined above in numbers 2-5, exclusive of 2, A.

C. The Present Legislation.

There is almost a unanimous agreement among post-Code authors that canon 894, with the exception of the more lenient discipline for the granting of absolution from the reserved sin, is taken over *ex integro* from pre-Code law. The Constitution *"Sacramentum*

Poenitentiae," which constitutes the source for the law enacted against the crime of false denunciations of the crime of solicitation, penalized not only the false denunciation of an innocent confessor, but also the false denunciation of an innocent priest if the latter was denounced *qua confessarius.*

Iorio is the only author to demonstrate that canon 894 with its reservation of the sin reserved *ratione sui* embodies only that portion of the old law which dealt with the false accusation of an innocent priest, the *falsa delatio qua sacerdos innocens accusatur.* The false denunciation of an innocent confessor, according to the same author, is not passed by in the Code, but has become the matter for a special and serious penalty, that of an excommunication reserved *speciali modo* to the Holy See.[61]

Iorio bases his deduction on the observation that canon 894 uses the word *sacerdos,* and contrasts that term with the word *confessarius* employed in canon 2363. In the light of a judicious application of the principles of interpretation a further change in the law appears. The word *confessarius* as employed in canon 2363 is to be given a strict interpretation.[62] In view of this strict interpretation which is to be accorded to the term *confessarius* as employed in canon 2363, only the *confessarius proprie dictus* can be meant. The *confessarius improprie dictus* and the priest not having confessional faculties, if they be falsely accused to have functioned as *confessarii proprie dicti* and to have supposedly committed the crime of solicitation, are comprised under the word *sacerdos* as employed in canon 894.

Because of the preexistence of the law now embodied in canons 894 and 2363, most of the canonists maintain that no change has been introduced with the promulgation of the Code. On the one hand they allow an exception for the milder discipline in the prospective granting of absolution from the reserved sin and for the presence of a new penalty of excommunication as enacted in canon 2363. But on the other hand, these canonists insist that the

61. Canons 894; 2363; *Compendium,* II, n. 582 bis, *Quaer.* 30°, Notanda I, b).

62. Leges quae poenam statuunt, . . . stricte subsunt interpretationi. — canon 19; In poenis benignior est interpretatio facienda. — canon 2219, § 1.

word *sacerdos* in canon 894 is a synonym for the word *confessarius* in canon 2363.[63]

Phrases like the following are found in nearly every manual of canon law: *dummodo denuntiatio fiat confessarii secus non habetur verum delictum sollicitationis.*[64] It appears that nearly all the authors interpret the word *confessarius* which is employed in canon 2363 in the double sense of:

1. a confessor *proprie dictus,* who *de facto* is exercising his his ministry as a confessor; and
2. a confessor *improprie dictus,* who possesses jurisdiction for the hearing of confessions, but does not function as a confessor, inasmuch as *de facto* he is simply operative in one of the sets of circumstances proximately connected with confession or intimately related to its administration.

According to the majority of the canonists, whether a *confessarius proprie dictus* or a *confessarius improprie dictus* be calumniated as guilty of the crime of solicitation, his denouncer would incur the excommunication enacted in canon 2363. Furthermore, they hold that the reservation of the sin as stated in canon 894 is in force, inasmuch as they contend that the delict mentioned in canon 2363 is coextensive with the sin which canon 894 reserves to the Holy See for absolution.

From their commentaries it is nowhere evident that these canonists include the following calumniators as subject to either or both of the juridical sanctions enumerated in canons 894 and 2363.

I. A. The hearing of a confession was not undertaken by a confessor *improprie dictus*;

63. Cf. Ferreres, *Casus Conscientiae,* II, 369, *Casus* XXXII; Vermeersch-Creusen, *Epitome,* III, n. 565; cf. also footnotes 1 and 34 of this chapter

64. Sipoș, *Enchiridion,* p. 1012; cf. also Cappello, *De Poenitentia,* n. 606, 3°; Sole, *De Delictis et Poenis,* n. 416; Cocchi, *De Delictis et Poenis,* n. 223, b; Cavigioli, *De Censuris,* n. 115; Regatillo, *Institutiones,* II, n. 1111; Salucci, *Il Diritto Penale,* II, n. 312; Pruemmer, *Manuale Theologiae Moralis,* III, n. 468, *Scholion* I; Beste, *Introductio in Codicem,* p. 960; Cerato, *Censurae Vigentes,* n. 79, c, e.

B. No provocation to sins of the flesh took place;

C. The calumniator however in his false report left the impression in the mind of the recipient of the denunciation that a confession did take place and that the crime of solicitation was committed during that alleged confession.

II. A. The confessor *improprie dictus* was not operative in any of the sets of circumstances described by the Constitution as occasions in which the attempted seduction to sins of impurity could become a crime of solicitation;

B. No solicitation took place;

C. The false delator accused the innocent confessor *improprie dictus* of having under those alleged circumstances sought to seduce the penitent to sins of the flesh.

III. A. A solicitation was perpetrated by a confessor *improprie dictus* but not in the act of hearing the confession, nor in any of the remaining circumstances specified by the Constitution;

B. The reporter however falsely accused the confessor *improprie dictus* of having been operative in those circumstances in which the sin would have to be construed as a crime of solicitation.

IV. In place of the phrase "a confessor *improprie dictus*" there is substituted in the foregoing three cases the phrase "a priest not having confessional faculties." Under that supposition the same false denunciations can result.

It is clear that in none of these four possible cases is a confessor-penitent relationship established. The element of confession or the circumstances which the law indicates as implying a close connection with confession are fancied and not factual. These four cases were however embraced under the juridical sanctions invoked in the pre-Code law.[65]

65. Berardi, *De Sollicitatione,* n. 349; Cf. *supra,* Section A and B of this present ARTICLE.

Since so many authors accept the word *sacerdos* as used in canon 894 in the sense of the word *confessarius* as used in canon 2363, they necessarily restrict the false denunciation of the crime of solicitation to a *confessarius stricte dictus,* or at best to a *confessarius improprie dictus* who *de facto* is operative in one of the circumstances postulated in the Constitution. Because of that interpretation they do not make provision for the incurrence of either the excommunication or the reservation of the papally reserved sin, when there is question of falsely accusing an innocent priest, that is, of a *confessarius improprie dictus* who did not hear confession, or of a priest who has no faculties for the hearing of confessions, but either of which is falsely denounced as having solicited the accuser in an alleged but fictitious confession.

Ferrerres maintains that no priest can commit the crime of solicitation unless the act is placed within the limits postulated in the Constitution "*Sacramentum Poenitentiae.*" It is equally impossible, then, to denounce any priest who was not operative in any of those circumstances. He assumes that only in the case in which the element of provocation to sins of impurity is falsified is the calumniator brought under the reserved sin and the excommunication. If the delator fabricates two falsehoods, first stating that a priest — either the confessor *improprie dictus* or the priest who has no faculties — heard the confession, and secondly, that during the alleged confession the solicitation took place, the informer would not have committed the delict of false denunciation. Ferrerres insists that the priest was not operative within the limits which the law specified for making the crime of solicitation possible; accordingly the emergence of a false accusation of solicitation is likewise not possible.[66]

False denunciations of this kind were penalized in the pre-Code law. All indications point to the assumption that these types of denunciations are punished also in the present law. When canon 894 draws such a sharp contrast with canon 2363 by purposely using the word *sacerdos* instead of the word *confessarius,* a change from the pre-Code law seems to result. Whereas the Constitution

66. Cf. *Casus Conscientiae,* II, 369, *Casus* XXXII.

"Sacramentum Poenitentiae" enacted only one penalty for two distinct transgressions, it is here respectfully contended that today the law invokes two juridical sanctions against two distinct transgressions. Canon 894 reserves the sin of a false accusation of an innocent priest to the Holy See, and canon 2363 excommunicates the false denunciator of an innocent confessor.

Since a twofold distinction has been made for the word *confessarius,* as one who is such *proprie dictus* or only *improprie dictus,* it will be necessary to ascertain whether the excommunication will be incurred by him who falsely denounces a confessor considered according to either of these two concepts. Consider the following possibilities:

I. A. The hearing of a sacramental confession is undertaken by a confessor *proprie dictus*;

B. No provocation to sins of impurity is attempted in that confession;

C. The penitent maliciously accuses his confessor of solicitation.

In this case there is a confessor- -penitent relationship. The false denunciation is such as to qualify the calumniator for the incurring of the excommunication. The word *confessarius* is taken in its strict sense.[67]

If it should happen that when the penitent has begun the confession the confessor discovers that he cannot grant absolution inasmuch as he lacks the specially required faculty; or he desires to study the solution of a difficult moral problem with a view to giving absolution or imparting correct counsel; or he finds the penitent improperly disposed for absolution; or he leaves the confessional for any other reason before granting absolution — in such instances the confessor can still be classified as a confessor *proprie dictus.* The confessor - penitent relationship is established as soon as the initial blessing of the confessor is imparted to the penitent. It was the accepted doctrine before the Code, and it is the teaching today, that the phrase *in actu sacramentalis confessionis* does not mean

67. Cf. canon 19; Iorio, *Compendium,* II, n. 582 bis, *Quaer.* 30°, Notanda I, c.

that the absolution must be imparted before the confessor - penitent relationship can become established.[68] If the penitent falsely denounces the confessor who interrupted the confession after it was seriously begun with the intention of obtaining absolution, he would denounce a *confessarius proprie dictus,* and the excommunication as enacted in canon 2363 would be incurred.

II. A. A confessor *improprie dictus* is operative in one of the circumstances outlined by the Constitution as making possible the crime of solicitation (except *in actu sacramentalis confessionis*);

B. No attempt was made to solicit the penitent in any of the specified sets of circumstances;

C. A false denunciator nevertheless denounces the priest as guilty of the act of solicitation.

Since no sacramental confession was made, the circumstance identified with the time immediately prior to the confession (*immediate ante confessionem*) does not suffice to establish the confessor - penitent relationship; on the other hand, the circumstance associated with the time immediately after the confession (*immediate post confessionem*) points rather to the already effected termination of this specific relationship. Again the circumstances connoted by the phrases, *occasione confessionis, praetextu confessionis,* and *in confessionali, sive in alio loco ad confessiones audiendas destinato, aut electo, cum simulatione audiendi ibidem confessionem,* never give rise to a confessor - penitent relationship, for in none of these is a sacramental confession ever instituted.

By applying the following principles of interpretation:

1. those canons which differ from their pre-Code counterpart must be interpreted according to the meaning of the words employed in those parts in which they differ;[69]

68. Cf. Berardi, *De Sollicitatione,* n. 49; St. Alphonsus, *Theologia Moralis,* lib. VI, n. 677; Rota, *Enchiridion,* n. 268; De Smet, *De Absolutione,* n. 72; Noldin-Schmitt, *De Sacramentis,* n. 375, 1; Cappello, *De Poenitentia,* n. 672; Iorio, *Compendium,* II, n. 576, *Quaer.* 1°, b); Coronata, *Institutiones,* IV, 542; Cerato, *De Delicto,* n. 41.

69. Canon 6, 3°.

2. ecclesiastical laws must be understood according to the proper meaning of the words considered in the context;[70]
3. all penal laws are subject to a strict interpretation;[71]
4. in the application of penalties the milder interpretation is to favor the delinquent;[72] and
5. a penalty decreed by law is not incurred unless the specific transgression has been consummated in accordance with the proper meaning of the terms used by the law;[73]

the conclusion is reached that canon 2363 penalizes with an excommunication only those persons who falsely denounce an innocent confessor *proprie dictus* as having solicited his penitent *in actu sacramentalis confessionis.*

The informer who falsely accuses a priest who has no faculties for the hearing of confessions, or a confessor *improprie dictus* who has jurisdiction but who did not exercise it during a confession, cannot come under the excommunication of canon 2363 because of the strict interpretation that is to be given to the word *confessarius.* It is precisely here where the law regarding the enacted reservation of the sin as stated in canon 894 has application. A change from the pre-Code law is to be noted. A true distinction exists between canons 894 and 2363. Canon 894 treats of the false accusation of an innocent priest whose falsely alleged act of solicitation is connected with a purely fictitious confession. That is true whether or not the calumniated priest has faculties for the hearing of confessions, provided only that he was not engaged in exercising his office as confessor. When the priest in question did not have confessional faculties, then no confessor - penitent relationship could be established, since no sacramental confession was heard. Hence only a priest (*sacerdos*) is denounced, but denounced as a confessor (*qua confessarius proprie dictus*). The reason for the more severe sanction against the false denunciation of an innocent *confessarius proprie dictus* than against the false accusation of an innocent priest is

70. Canon 18.
71. Canon 19.
72. Canon 2219, § 1.
73. Canon 2228.

apparently to be sought in the fact that an objective abuse of the sacrament is inherent in the fact that the false denunciation is leveled against the confessor in his very status of confessor.[74]

It is a common practice among Catholics who regularly confess to the same confessor to designate him as their confessor. If such a confessor is falsely denounced by one of his erstwhile penitents, would he be denounced as a confessor or as a priest? If Ada falsely denounced Henry of solicitation by charging that the crime occurred when she made her confession on December 5, whereas Henry at that time was actually many miles from the place where the alleged solicitation is described as having occurred, Henry would be falsely denounced as a *confessarius improprie dictus.* There was definitely no confessor - penitent relationship established in the case. Ada could not be under the excommunication of canon 2363. She did not denounce a *confessarius proprie dictus,* but rather a priest to whom she gave the designation of a *confessarius proprie dictus* in her false report. On the other hand, if Ada did go to confession to Henry on December 5, and Henry conducted himself as a worthy and an honorable confessor, but Ada falsely denounced him as having sought to seduce her to sins of the flesh, she has denounced a *confessarius proprie dictus.* Granted that Ada was not in ignorance regarding the enactment and the nature of the censure, and that she was without any benefit of other excuses as furnished by the law, the excommunication stated in the law of canon 2363 would be in effect.

Since there is a true distinction between the word *sacerdos* occurring in canon 894 and the term *confessarius proprie dictus* contained in canon 2363, the two sanctions for their respective transgressions cannot be said to coalesce, as two distinct acts are involved. It is wrong to state that whoever is under the excommunication enacted in canon 2363 for the false denunciation of an innocent confessor is at the same time subjected to the reserved sin mentioned in canon 894; or that if the culprit is absolved from the excommunication or has escaped the contraction of the excommunication

74. "Ratio maioris severitatis pro sanctione poenali de qua in can. 2363 repetenda videtur ex obiectivo abusu ipsius sacramenti. — Iroio, *Compendium,* II, 418, footnote, (1).

in consequence of the presence of ignorance or through some other excuse as furnished in the penal law, then the reservation of the sin according to the decree of canon 894 is in force; or that if the reservation from sin ceases by the applied operation of canon 900, then the excommunication as enacted in canon 2363 is still in force. As a person, when he is *ipso facto under* excommunication *speciali modo* reserved to the Holy See for having laid hands of violence upon a bishop cannot at the same time be said to incur an excommunication reserved to the Ordinary for the reason that the bishop is at the same time a cleric,[75] so there can be no coalescing of the two separate effects which flow from the separate laws of canons 2363 and 894, namely the reservation together with the excommunication.[76]

COROLLARY

D. The False Denunciation Of An Innocent Bishop.

Before the Code canonists were undecided whether bishops who were guilty of the crime of solicitation were to be denounced. Because of the phrase, "*cuiuscumque dignitatis et praeeminentiae,*" contained in the Constitution "*Sacramentum Poenitentiae,*" St. Alphonsus,[77] Berardi,[78] Palmieri,[79] and Kaiser[80] maintained that the obligation to denounce those who were guilty of solicitation touched the denunciation of bishops as well as of priests. Rota[81] and Ballerini[82] denied that bishops were to be denounced, since they themselves were inquisitors and therefore were not subject to trial by other inquisitors. Since the appearance of the Code the opinion of canonists is about equally divided. Vermeersch-Creusen,[83] Cappello,[84]

75. Cf. canon 2343, §§ 3, 4.
76. Iorio, *Compendium,* II, 419, footnote (2).
77. *Theologia Moralis,* lib. VI, n. 685.
78. *De Sollicitatione,* n. 6.
79. *Opus Theologicum,* V, n. 1090, footnote (a).
80. "De obligatione denunciandi confessarios sollicitantes," — *Analecta Ecclesiastica,* VI (1898), 503.
81. *Enchiridion,* n. 263.
82. *Opus Theologicum,* V, n. 1090.
83. *Epitome,* III, n. 603.
84. *De Poenitentia,* n. 689, 2.

Cerato,[85] Pighi,[86] and the Praxis[87] of the Holy Office uphold the view that bishops are to be denounced, not merely in consequence of the demand made by natural law itself, but also in view of the prescription of the positive law. Arregui,[88] Ferreres,[89] De Smet,[90] Iorio,[91] Noldin-Schmitt,[92] and Coronata,[93] relying on the enactment of canon 1557, § 1, 3°, which reserves to the Holy Father the right to judge bishops in criminal matters, maintain that they need not be denounced. The Holy Office loses its competence in cases of solicitation when bishops are implicated, and therefore none of its officials is competent to receive a judicial denunciation. The same authors also base an argument on the choice of the word *sacerdos* in canon 904, which states that solicited penitents are to denounce the *sacerdos* who allured them. In their mind the difference in meaning between the word *sacerdos* and the *episcopus* warrants the conclusion that the denunciation of the *episcopus* is not a duty established in the law. A *dubium iuris* exists. Accordingly the more favorable opinion may safely be followed. If an obligation arises from the natural law, the denunciation cannot be judicially received by the Holy Office unless the Holy Father dispenses from the norm of canon 1557, § 1, 3°, and designates the Holy Office as a competent reviewer of the judicial denunciation.[94]

If any person, then, should dare to approach the Holy Father in order falsely to accuse a bishop of the crime of solicitation, would such an accusation entail the reservation mentioned in canon 894, or would it give rise to the excommunication enacted in canon 2363? Without making any distinctions Cerato asserts that the

85. *De Delicto,* n. 14, 4.
86. *Cursus Theologiae Moralis,* III, n. 396.
87. Cf. Cappello, *loc. cit.*
88. *Summarium,* n. 653.
89. *Compendium,* II, n. 692, b).
90. *De Absolutione,* n. 83.
91. *Compendium,* II, n. 581, *Quaer.* 19.
92. *De Sacramentis,* n. 376.
93. *Institutiones,* IV, 539.
94. Cf. Iorio, *Compendium,* II, n. 581, NB); Coronata, *Institutiones,* IV, 539, footnote 6; Cappello, *De Poenitentia,* n. 689, 2.

false denunciator would be subject to the reservation of his sin as implied in canon 894.[95]

If it be assumed that the bishop did not hear the confession of the calumniator, or that he did not simulate the hearing of a confession in any of the various circumstances postulated in the Constitution *"Sacramentum Poenitentiae,"* but that the informer maliciously stated that a confession did take place and that the crime of solicitation did occur, the excommunication as enacted in canon 2363 would not be incurred. This conclusion is attained in view of the strict interpretation that must be given to the word *confessor.* Since the bishop was not a confessor for the denunciator, no confessor - penitent relationship was established, and no *confessarius proprie dictus* was denounced.

Since there is question of penal matters, the word *sacerdos* must also be accepted in its strict connotation. The terms *sacerdos* and *episcopus* are neither identical nor convertible. Hence the deduction that the delator also escapes the reservation of the sin which reservation is established when an innocent *sacerdos* has been denounced.[96]

Granted however that the bishop did hear the confession of the calumniator, and thereupon the latter made a judicial denunciation of the fictitious crime of solicitation, one must conclude that the delinquent's act entailed the excommunication enacted in canon 2363. The bishop in his capacity of confessor institutes a confessor - penitent relationship. The office of confessor is common to bishops and to priests. It is the office that is criminally abused when a false denunciation of the crime of solicitation is reported. It is immaterial, then, whether the agent who exercises the office is a priest or a bishop.[97]

E. Conclusion.

From the presentation of the foregoing arguments it appears that the legislator had not only a distinct penalty in view when he

95. *De Delicto,* n. 14, 4.

96. Cf. Iorio, *Compendium,* II, 419, n. 582 bis, *Quaer.* 30°, NB. Resolves, 3°, 4; ibid., II, 414, footnote (1).

97. Cf. Iorio, *Compendium,* II, 414, footnote (1).

made canon 2363 part of the law of the Code, but also a distinct transgression. To point to an identification of the laws of canon 894 and canon 2363, the lawgiver would have to indicate that identity more clearly by using at least synonymous terms in the respective canons. While in the pre-Code law there were to be recognized two distinct transgressions but only one and the same juridical sanction against them, it is submitted here that there are today to be recognized the same two distinct transgressions, but each with its own restraint or penalty. The false denunciation of an innocent *confessarius proprie dictus* involves its culprit in an excommunication reserved *speciali modo* to the Holy See. The false accusation of an innocent *sacerdos*, that is of a *confessarius improprie dictus*, or of a priest who has no jurisdiction for the granting of sacramental absolution, gives rise to a sin which in and for its absolution is reserved to the Holy See.

CHAPTER IV

THE DENUNCIATIONS

Article 1. The Recipient of the Denunciation

Nearly all of the canonists who contend that there is a duality of transgressions implied by the wording of canons 894 and 2363 base their reason for that deduction on the observation that the Code presents the use of diverse clauses in the respective canons. Canon 894 employs the phrase *apud iudices ecclesiasticos* and canon 2363 uses the phrase *apud Superiores*.[1] The majority of the authors however favors the view that this difference in the phrases evinces simply a material distinction, and by no means a formal one. The two phrases are therefore interchangeable.[2]

It is common knowledge that in ecclesiastical law judges are distinct from superiors. Incidentally, of course, it may happen that physically they are the same persons. The Holy Father is a superior and at the same time a judge.[3] The same is true of all local Ordinaries with the exception of the vicars general. The latter are superiors, but they are not judges.[4] The major superiors of religious orders or of congregations as well as the minor superiors and all persons enumerated in canon 198 are designated as superiors.[5] Not all of these superiors however are judges. Except for the major superiors in clerical religious orders or in exempt religious congregations, all other religious superiors are excluded as judges.[6] The *officialis* of canon 1573 is a judge, but nowhere in the Code is he classified as a superior. Since the crime of solicitation

1. Cf. authors cited in Chapter III, footnotes (3-12)
2. Cf. authors cited in Chapter III, footnote 1.
3. Cf. canons 449, § 1; 198, § 1; 1557, § 1, 1°, 2°, 3°; 1569.
4. Cf. canons 1573; 2220, § 2; S. C. de Sac., instr. 15 aug. 1936, art. 3, § 2 — *AAS,* XXVIII (1936), 313; canon 1940 collated with canon 1573; Cf also Wernz-Vidal, *Ius Canonicum* VI, 721; T. Muniz, *Procedimientos Ecclesiasticos* (2. ed., 3 vols., Sevilla: Imp. y Lib. de Sobrino de Izquierdo, 1925), III, n. 561, and footnote 4; Beste, *Introductio in Codicem,* p. 827; Coronata, *Institutiones,* III, 391.
5. Cf. canon 488, 8°.
6. Cf. canons 1579, §§ 1, 2; 654-688; 2220, § 1.

is reserved for judgment to the tribunal of the Holy Office, not even the *officialis* is a competent judge to review judicial denunciations which involve the crime of solicitation.[7] Only those persons are competent to review judicial denunciations of the crime of solicitation whom the tribunal of the Holy Office designates. The judgment of priests guilty of the crime of solicitation is reserved to its competence, and to those inferior tribunals to which it issues special instructions. All other persons who attempt to review such a denunciation do so in a non-judicial manner, even though they employ the formalities specified in canon 1936. Needless to say, a non-judicial denunciation is merely a simple denunciation, and in no manner is it fitted and in no way does it suffice for the instituting of a judicial process with a view to convicting the reported confessor.

The persons who are competent in law to review judicial denunciations of the crime of solicitation are the Holy Father,[8] the judges of the tribunal of the Holy Office or of those inferior courts delegated by it,[9] and all local Ordinaries.[10] That local Ordinary in whose diocese the solicited person has his domicile or quasi domicile is to review the denunciation. The penitent, however, is given the option to inform the confessor's local Ordinary, or the local Ordinary of the place where the solicitation was perpetrated.[11] Besides the Holy Office only that local Ordinary in whose diocese the guilty confessor has his domicile is competent to begin the judicial process by ordering the inquest, citing the reported confessor, and pronouncing sentence.[12]

A copy of the denunciation is always to be forwarded to the local Ordinary of the guilty confessor and to the Holy Office. The

7. Cf. canons 247, § 2 collated with canon 1555, §§ 1, 2; S. C. S. Off., instr. 20 febr. 1866, nn. 6, 7 — *Fontes,* n. 990.
8. Canon 1569, § 1; Cf. Coronata, *Institutiones,* IV, 571; Iorio, *Compendium,* II, n. 583.
9. Cf. S. C. S. Off., instr. 20 febr. 1866, n. 6 — *Fontes,* n. 990.
10. Canon 904.
11. Cf. Iorio, *Compendium,* II, n. 583, *Quaer,* 31°; Blat, *Commentarium,* lib. III, Pars I, 272; De Smet, *De Absolutione,* n. 96; Cerato, *Censurae Vigentes,* n. 79, d; Aertnys-Damen, *Theologia Moralis,* II, 287.
12. Jone, *Gesetzbuch,* II, 137; Lega, *De Iudiciis,* IV, nn. 539, 542; Aertnys-Damen, *Theologia Moralis,* II, 287, 289.

Holy Office has a right to possess the information to ascertain whether other denunciations against the same confessor have been made directly to its office.[13]

Included among the local Ordinaries are all the persons classified in canon 198, § 1. The *Capitula,* therefore, and the Vicars Capitular are qualified officials.[14] By special delegation of the Holy See all nuncios, internuncios, and Apostolic Delegates have been empowered to review such denunciations.[15] Besides all of the foregoing persons, their delegated substitutes too become competent officials.[16]

Though the *Superiores Regulares* are judges in the proper sense, they are excluded from all canonical causes that are reserved to the Holy Office. Alexander VII (1655-1667) on July 8, 1660 forbade them to review judicial denunciations of the crime of solicitation though these denunciations were submitted by their subjects. He furthermore decreed that they were not to refuse permission to any of these subjects who were commanded by their confessors to make these depositions to the inquisitors or to the local Ordinaries.[17] On May 15, 1901, the Holy Office reiterated this decree of Alexander VII.[18] The decree has been incorporated in canon 501, § 2, and is the controlling law today.

In view of the words *"debet sacerdotes... denuntiare loci Ordinario"* as they occur in canon 904, does it follow that the vicar general is empowered to review a judicial denunciation of the crime of solicitation? Canon 198 includes him in its enumeration of local Ordinaries. In pre-Code days not even a mandate from his own local Ordinary could bestow upon him the unrestricted right

13. S. C. S. Off., instr., 6 aug. 1897 — *Fontes,* n. 1190; Jone, *loc. cit.;* Cappello, *De Poenitentia,* n. 699, 9; Aertnys-Damen, Lega, *locc. citt.*
14. Cf. Pius IX, const. *Romanus Pontifex,* 28 aug. 1873 — *Fontes,* n. 565; *ASS,* VIII (1873), 401, 402; Rota *Enchiridion,* n. 408; Coronata, *Institutiones,* IV, 572; Cappello, *De Poenitentia,* n. 696, 3°.
15. Vermeersch-Creusen, *Epitome,* I, Appendix, I, n. 18; Arregui, *Summarium,* Appendix, p. 604, n. 18; Cappello, *De Poenitentia,* n. 696, 3.
16. S. C. S. Off., instr. 20 febr. 1866, n. 6 — *Fontes,* n. 990.
17. Const. *"Licet alias"* — *Bullarium* XVI, 582, 583. This Constitution cites Paulus V, const. *"Romanus Pontifex",* 1 sept. 1606, § 2, as responsible for the law. — *Fontes,* n. 194, pp. 371-373.
18. *Fontes,* n. 1254.

to accept or to delegate others to accept judicial denunciations. Like any other ecclesiastic, he could be appointed the delegate of the local Ordinary to review a formal deposition in an individual case. On July 14, 1753, the Holy Office denied the vicar general the right to review or to delegate others to review the judicial denunciation of a guilty confessor.[19]

By means of recource to the Holy Office, however, a special indult could be obtained, which indult would permit the vicar general to review and to delegate others to review the judicial denunciations. On March 20, 1901, an unamed archbishop applied to the Holy Office for the concession that he in his absence might be permitted to delegate his vicar general for reviewing these denunciations. In granting him this request the Holy Office alluded to the prohibition enacted in the year 1753, and Cardinal Gennari added his personal comment, stating that bishops and not their vicars general are the natural inquisitors.[20]

Despite the fact that canon 904 mentions local Ordinaries as the competent reviewers of judicial denunciations, the vicar general is excluded. The canon is a restatement of the corresponding law in pre-Code days, and according to canon 6, 2°, is to be interpreted according to the pre-Code norms of interpretation. Canon 904 itself demands that the authentic norms that governed the interpretation of the Constitution *"Sacramentum Poenitentiae"* be still in effect.[21]

The special permission of the Holy See is no longer required for empowering the vicar general to act in the name of his local Ordinary when the crime of solicitation is involved. Canon 2220, § 2, though it does not specifically treat of reviewing judicial denunciations, states that vicars general cannot inflict penalties without a special mandate. Since the judicial denunciation is eventually destined for the imposition of the penalties specified in canon 2368, § 1, the vicar general must be excluded from accepting and

19. This decree can be found in Giraldi, *Expositio,* II, 643, n. XVIII; cf. also De Smet, *De Absolutione,* n. 188.
20. *ASS,* XXXIII (1901), 553; *Il Monitore Ecclesiastico,* XIII (1901), 6, 7; Coronata, *Institutiones,* IV, 572, footnote (12).
21. Cf. Jone, *Gesetzbuch,* II, 126, e.

reviewing such denunciations. The presence of the phrase *"sine mandato speciali"* has been accepted by canonists as implying that the decrees of canons 1753 and of 1901 have been revoked. Any local Ordinary, when impeded, or absent, can, without a papal indult, delegate his vicar general to review the denunciations.[22]

Article 2. The Ordinary Judicial Denunciation

In view of the special Instruction of the Holy Office pertaining to the form a judicial denunciation is to take, and of the exceptions allowed by the same Office when extraordinary difficulties present themselves, authors generally divide the denunciation into the following classes:

A. the judicial denunciation:
   a. the ordinary judicial denunciation,
   b. the extraordinary judicial denunciation;

B. the irregular denunciation;

C. the simple denunciation.[23]

In the judicial denunciation the penitent is to appear personally before a competent official to manifest to him the crime of solicitation. This must be done in the presence of an ecclesiastical

22. De Smet, *De Absolutione,* n. 94; Jone *Gesetzbuch,* II, 137; De Meester, *Compendium,* III, Pars, II, 268; Chelodi, *Ius Poenale,* n. 88; Sipos, *Enchiridion,* p. 1012; Cappello, *De Poenitentia,* n. 696, 3. Cerato (*De Delicto,* n. 119) speaks of the vicar general receiving a simple denunciation by letter or by messenger, but not a judicial one. Coronata (*Institutiones,* IV, 573), relying on the Instruction of the Holy Office of June 8-9, 1922, as well as on canon 2220, § 2, permits the vicar general, after receiving a special mandate from his local Ordinary, to review the denunciation and also to begin the preliminary inquest (*ad faciendas diligentias*).

23. Cf. S. C. S. Off., instr. 20 febr. 1866, nn. 1-15 — *Fontes,* n. 990; Berardi, *De Sollicitatione,* n. 136; Rota, *Enchiridion,* nn. 414-418; Many, "De Peccato Sollicitiationis," — *Le Canoniste,* XVIII (1895), 720; Berardi, *Theologia Moralis,* V, nn. 635-639; Cerato, *De Delicto,* nn. 116, 1, 118, 1, a, 2; De Smet, *De Absolutione,* n. 97, I, a, II, b; Cappello, *De Poenitentia,* nn. 698, 7°, 701, 1-6; Coronata, *Institutiones,* IV, 569; Iorio, *Compendium,* II, n. 583, *Quaer.* 31°, Notanda I.

notary.[24] Not only is the penitent placed under oath to tell the truth and to keep secrecy, but the officials too must take the oath to keep the report secret. For the taking of this oath the Instruction of 1866 demanded that even those priests who made denunciations of the crime of solicitation had to touch the gospels when taking this oath.[25] Though canon 1622 accords to a priest the privilege to touch his breast when he takes an oath, the Instruction of the Holy Office issued on June 8-9, 1922, demands that the norm of the 1866 Instruction be retained.[26] After the denunciation is completed, both he who brings the charge and the officials who review it, sign their names to the document upon which the denunciation is made.[27]

Article 3. The Extraordinary Judicial Denunciation

The Holy Office exercises great solicitude that the crime of solicitation never remain unpunished. Whenever difficulties prevented the fulfillment of the rigorous norms outlined for the normal judicial denunciation, it was ready to relax them somewhat by allowing all officials legitimately empowered to review denunciations to dispense from some of the formalities. Usually this entailed foregoing the services of the notary and delegating a confessor to review the report privately.[28]

24. S. C. S. Off., instr., 20 febr 1866, n. 6 — *Fontes,* n. 990; De Smet, *De Absolutione,* n. 97.
25. *Ibid.,* n. 14 — *Fontes,* n. 990.
26. This Instruction was approved by Pius XI on June 8, 1922, and released on June 9, 1922, under the direction of Cardinal Merry del Val. On the fly leaf of this Instruction appear the following words: "*Instructio* servanda diligenter in archivo secreto Curiae pro norma interna, nec publicanda nec ullis commentariis *augenda.*" In the main this Instruction of 1922 is very similar to the previous Instructions issued by the Holy Office in 1866, 1890 and 1897. It was necessary however to introduce changes in order to adapt the various norms to the prescriptions of the Code.
27. S. C. S. Off., instr., 20 febr. 1866, n. 6 — *Fontes,* n. 990; Cf. also Lega, *De Iudiciis,* IV, n. 540; Rota, *Enchiridion,* n. 407; Cerato, *Censurae Vigentes,* n. 45; Berardi, *De Sollicitatione,* n. 137; Aertnys-Damen, *Theologia Moralis,* II, 288, III.
28. S. C. S. Off., instr., 20 febr. 1866, n. 8 — *Fontes,* n. 990; Cf. also Berardi, *Theologia Moralis,* V, n. 638, 1°; Blat, *Commentarium,* lib.

Whenever persons, who are dependent on others, find it inconvenient, if not impossible, to make a judicial denunciation the extraordinary concession is readily made. The usual examples given by authors are: the cases of women religious who cannot leave their convent because of the restrictions of the cloister; of a daughter who cannot leave her parental home without arousing suspicion on the part of her mother; of servants who find it embarrasing to ask for permission to leave their employ even for a short while; of persons beset with sickness or with any other physical or moral impediment that prevents a personal appearance before the judge.[29]

The Holy Father, the officials of the Holy Office, the local Ordinary, the nuncios, the internuncios, the Apostolic Delegates, and also vicars general when they have a special mandate to review the judicial denunciation, may grant this dispensation. A special formula to be used for this extraordinary manner of accepting and reviewing judicial denunciations was drawn up by the Holy Office.[30]

Pre-Code authors were not in agreement whether the denunciation to be reviewed by a delegated confessor without the intervention of a notary was to be accepted in the confessional or outside it. Berardi, citing Scavini (1790-1869) and Frassinetti (1803-1868) in support, favored the use of the confessional.[31] Gury (1801-1866)[32] and Rota[33] preferred that it be reviewed outside the confessional. The Instruction of 1922 suggests that the confessional

III, Pars I, 277; Iorio, *Compendium,* II, n. 583, *Quaer.* 31°, Notanda I, a); De Smet, *De Absolutione,* n. 97, II; Cappello, *De Poenitentia,* n.701, 3, 7; Cerato, *De Delicto,* n. 118, 1, b.

29. Cf. St. Alphonsus, *Theologia Moralis,* lib. VI, n. 699; Ballerini-Palmieri, *Opus Theologicum,* V, n. 1151.
30. The 1866 Instruction as reported in *Fontes,* n. 990, did not reproduce this formula. It can be found in *ASS,* III (1867), 505, 506; Giraldi (*Expositio,* II, 643, n. XVIII) and Berardi (*De Sollicitatione,* nn. 146-148) also furnish formulas. In the appendix of the Instruction of June 8-9, 1922 another formula is found.
31. *De Sollicitatione,* n. 147.
32. *Compendium,* II, n. 598, 4°.
33. *Enchiridion,* n. 447.

be used. Without vitiating the judicial denunciation the delegated confessor can also dispense the penitent from affixing his signature to the document bearing his statement.[34]

Still further relaxations are tolerated by the Holy Office in the event that the extraordinary judicial denunciations is incapable of execution. The penitent is directed, either personally or through the kindness of another, to consult the Holy Office or the local Ordinary for additional advice, *pro opportunis provendentiis consuluerit... et deinde se gerat iuxta instructionem quam erit acceptura.*[35]

Upon the arrival of the letters or the messenger of the penitent seeking further instruction on procedure the Holy Office is wont to respond with one of the following suggestions:

1. it orders the denunciation to be sent by mail;
2. it designates the rural dean or some other ecclesiastic as its delegate to review the deposition judicially;
3. it commands the local Ordinary to go to the home of the penitent to review the denunciation;
4. it delegates the penitent's confessor to review it without the services of a notary;
5. it excuses the penitent for this one occasion from making a deposition if the circumstances warrant such a total dispensation.[36]

34. Rota, *op. cit.*, n. 444; Berardi, *loc. cit.;* Many "De Peccato Sollicitationis," — *Le Canoniste,* XVIII (1895), 711.
35. S. C. S. Off., instr. 20 febr. 1866, n. 7 — *Fontes,* n. 990; Rota *Enchiridion,* n. 437; Coronata, *Institutiones,* IV, 569, footnote 5. Cerato (*De Delicto,* n. 116) misinterprets this Instruction. He maintains that a simple denunciation is acceptable to the Holy Office. Instruction (n. 7) clearly states that the letter or the messenger are to be sent solely for the sake of obtaining information on procedure, and are not to make the denunciation.
36. Cf. Berardi, *De Sollicitatione,* n. 160; Rota, *Enchiridion,* n. 455; Lehmkuhl, *Theologia Moralis,* II, n. 1257; Many, "De Peccato Sollicitationis," — *Le Canoniste,* XVIII (1895), 711; Berardi, *Theologia Moralis,* V, nn. 638, 1°-4°, 653; Ballerini-Palmieri (*Opus Theologicum,* V, n. 1151) and D'Annibale (*Summula,* III, n. 368, footnote 20)

Article 4. The Simple Denunciation

The Instructions of the Holy Office insist on judicial denunciations. Occasionally denunciations are brought to its tribunal by means of letter or through a messenger. Such denunciations are referred to as simple denunciations.[37] All anonymous letters and letters that contain fictitious names, or letters that reveal the true names of the denunciators but fail to indicate their return address, are suspected as calumnious.[38]

It is the practice of the Holy Office to accept simple denunciations provided that they are properly signed and indicate a return address. A competent delegate will be dispatched to approach the writer to have him put the simple denunciation into legal form.[39] Though the simple denunciation is never acceptable as a means for instituting a judicial trial, it can be used as proof in the trial of a confessor who has been judicially denounced by others, *ut probatione minus idonea alias probationes coadiuvet.*[40] Since the Code has introduced canons 1942, § 2, and 1645, § 4, even anonymous letters having a bearing on the crime of solicitation can be used as adminicular proof. The *Pagella* of 1922 refers to this fact. It denotes a change from the Instruction of 1866 which stated,

referred to the situation in which such outright dispensations were granted. Cf. also *Fontes,* n. 787; *Collectanea,* n. 308; Giraldi, *Expositio,* II, 640.

37. Benger, *Pastoral-theologie,* III, 439, f; Berardi, *De Sollicitatione,* nn. 152, 162; D'Annibale, *Summula,* III, n. 369; Craisson, *Manuale,* III, n. 3888; Rota, *Enchiridion,* n. 419; Coronata, *Institutiones,* IV, 569; Cappello, *De Poenitentia,* n. 701, 4, 6. De Smet (*De Absolutione,* n. 123) calls the simple denunciation *aequivalenter juridica* in so far as it can serve the bishop as a basis for imposing a suspension *ex informata conscientia.*
38. S. C. S. Off., instr. 20 febr. 1866, n. 6 — *Fontes,* n. 990; Rota, *Enchiridion,* n. 419; Berardi, *De Sollicitatione,* nn. 152, 162.
39. Cf. Albitius, *De Inconstantia in Fide,* cap. 35, n. 21; D. Bouix (1808-1870), *De Iudiciis Ecclesiasticis* (2 vols. in 1, Parisiis, 1855), II, 498; Potestas, *Examen,* II, Pars III, n. 599; Bucceroni, *De C. "Sac. Poenit.",* n. 45; Coronata, *op. cit.,* IV, 569; Aertnys-Damen, *Theologia Moralis,* II, n. 427; Wouters, *Manuale,* II, n. 426, *Scholion* I, III, nota.
40. Berardi, *De Sollicitatione,* n. 163.

"*Denunciationes anonymae contra sollicitantes ad turpia nullam vim habent. .*"[41]

Classified in the same category as simple denunciations are the irregular or illegitimate denunciations. Whenever a condition necessary for the valid procedure in the reviewing of a denunciation has been overlooked or culpably neglected, the deposition is defective and hence called irregular. The denunciation can become irregular if:

1. the penitent fails to take the oath to tell the truth or to keep secrecy;
2. the delegate and (or) notary have no document to prove their delegation;
3. the delegate and (or) notary fail to take the oath of secrecy;
4. the signatures are not affixed to the deposition;
5. the delegate brings the deposition orally to the local Ordinary or to the Holy Office;
6. the deposition is made to a *Superior Regularis*, to a vicar general, to a rural dean, or to any other priest who has no delegation from the local Ordinary or from the Holy Office to review the denunciation.[42]

It is evident that if dispensations from the affixing of the signature or from compliance with other formalities are obtained, the denunciation will not be vitiated. The transcript of the document authorizing the dispensation is to accompany the denunciation.[43] Failure through oversight or neglect to comply with any of the enumerated formalities will invalidate the deposition and occasion a deferring of the judicial prosecution. If the prosecution is never-

41. *Fontes,* n. 990, n. 6.
42. Cf. Berardi, *De Sollicitatione,* nn. 150, 151; Rota, *Enchiridion,* nn. 390, 411; Jone, *Gesetzbuch,* II, 126, e; Cerato, *De Delicto,* n. 118, 2, 3; Coronata, *Institutiones,* IV, 574, footnote 5 (continued from p. 573).
43. Cf. Maurus Kaiser, "De obligatione denunciandi confessarios sollicitantes," — *Analecta Ecclesiastica,* VI (1898), 502; Many, "De Peccato Sollicitationis," — *Le Canoniste,* XVIII (1895), 711; Wouters, *Manuale,* II, n. 426, *Scholion,* I, n, III, nota.

theless commenced before the denunciation is put into legal form (*in forma*) the trial will be without judicial effect.[44]

Article 5. The Local Ordinary Reviewing the Denunciation as a Superior

The question may be raised whether the local Ordinary, a superior and at the same time a judge, has the option to review a denunciation of the crime of solicitation as an evangelical denunciation or as a judicial denunciation. Blat,[45] Motry,[46] Tanquerey,[47] Cerato,[48] De Smet,[49] Merkelbach[50] and the anonymous writer in *Il Monitore Ecclesiastico,*[51] take it for granted that he can review it as an evangelical denunciation. They are of the opinion that, whenever the local Ordinary reviews a false denunciation *qua Superior,* the calumniator will incur the excommunication enacted in canon 2363, but when he reviews it *qua iudex* the denunciator's sin will become reserved to the Holy See as prescribed by canon 894.

Coronata thinks that the local Ordinary can determine in each case whether to accept and review the denunciation judicially or paternally.[52] Bucceroni (1841-1918) mentioned that it was a common practice in many places to have bishops review the denunciations without the formalities of law, that they might impose a mild penalty, especially for the first offense. He doubted, however,

44. "2 Praeceptum huiusmodi, uti omnia quae ad huius Supremi Tribunalis procedendi rationem spectant, strictissimi iuris censendum est, ita ut, eo neglecto, ad ulteriora procedi nequeat." — S. C. S. Off., instr. 6 aug. 1897 — *Fontes,* n. 1190. The Instruction of June 8-9, 1922, demands that its norms be followed to the very finger tips, ". . . ut ad unguem servent et servare faciunt. . ." wrote Cardinal Merry del Val when he released it.
45. *Commentarium,* lib III, Pars I, 260.
46. *Diocesan Faculties,* pp. 110, 116, footnote (70).
47. *Synopsis,* I, n. 455, 1°.
48. *De Delicto,* n. 129, adn. 1; *ibid.,* n. 118, 2, n. 131, 3; *Censurae Vigentes,* n. 79, adn.
49. *De Absolutione,* nn. 110, 123, 2.
50. *Summa,* III, 643, C, b.
51. "Il Codice di Diritto Canonico: Riassunto e Dilucidazioni," XXXI (1919), 149; Cf. also Badii, *Institutiones Iuris Canonici,* II, n. 368, d).
52. *Institutiones,* IV, 574.

whether that was a lawful procedure in view of the unusual difficulty involved in obtaining proof of guilt. He seriously doubted that such a practice could ever obtain the force of law through custom.[53] Rota[54] and Kaiser[55] definitely denied that the local Ordinary had the option.

Iorio suggests that the local Ordinary give a paternal and even a judicial admonition. In favoring such a procedure he relies on an antiquated decree of the Holy Office, which recommended that local Ordinaries wait until a second and even a third denunciation had been received before they started the inquest.[56] The Instruction of 1897 revoked that recommendation and ordered that as soon as a denunciation was received the local Ordinaries were to proceed to the special inquest to find the indications of guilt.[57] According to Aertnys-Damen the suggestions of the 1897 Instruction are still followed today.[58]

There are many canonists who maintain that a penitent will escape the penalty of excommunication by bringing a simple denunciation of a crime of solicitation to the local Ordinary, inasmuch

53. *De C. "Sac. Poenit."*, nn. 47, 53.
54. *Enchiridion,* n. 418.
55. "De obligatione denunciandi confessores sollicitantes," — *Analecta Ecclesiastica,* VI (1898), 502.
56. *Compendium,* II, 415, *Quaer.* 23°, Resp. NB. Cf. also S. C. S. Off., decr 6 iulii 1835 — "Instruction de la S. Congregation de l'Inquisition Touchant la Denonciation des Confesseurs," *NRT,* VIII (1876), 352, S. C. S. Off., instr. 20 febr. 1866 — *Fontes,* n. 990, n. 10.
57. "5 Ordinarius igitur toties quoties aliquam de infando sollicitationis crimine denunciationem acceperit, illico ad diligentias peragendas procedet. . ." — S. C. S. Off., instr. 6 aug. 1897, *Fontes,* n. 1190.
58. "Denuntiatione qualibet accepta, Ordinarius tenetur sub gravi eam quamprimum communicare cum promotore justitiae qui declarare debet an crimen sollicitationis adsit vel non, et si Ordinarius ab eo dissentiat, intra decem dies rem deferre ad S. Officium. Si Ordinarius et promotor justitiae in unum consentiunt, vel utcumque promotor justitiae recursum ad S. Officium non faciat, tunc Ordinarius, si delictum sollicitationis non adesse decreverit, acta in archivo secreto reponenda mandet; . . . si vero adesse censuerit, illico ad inquisitionem procedat." — *Theologia Moralis,* II, n. 427, V. Cf. also canon 1942, § 1.

as canon 2368, § 2, uses the words *"qui scienter omiserit."*[59] The penitent will hardly be expected to know what constitutes a simple denunciation and a judicial denunciation. He will however be obliged to make the deposition judicial when the local Ordinary calls upon him to do so. De Smet,[60] Merkelbach,[61] Cerato[62] and Jone[63] advise that a simple denunciation of the crime of solicitation precede the judicial denunciation. The fact that it is the *praxis* of the Holy Office to accept simple denunciations as long as the letters are properly signed and indicate a return address, in no way implies that the simple denunciation satisfies the obligation imposed by the word *denuntiare* employed in canons 904 and 2368, § 2. The Holy Office will never act on such simple denunciations until they are put *in forma*;[64] and likewise will not honor them as having probative value unless other judicial denunciations against the same confessor have been previously made.

Though the various Instructions emanating from the Holy Office do not prohibit the local Ordinaries from reviewing evangelical denunciations instead of judicial ones — they are silent about the matter — the general import is that simple denunciations cannot serve as a basis for instituting a criminal process calculated to punish the reported confessor. For a local Ordinary, after reviewing a simple or an evangelical denunciation, to order a special inquest, to examine character witnesses, to cite the accused con-

59. Iorio, *Compendium,* II, n. 583, *Quaer.* 31°, Notanda II; Aertnys-Damen, *Theologia Moralis,* II, 288; Ferreres, *Compendium,* II, n. 701, 3°; De Smet, *De Absolutione,* nn. 99, 100, 123; Cerato, *De Delicto,* n. 118, 3; Coronata, *Institutiones,* IV, 569, 573, footnote 5 (continued on p. 574); Cappello, *De Poenitentia,* n. 701, 6.

60. *loc. cit.*

61. *Summa,* III, n. 645, B, 2, a), b).

62. *De Delicto,* n. 101,; *Censurae Vigentes,* n. 45.

63. *Gesetzbuch,* II, 135.

64. ". . . urgenti gravi omnino ac prorsus extraordinaria causa, denuntiatio etiam fieri poterit per relationem a denuntiante scriptam, dummodo tamen coram loci Ordinario ejusve delegato ac notario si adsit, jurejurando postea confirmetur et subsignetur." — Aertnys-Damen, *Theologia Moralis,* II, 288, IV; Berardi, *De Sollicitatione,* n. 163; Coronata, *Institutiones,* 569; D'Annibale, *Summula,* III, n. 369; Rota, *Enchiridion,* nn. 418, 419.

fessor, and to pronounce judgment against him, would leave the entire procedure without valid juridical effect.[65]

Whenever the local Ordinary proceeds in a case involving solicitation he must adhere to the norms prescribed by the Holy Office.[66] Since these norms are so emphatic in commanding the local Ordinary to review the denunciation of the crime of solicitation judicially in order to be able to proceed immediately to the gathering of information leading to a formal accusation, there is little reason to believe that the local Ordinary has any option in the matter. On the contrary he must accept and review the denunciations judicially rather than evangelically. This conclusion is confirmed by a decree in the *Fonti* as affecting Orientals, according to which decree the solicited persons cannot be content with a denunciation made to their superior *sub sigillo confessionis;* rather they are commanded to make it judicially so that the *promotor iustitiae* can draw up his indictment (*illos iudicialiter denunciare debent, ad effectum ut fiscus procedere possit*).[67]

Canonists usually stay within the limits of the law when they recommend the application of penal remedies for priests reported as guilty of the crime of solicitation. Wouters (1864-1933) mentions that whenever the local Ordinary reviews a denunciation of the crime of solicitation, but recognizes that the crime as defined in law is not present, he may admonish and even punish the priest, not as one guilty of solicitation, but as one guilty of the definitely recognized or certainly established improprieties.[68] In their endeavor to forestall future transgressions, canonists acknowledge to local

65. Cf. S. C. S. Off., instr. 20 febr. 1866, nn. 6, 11, 12 — *Fontes,* n. 990; 6 aug. 1897, nn. 2, 5 — *Fontes,* n. 1190; canons 247, §2; 1555, §1; ". . . quia denunciatio, nisi iuridica fuerit, ad procedendum et sententiam ferendam non valet;. . ." — Cerato, *De Delicto,* n. 118, 2. The 1922 *Pagella* likewise intimates this when it prescribes that its norms are to be followed *ad unguem.*

66. Cf. canon 247, §2, collated with canon 1555, §1; Cappello, *De Poenitentia,* n. 721, 1, 2.

67. *Sacra Congregazione "pro Ecclesia Orientali," Codificazione Canonica Orientale Fonti* (XV Fasciculi, Romae: Tipographia Poliglotta Vaticana, 1931-1933), Fasc. II, Parte Seconda, p. 607.

68. *Manuale,* II, n. 426, Scholion, I, n. IV, 2, a).

Ordinaries the right to inflict a penal remedy, but only after the crime of solicitation has been denounced judicially and when at the same time the *indicia criminis* are not sufficiently grave to warrant an accusatory action by the *promotor institiae.*[69]

Article 6. The Privilege of the Vicars Apostolic

In pre-Code days only one exception whereby a local Ordinary could inflict penalties *extra iudicii ordinem* upon a priest reported guilty of the crime of solicitation was tolerated. In 1775 Pius VI (1775-1799) permitted a Vicar Apostolic of Cochin China to relax the solemnities of the procedure. Whatever process he chose was acceptable to the Holy Office, provided that the Vicar's judgment and prudence safeguarded justice so that no innocent confessor would be punished. This concession was granted because of the difficulties of travel to which the penitent would be subjected if obliged to make a judicial denunciation, and also because of the difficulty in obtaining proofs according to the rigorous inquisitorial process.[70]

This indult was incorporated in the Instruction of 1866,[71] and in 1883 the Sacred Congregation for the Propagation of the Faith extended it to all Vicars Apostolic.[72] As a consequence simple denunciations brought to the attention of the Vicars Apostolic could be acted on by them. The document that granted them the privilege to proceed *extra iudicii ordinem* did not include a penalty for the non-judicial false denunciations. Only the judicial false denunciations were under the inhibitive sanction which constituted them as reserved sins.

69. ". . . si satis indicia habentur, sed non sufficientia ad actionem accusatoriam, monendus est reus, vario modo, pro varietate casus. . ." — Aertnys-Damen, *Theologia Moralis,* II, 289, n. 428, II; Cf also Coronata, *Institutiones,* IV, 557; Wouters, *Manuale,* II, n. 426, Scholion, I, n. V, 3; Cappello, *De Poenitentia,* n. 716, 9; De Smet, *De Absolutione,* n. 116; Sole, *De Delictis et Poenis,* n. 87; canons, 2307; 1946, § 1, 2°.
70. Cf. S. C. de Prop. Fide, instr. (ad Vic. Ap. Cochinchin), 26 aug. 1775 — *Collectanea,* n. 509; *Fontes,* n. 4568.
71. N. 15 — *Fontes,* n. 990.
72. S. C. de Prop. Fide, litt. encycl. 25 iul. 1883 — *Fontes,* n. 4902; *Collectanea,* n. 1604.

Blat avers that the Church has added the penalty of canon 2363 to supplement the already existing inhibitive sanction with reference to false judicial denunciations.[73] The more generic term *Superiores* had to be used in canon 2363 instead of the term *iudices* to include the simple, non-judicial denunciations that were made to those *Superiores* who were privileged to act upon them. This observation of Blat stands or falls on the historic reality of whether it was the purpose, the *ratio legis,* of canon 2363. Granted that this had been the mind of the legislator, the norm of canon 2363 could then not be extended to all superiors indiscriminately. It would have to be limited to those *Superiores,* the Vicars Apostolic namely, who enjoy the privilege to inaugurate a less formal process against the denounced confessors. The force of the excommunication could not affect the denunciators if they brought a simple denunciation *apud Superiores* who cannot act *extra iudicii ordinem.* The very last sentence in n. 15 of the Instruction of 1866 cautioned that the concession could not be considered common. Without a papal indult it could not be invoked.[74] Though extended in 1883 to all Vicars Apostolic, it did not become a common privilege for other local Ordinaries. Later Instructions of the Holy Office did not extend the indult any further. The *Pagella* of 1922 is silent about it.

Article 7. The Suspension *"EX INFORMATA CONSCIENTIA"*

Though foreign to this study, a brief resume of the opinions whether a suspension *ex informata conscientia* for a simple denunciation of the crime of solicitation is permissible or feasible is in order. The purpose is to discover whether a false denunciation which the local Ordinary uses as a basis for his suspension will bring into operation against the calumniator the sanctions enacted

73. ". . .Ut ergo falsas omnes huiusmodi denunciationes [factas extra iudicii ordinem apud Vicarios Apostolicos] omnino scelestas puniret S. Mater Ecclesia efficacius condidit novum canonem sub "Titulo de crimine falso ultimum,. . ." — *Commentarium,* lib. V, n. 204.

74. "15. . . . Iam vero quisque videt hanc indulgentiam pro locis adeo dissitis, ac disporatis factam, neque omnibus esse communem, neque absque Apostolicae Sedis auctoritate iure posse ubivis induci." — *Fontes,* n. 990.

in canons 894 and 2363. Planchard was the outstanding canonist who before the Code upheld the opinion that this extraordinary means of punishing the guilty confessors could be resorted to by the local Ordinary. The process outlined by the Instruction of the Holy Office could be considered as sufficiently difficult to warrant the use of the suspension *ex informata conscientia.*[75]

Since the Code De Smet has become the chief proponent of that view. His defense is based on the grounds that all the elements demanded by the canons on suspension *ex informata conscientia* are verified in cases of solicitation. Canon 2191, § 1, restricts the use of the penalty to an occult crime. The crime of solicitation qualifies for this condition. The *grave incommodum* referred to in canon 2186, § 1, is present, since the application of the rigorous norms of the *Pagella* is arduous. The regulations on suspension *ex informata conscientia* do not *nominatim* forbid its application to cases of solicitation, but rather include it, inasmuch as the *fontes* listed for canon 2191 refer to a case in which the Congregation of the Council upheld a sentence of suspension *ex informata conscientia* imposed by a local Ordinary for the crime of solicitation.[76] Finally there is the observation of De Smet[77] and of Bucceroni[78] that it is not an uncommon practice for local Ordinaries to abstract from the Instructions of the Holy Office in cases of solicitation and to employ instead the suspension *ex informata conscientia.* De Smet concludes that while the suspension *ex informata conscientia* constitutes an extraordinary measure (*modus*) in most criminal cases, it becomes an ordinary one in the cases which involve the crime of solicitation.[79]

Most of the canonists who have given the question a thought take exception to the opinion of Planchard and De Smet. Cappello admits

75. "Procedure Contre les Sollicitants," — *NRT,* XXIII (1891), 621.
76. S. C. S., Lucionen, 8 apr. 1848, ad 2 — *Thesaurus Resolutionum S. Congregationis Concilii* (167 vols., Romae, 1718-1908), CVIII, 135, 165, ad I. In the resolution referred to, the crime of solicitation in its strict meaning was not at all considered. Rather other excesses against the virtue of purity were punished.
77. *De Absolutione,* n. 123, 2; *ibid.,* n. 110, 3.
78. *De C. "Sac. Poenit.",* nn. 47, 53.
79. *Op. cit.,* n. 110, 2.

the force of the argument that favors De Smet's contention, but he opposes it nevertheless. He argues that unless the detailed instructions of the Holy Office were resorted to it would be too difficult, if not even impossible, to gather proof regarding the guilt of the denounced confessor.[80] Cerato considers the act illicit, but acknowledges that the sentence would be valid. An appeal against it could be lodged with suspensive effect.[81] Wernz (1842-1914),[82] Heiner (1849-1919)[83] and Lega (1860-1935)[84] were the pre-Code authors who denied its use to local Ordinaries in cases pertaining to solicitation. Following the same opinion among post-Code commentators, besides Cappello and Cerato already alluded to are Sole,[85] Pistocchi,[86] Cocchi,[87] Coronata,[88] and Salucci.[89]

Iorio summarized the appraisal of the respective opinions by concluding that it is certain doctrine that the local Ordinary cannot licitly use the suspension *ex informata conscientia,* and that it is also probable that he cannot resort to it validly, *certo quoad liceitatem. . . probabiliter quoad validitatem.*[90] Though not directly considering this extraordinary means of penalizing a denounced confessor, Coronata cautions that a prudent superior should never punish a denounced priest unless the denunciation is judicially reviewed, or if the denunciation was accepted in a simple manner, he should first seek confirmation of it in a judicial manner, lest he expose an innocent priest to the danger of being submitted to an unjust penalty.[91]

Should a local Ordinary however rely on the slight probability

80. *De Poenitentia,* n. 720, 3.
81. *De Delicto,* n. 128.
82. *Ius Decretalium,* VI, n. 472.
83. *De Processu Criminali Ecclesiastico* (Latine vertit ac Denuo edidit Dr. Arthurus Wynen, Romae: Fridericus Pustet, 1912), p. 167.
84. *De Iudiciis,* IV, 550.
85. *De Delictis et Poenis,* n. 424.
86. *I Canoni Penali,* pp. 236, 237.
87. *De Delictis et Poenis,* n. 235, a).
88. *Institutiones,* IV, 557, footnote 3.
89. *Il Diritto Penali,* II, 272, 274.
90. *Compendium,* II, 422, *Quaer.* 34.°.
91. *Op. cit.,* IV, 574, in footnote 5 (continued from p. 573).

that allows him to use the suspension *ex informata conscientia,* then upon the receipt of a simple denunciation by letter or by messenger he would have to begin to gather proofs of guilt by ordering a simple inquest to present to the Holy See in the event that a recourse be made by the suspended confessor.[92] Based on the supposition that the local Ordinary can proceed to punish the denounced confessor by invoking the extraordinary measure of the suspension *ex informata conscientia* De Smet concluded that a false denunciation brought to the local Ordinary without benefit of the judicial procedure will be subject to the law's inhibitive sanction in the same manner as the judicial false denunciation. If this sanction were not attached to the simple denunciation, he avers, many false denunciations would escape punishment, especially in those instances in which bishops proceed against the reported confessors by means of the suspension *ex informata conscientia.*[93]

Since the procedure governing the penalization of the crime of solicitation, including the manner of introducing it by a judicial denunciation, is reserved to the Holy Office and to the inferior courts delegated by it, the prescriptions of canon 1555, § 1, are in force. This canon regulates that no other norms than those indicated by the Holy Office have any validity in processes affecting this crime. Through the application of the principle of canon 19, namely that in penal matters the law is to receive a strict interpretation, and through compliance with the norms of the Instruction of the Holy Office of June 8-9, 1922, those persons who are capable in law to review denunciations concerning the crime of solicitation must accept them judicially, that is as judges, the conclusion follows that the *Superiores* who receive mention in canon 2363 are synonymous with the *iudices ecclesiastici* whom canon 894 contemplates.[94]

92. Cf. canons 1939, § 2, 2194; Coronata, *op. cit.,* III, 387.
93. *De Absolutione,* n. 123, 2.
94. Cf. Raus, *Institutiones,* p. 412, b; Pistocchi, *I Canoni Penali,* p 213; Vermeersch-Creusen, *Epitome,* III, n. 565; Wouters, *Manuale,* II, n. 427, footnote 4 on p. 335; Cappello, *De Poenitentia,* n. 606, 5°; Jone, *Gesetzbuch,* II, 126, d); Sole, *De Delictis et Poenis,* n. 416; Coronata, *Institutiones,* IV, 503; Chelodi, *Ius Poenale,* n. 88; Claeys Bouuaert-

Though canon 2363 introduces a new penalty for the false denunciation of the crime of solicitation, it cannot be demonstrated that the *Superiores* to whom the false denunciation is made are any other that the officials mentioned in canon 894, or simply the *loci Ordinarii* of canon 904. Nor can it be demonstrated that the *loci Ordinarii* can receive the denunciation in a paternal or evangelical rather than in a judicial manner.

Article 8. The Contrast Between "Accusation" in Canon 894 and "Denunciation" in Canon 2363

A. Pre-Code Law And Its Interpretation.

Canon 894 uses the words, *"Unicum peccatum... reservatum... est falsa delatio, qua sacerdos innocens accusatur..."*, while canon 2363 has these, *"Si quis... confessarium... apud Superiores falso denuntiaverit."* Does the word "accusation" used in canon 894 take on the meaning that obtains for the term in canon law today? Did the words *falso insimulare and calumniare* which were employed in the Constitution *"Sacramentum Poenitentiae,"* the source for these two canons, imply the same juridical connotation attached to the words *accusare* and *denuntiare* in the law before the Code?

Canon 1934 speaks of an accusation in criminal processes. The right to present a criminal accusation is exclusively reserved to the *promotor iustitiae*. Although the practice known in history as the *actio popularis*, that is, the right of any private citizen not prohibited in law to bring a criminal charge to court, had not been resorted to in ecclesiastical procedure for many centuries, the prescription of canon 1934 was the first written legislation that outlawed it.[95]

Simenon, *Manuale*, II, n. 142, footnote (1); Salucci, *Il Diritto Penali*, II, n. 314; Cocchi, *De Delictis et Poenis*, n. 222; Pruemmer, *Manuale Theologiae Moralis*, III, n. 513.

95. "Verum hodie, quum accusationis forma non adhiberi soleat in foro eccl [esiastico]; — Lega, *De Iudiciis*, IV, 189, 200, 110-112; Bouix, *De Iudiciis*, II, 3, 11; Schmalzgrueber, *Ius Ecclesiasticum Universam*, lib, V, tit. 1, nn. 26, 37; Del Bene, *De Officio*, Pars I, *Dub.* XV, n. 18; Ferraris, *Prompta Bibliotheca*, I, 87, n. 4, ad v. *accusator;* Wernz, *Ius Decretalium*, V, 63, n. 882 Scholion, I; *ibid.*, n. 820; Coronata, *Institutiones*, III, 381; Vermeersch-Creusen, *Epitome*, III, 260.

Accusation is defined as a judicial action by which an alleged culprit is brought before a competent judge for the sake of securing his punishment.[96] The *promotor iustitiae* is forbidden to bring an accusation to the judge unless he has probable evidence of guilt. This evidence can come to his notice through notoriety of the crime, or also as a result of a general or a special inquisition, or finally through a denunciation.[97] In the decades preceding the promulgation of the Code criminal accusation had the same connotation it has today, though its use was not restricted to the *promotor iustitiae*. Besides manifesting the crime and its perpetrator to the judge for the sake of vindicating justice, the accuser also had to supply all the proofs of guilt. He became a plaintiff (*actor*) in the trial.[98]

Instead of the introduction of criminal trials by means of accusations, the simple and the judicial denunciations were substituted. These denunciations relieved the delator of the burden of supplying the proofs himself, and freed him of the obligation of submitting to the dreaded *poena talionis* if he failed in his prosecution.[99] He was however expected to point out all indica-

96. Cf. Coronata, *Institutiones,* III, 381; Iosephus Noval, *Commentarium Codicis Iuris Canonici Libri IV Processibus, Pars I De Iudiciis* (Augustae Taurinorum-Romae: Marietti, 1920), nn. 762, 765, 376; Vermeersch-Creusen, *Epitome,* III, 259.

97. Cf. canons 1939; 1946-47; 1954-55; Cf. Wouters, *Manuale,* II, n. 426, Scholion I, n. V, 4; Aertnys-Damen, *Theologia Moralis,* II, n. 428; Claeys Bouuaert-Simenon, *Manuale,* III, 275; Coronata, *Institutiones,* III, 382, and footnote 1; Vermeersch-Creusen, *Epitome,* III, 260.

98. Cf. Lega, *De Iudiciis,* IV, 185; F. Roberti, "De Iure Denuntiandi Nullitatem Matrimonii — Animadversiones," — *Apollinaris,* III, (1930), 248.

99. The *poena talionis* consisted in the imposition of the same punishment upon the plaintiff in a criminal process that would have befallen the defendant had the latter been convicted in the trial. As soon as the plaintiff had signed the brief (*libellus*) he became liable to the *poena talionis* if he defaulted in prosecuting his case, or if he failed to convict the defendant. Cf. C. 2, C. II, q. 3: — *Decretum Gratiani emendatum et notationibus illustratum una cum glossis* (Romae: 1582); Philippus Jaffe (1819-1870), *Regesta Pontificum Romanorum ab condita Ecclesia ad annum post Christum natum MCXCVIII* (2. ed., cura G. Wattenbach, F. Kaltenbrunner, P. Ewald, S. Lowenfeld,

tions of guilt, to name witnesses, and to produce documents that would lead to conviction. These were delivered into the hands of the *promotor fiscalis,* or to the judge who was to pass judgment on the worthiness of the case, for the sake of guiding him in deciding whether to proceed to an inquest or to reject the denunciation.[100]

The denunciator did not enter the judicial trial as a plaintiff. He merely sought the services of the judge or of the *promotor fiscalis,* and presented to him the indications of guilt. The accuser on the other hand took part in the criminal process as the plaintiff.[101] The chief difference between an accusation and a judicial denunciation consisted in this that the accusation was a judicial act whereas the denunciation was extra-judicial. The accusation opened the criminal process, the denunciation introduced the special inquisition to determine whether sufficient proofs of guilt were on hand to indict the culprit.[102]

Denunciation was defined by pre-Code authors as the manifestation of a crime to a superior with a view to seeking public correction or punishment of the crime, without however assuming the burden to prove the charge.[103] Today it is defined as the

2 vols., Lipsiae: Veit et Comp., 1885-1888), JK, n. 247; Jean Hardouin (1646-1729), *Acta Conciliorum et Epistolae Decretales ac Constitutiones Summorum Pontificum* (12 vols., Parisiis, 1714-1715), I, 811, canon 6; Pope Julius III (1550-1555) on February 1, 1554, issued a command to have all blasphemers in the city of Rome denounced to the inquisitors, and he approved the *poena talionis* as a penalty for those informers who falsely accused anyone of this crime — Const. *"In multis,"* n. 11, *Bullarium,* VI, 480. Pope Pius V (1566-1572) on April 1, 1566, in his Constitution *"Cum primum,"* prescribed the same penalty for false denouncers of simony, blasphemy, and rape (stuprum). — *Bullarium,* VII, 437, nn. 13-14.

100. C. Reiffenstuel, *Ius Canonicum,* lib. V. tit. 1, n. 94, V; Wernz, *Ius Decretalium,* V. n. 838.
101. Cf. Berardi, *De Sollicitatione,* n. 249; Lega, *De Iudiciis,* IV, 185; Roberti, *loc. cit.*
102. Lega, *De Iudiciis,* IV, 157, 185; Wernz, *Ius Decretalium,* V, n. 840; Del Bene, *De Officio,* I, Pars I, *Dubitatio* XV, nn. 7, 8; Sigismund Scaccia (18th century), *Tractatus de Iudiciis* (3. ed., 2 vols., Coloniae Agrippinae, 1738), I, cap. LXXI, n. 2.
103. Lega, *op. cit.,* IV, 157, 185; Wernz, *op. cit.,* V, n. 833.

manifestation of a crime to a Superior with the intention that it prepare the way for a criminal action.[104] Occult crimes were brought to the attention of the judge by means of a simple denunciation in order that he might protect the common good.[105] The various Instructions of the Holy Office outlining the manner of denouncing persons guilty of solicitation did nothing more than crystalize the norms of the inquisitors that had been in vogue for several centuries.[106]

Because of the unusual circumstances that attended the crime of solicitation it would have been difficult, perhaps impossible, to obtain legal proof to convict a guilty priest if the *actio popularis* had been resorted to. An accusation in its legal connotation was never entertained by the inquisitors when they demanded that penitents accuse confessors who solicited them in confession. The Constitution *"Universi"* of Pope Gregory XV, issued on August 30, 1622, spoke of denunciations, not of accusations.[107] Benedict XIV (1740-1758) reiterated this obligation, and spoke of denunciations.[108] In order to guide the local Ordinaries the better in their efforts to punish confessors guilty of the crime of solicitation, the Holy Office published four Instructions, the first on February 20, 1866,[109] the second on July 20, 1890,[110] the third on August 6, 1897,[111] and the last on June 8-9, 1922. On the title page of this most recent Instruction Cardinal Merry del Val gave directions that the Instruction was not to be published, nor to be commented on in manuals of Canon Law (*nec publicanda nec ullis commentariis*

104. Cf. Muniz, *Procedimientos Eclesiasticos,* III, 549; Coronata, *Institutiones,* III, 382; Cf. also canon 1935, § 1.

105. Berardi, *De Sollicitatione,* n. 249; Lega, *De Iudiciis,* IV, 209; St. Alphonsus, *Theologia Moralis,* lib. IV, n. 247.

106. Cf. Giraldi, *Expositio,* II, 640; Del Bene, *De Officio,* I, *Dubitatio* XVI, n. 1, *Dubitatio* CLXXXIII, n. 5; S. C. S. Off., decr. 10 martii 1677 — Ferraris, *Prompta Bibliotheca,* III, 122, ad vv. *Denunciatio quoad delicta spectantia ad S. Officium,* n. 1.

107. § 4 — *Fontes,* n. 201; *Bullarium,* XII, 729, § 4.

108. Const. *"Sacramentum Poenitentiae,"* 1 iun. 1741 — Document V in the Code.

109. *Fontes,* n. 990.

110. *Fontes,* n. 1123.

111. *Fontes,* n. 1190.

augenda). It is to be found only in the secret archives of diocesan chanceries (*Instructio servanda diligenter in archivo secreto Curiae pro norma interna*). In none of these four Instructions is an accusation by the penitent considered. Only the judicial denunciation is alluded to. A judicial denunciation was the occasion that prepared the way for a special inquest (*diligentias circa denunciatum eiusque denunciantes peragere*),[112] and for the eventual accusation that was drawn up by the *promotor iustitiae.* This judicial denunciation, though never directly called an accusation, by reason of its ultimate purpose could be termed the equivalent of an accusation. It is in this sense that the word *accusatur* of canon 894 is used. Moersdorf calls its use in that canon "*untechnisch.*"[113] Aertyns-Damen[114] and Wouters[115] clearly indicate that there is a distinction between the initial denunciation made to the local Ordinary and the accusation that is eventually drawn up by the *promotor iustitiae.* The delator can be said to form one juridic personality with the *promotor iustitiae* for he must assist him in presenting proofs for the judicial establishing of the crime.[116] If the indications of guilt brought by the informer are such that there is no basis for an inquest, or if after the *diligentiae* have been made there are not on hand sufficient reasons for the drafting of an accusation, the process must be closed and the acts placed in the secret archives or destroyed, according as the *indicia* point to a probable guilt or to a plausible innocence.[117]

Many canonists maintain that the delict of solicitation is an example of the obligation imposed by canon 1935, § 2 to make a judicial denunciation.[118] Though the Code has in canon 1936

112. S. C. S. Off., instr. 6 aug. 1897, n. 3 — *Fontes,* n. 1190.
113. Klaus Moersdorf, *Die Rechtssprache des Codex Juris Canonici — Goerres-Gesellschaft: Veroeffentlichungen der Sektion fuer Rechts — und Staatswissenschaft* (Koeln, 1908-1910, Paderborn, 1910 — Verlag Ferdinand Schoningh, Heft 74, 1937), p. 317, 3, b.
114. *Theologia Moralis,* II, nn. 427, V, 428, III.
115. *Manuale,* II, n. 426 Scholion I, n. V, 1. Cf. canon 1946.
116. Cf. canon 1937.
117. Cf. canons 1946; 1954-56; Cf. Wouters, Aertnys-Damen, *locc. citt.*
118. Regatillo, *Institutiones,* II, n. 732; Eichmann, *Das Strafrecht,* n. 72; Coronata, *Institutiones,* III, 385; Beste, *Introductio in Codicem,* p. 826. Cf. also canons 904 and 2368, § 2.

enacted special norms for the making of judicial denunciations, no deduction can be made that these norms are to be employed for the reporting of crimes of solicitation as Cerato[119] and Augustine maintain.[120] Though the crime of solicitation be occult, nevertheless the norms used for the procedure against public crimes could most appropriately be applied in the procedure against such crimes of an occult nature.[121] Still despite the fittingness of these norms, the form of denunciation as mentioned in canon 1936 cannot be substituted for the judicial denunciation demanded by the Holy Office, unless the officials who are mentioned in canon 1936 are individually delegated to review the denunciation. The denunciation which is spoken of in canon 1936 is in all respects a judicial one for public crimes,[122] but for the occult crime of solicitation it is regarded only as a simple denunciation, or a denunciation that is not *in forma.* No one will deny that the crimes of solicitation and all the circumstances attending them are occult by their very nature. The delict of false accusation on the other hand is not occult, but the matter of which it treats is occult. If a false denunciation regarding the crime of solicitation be made through compliance with the procedural norms of canon 1936, that is, made either in writing or orally, to the local Ordinary, the chancellor, the vicar forane, or the pastor,[123] but is not confirmed in the manner pre-

119. *De Delicto,* n. 129, adn. 4, and n. 116; in his work *Censurae Vigentes* (n. 79, d) Cerato does not recognize the denunciation made in accordance with canon 1936 as fulfilling the meaning of the word *denuntiaverit* mentioned in canon 2363. This is a contradiction of his doctrine in *De Delicto, locc. citt.*

120. *Commentary,* IV, 318, 319; in *Commentary,* VIII, 424, while commenting on canon 2363, Augustine insists that the norms of the Holy Office relative to the manner of bringing denunciations to the local Ordinary are to be employed. This too is an unexplainable contradiction.

121. Cf. Wouters, *Manuale,* II, 426, Scholion I; Aertnys-Damen, *Theologia Moralis,* II, n. 427; Motry, *Diocesan Faculties,* n. 117, footnote (75).

122. Canon 1933, § 1. Delicta quae cadunt sub criminali iudicio sunt delicta publica.

123. Beste (*Introductio in Codicem,* p. 826) includes also the *promotor iustitiae,* since the denunciator must bring his proofs to him eventually.

scribed by the tribunal of the Holy Office, it cannot serve as a basis for an accusation by the *promotor iustitiae.*[124]

Whereas the Constitution "*Sacramentum Poenitentiae*" used the words *innoxios sacerdotes falso insimulare* and *innocentes confessarios impie calumniando,*[125] those terms have now become *falsa delatio qua sacerdos innocens accusatur* in canon 894, and *Si quis confessarium falso denuntiaverit* in canon 2363. The word *insimulare* in its legal sense is a perfect synonym for *accusare,*[126] and the word *calumniari* a synonym for *falso insimulare* or *falso accusare.*[127]

The words *falso insimulare* and *caluminari* in a juridical sense meant to act in bad faith as a plaintiff in court. Pre-Code jurisprudence however never attached that legal connotation to these two terms employed in the Constitution "*Sacramentum Poenitentiae.*" Pre-Code canonists were unanimous in accepting the phrases *falso insimulare* and *impie calumniando* as denoting a judicial denunciation rather than a criminal accusation.[128] In his Com-

124. "Denuntiatio. . . iudicialis esse debet, ut delictum committatur. Iudicialis autem est quae fit: 2° modo ad processum instituendum apto." — Vermeersch-Creusen, *Epitome,* III, n. 565, 1, 2°, 2°; Jone, *Gesetzbuch,* III, 520; Cipollini, *De Censuris,* p. 128; Augustine, *Commentary,* VIII, 424.

125. § 3 — Document V in the Code.

126. "Insimulat: quod proprie notat in aliquem simulate agere, et sumitur pro accusare et criminari. . ." — Rota, *Enchiridion,* n. 104, 7°; Cf. also Rudolf Koestler, *Woerterbuch zum Codex Iuris Canonici* (Muenchen: Friedrich Pustet, 1927-1929), p. 191; *ibid.,* p. 20, 3); Dom. Carolus Dufresne Du Cange, *Glossarium ad Scriptores Mediae et Infimae Latinitatis* (10 vols., Paris. 1733). *Glossarium Novum ad Scriptores Medii Aevi cum Latinos tum Gallicos, seu Supplementum ad auctiorem Glossarii Cangiani Editionem collegit et digessit D. P. Carpientier* (10 vols., Vols. VII-X, D. P. Carpientier, Paris, 1766), III, column 1466; Jacob Facciolati, *Totius Latinitatis Lexicon,* consilio et cura Jacobi Facciolati, opera et studio Aegidii Forcellini, editit Jacobus Bailey (2 vols., London, 1828), I, 989.

127. Cf. Koestler, *op. cit.,* p. 57; Schmalzgrueber, *Ius Ecclesiasticum,* lib. V, tit. 2, n. 1; Reiffenstuel, *Ius Canonicum,* lib. V, tit. 2, n. 1; Ferraris, *Prompta Bibliotheca,* I, 88, n. 24; Ducange, *op. cit.,* II, column 57; *ibid.,* VII, columns 728, 729.

128. Rota, *Enchiridion,* n. 104, 7°; Berardi, *De Sollicitatione,* n. 359, 3°;

mentary on the Constitution *"Sacramentum Poenitentiae"* Bucceroni explained that the judicial denunciation was insisted on rather than the simple one, in order to prevent calumnies which might otherwise so easily be resorted to by persons who desired to avenge themselves against innocent priests, and which might cause great detriment to the clerical state and to religion.[129]

As a penitent could not bring a report of a factual crime of solicitation to court as a plaintiff, so it was impossible in the same capacity to present a charge of a fancied solicitation. All authors understood the words *falso insimulare* and *impie calumniando* to mean a denunciation made in accordance with the Instructions of the Holy Office, so that, unless the false denunciations were made judicially, the reserved sin would not be in force. The same formalities that the Holy Office prescribed for reporting a factual crime of solicitation were postulated by the commentators in the false denunciations of an innocent confessor if the sin was to become a reserved sin. No reservation of sin followed unless the false denunciation was made to the same officials who were competent for reviewing the deposition of a true crime. Anonymous denunciations were not recognized as sufficient to subject the deponent to the inhibitive sanctions of the law,[130] nor the vitiated or defective

Ballerini-Palmieri, *Opus Theologicum,* V, n. 1155; Hollweck, *Die kirchlichen Strafgesetze,* p. 280; Many, "De Peccato Sollicitationis," — *Le Canoniste,* XVIII (1895), 720, 3; Santi, *Praelectiones,* lib. V, tit. 2, n. 4; *ibid.,* Appendix, p. 232, n. III, 1°; Noldin, *De Sacramentis* (5. ed., 1904), n. 393, 5; Bucceroni, *Institutiones,* II, n. 1279; Gury, *Compendium,* II, n. 596. Rota (*loc. cit.*) mentioned that the false denunciation could be made orally or in writing provided that the document contained the writer's signature, through a messenger, or by anonymous letters. In n. 116 (*op. cit.*) he states that the denunciation must be made judicially: ". . . Notandum porro, quod cum hic agatur de casu qui ex natura sua, ad effectum saltem reservationis, non completur, nisi in judicio, agitur enim de accusatione apud judices. . ."

129. n. 45.

130. Berardi, *De Sollicitatione,* n. 359, 3°; Hollweck, *Die kirchlichen Strafgesetze,* p. 280; Many, "De Peccato Sollicitationis," — *Le Canoniste,* XVIII (1895), 720.

false denunciations, much less the simple denunciations and those made to incompetent officials.[131]

B. The Present Law And Its Interpretation.

With the promulgation of the Code and the embodiment of the law on false denunciations of the crime of solicitation in canons 894 and 2363 the word *accusare* as used in canon 894 is accorded the same interpretation that obtained in pre-Code jurisprudence. Even those canonists who see a distinction between the transgressions listed in canons 894 and 2363 agree with those who consider the transgression in the two canons to be identical, namely, that the accusation mentioned in canon 894 is not the legal accusation understood by canon 1934, but rather the formal or judicial denunciation made in accordance with the special Instructions of the Holy Office.[132] Even Cerato, the chief proponent of the theory that a simple denunciation suffices for the incurring of the excommunication enacted in canon 2363, is in agreement with other authors in holding that the denunciation mentioned in canon 894 must be a judicial one and hence must have complied with the

131. Many, *loc. cit.*

132. Cf. Jone, *Gesetzbuch,* II, 126, d); Vermeersch-Creusen, *Epitome,* III, n. 565; Coronata, *Institutiones,* IV, 504; Salucci, *Il Diritto Penali,* II, n. 315; Cocchi, *De Delictis et Poenis,* n. 222; De Smet, *De Absolutione,* n. 123; Cerato, *De Delicto,* n. 131, 2, 3; Wouters, *Manuale,* II, n. 427; Beste, *Introductio in Codicem,* p. 960; Cappello, *De Poenitentia,* n. 604, 1, 2°; Claeys Bouuaert-Simenon, *Manuale,* II, n. 142; Iorio, *Compendium,* II, n. 582 bis, *Quaer.* 30°, Notanda I, B), 1); Ferreres, *Compendium,* II, n. 689, *Quaer,* 12; Wernz-Vidal, *Ius Canonicum,* VII, n. 500; Davis, *Moral and Pastoral Theology,* III, 406. In addition to the false judicial denunciation De Smet (*loc. cit.*) speaks of the *denuntiatio aequivalenter juridica,* which in substance is nothing more than a simple denunciation accepted by the local Ordinary acting in his capacity as superior. According to De Smet the local Ordinary, if he so chooses, may proceed with the imposition of a suspension *ex informata conscientia.* De Smet stands alone in defending the opinion that the false denunciator becomes subject to the reservation mentioned in canon 894 or incurs the censure enacted in canon 2363, by bringing a simple false denunciation to the local Ordinary. De Smet considers the two canons as treating one and the same kind of transgression. In view

special procedural rules prescribed by the Holy Office for the making of a denunciation, if the reservation is to set in.[133]

Canon 1934 precludes the *actio popularis.* There is no possible opportunity for any person except the *promotor iustitiae* to accuse any one falsely in a criminal process. To defend the theory that canon 894 is so restricted that it is to convey the impression that if the *promotor iustitiae* himself should falsely accuse a priest of solicitation his sin would be reserved to the Holy See for absolution would be contrary to pre-Code interpretation, and hence would entail a violation of the norm regarding the doctrinal interpretation, as explained in canon 6, 2°. The word *delatio* stands in apposition to the word *accusatur.* The *promotor iustitiae* does not bring the *delatio* by which an innocent priest is accused. He merely draws up the indictment after the denunciation has been made. There can be no doubt that the word *accusatur* in canon 894 is not to be understood in the sense of the accusation which receives mention in canon 1934. It has the connotation of a judicial denunciation. This supposition alone will allow harmony between the word *accusatur* and the Instruction of the Holy Office of June 8-9, 1922.

Canon 2363 has introduced a new penalty for the false denunciation of an innocent confessor. There is little reason to believe that a new method of bringing that false denunciation to the superiors has been introduced. The opinion of the authors in their interpretation of the pre-Code manner postulated for the false denunciation of an innocent confessor is to continue to be the guiding norm for the interpretation of the present law. The word *denuntiaverit* in canon 2363 cannot be governed by the norms of canon 1936, for canon 2363 treats of a crime the judgment of which is reserved exclusively to the Holy Office. The norms of this

of the very clear Instructions of the Holy Office, of the pre-Code interpretation of the words *falso insimulare* and *impie calumniando,* and of the application of canon 6, 2°, which demands that the present law is to be accepted according to the pre-Code interpretation whenever it is taken over *ex integro,* the singular interpretation of De Smet is hardly tenable.

133. *De Delicto,* n. 131, 3,; *ibid.,* n. 118, 2, 2, 3.

tribunal demand that a judicial denunciation be made in all instances where the crime of solicitation is involved. The selection of the word *denuntiaverit* by the legislator for canon 2363 is a better choice than the word *accusatur* for canon 894.

The phrases *falso insimulare* and *impie calumniando* of the Constitution "*Sacramentum Poenitentiae*" were accepted as restricted to judicial denunciations by all pre-Code canonists, and their interpretation, according to the rule of canon 6, 2°, is not to be discarded. These men were guided to their conclusions by number six of the Instruction which the Holy Office issued on February 20, 1866.[134] That Instruction spoke of the denunciation of a factual solicitation. It was not directly concerned with false denunciations. Yet that norm which demanded judicial denunciations for the true crimes of solicitation was accepted by the authors as indicative also of the form in which a false denunciation had to be made if the false denunciation was to give rise to the application of the juridical sanctions invoked against it. In 1922 the Instruction of 1866 was revised and sent to all the curias of local Ordinaries. No change that affected the manner of reporting the crimes of solicitation to the Holy Office or to local Ordinaries was made.[135]

Since in a false denunciation there is at least an indirect association with the crime of solicitation, the manner in which falsely made denunciations will give rise to the application of the sanctions against them is governed by the new Instruction. Inasmuch as the directions of the Holy Office were unanimously accepted by pre-Code authors to determine how false denunciations had

134. *Fontes,* n. 990.

135. For the sake of making the Instruction correspond with the substantial changes that had been introduced by the Code a few corrections and revisions however, had to be introduced. N. 11 in the Instruction of 1866 compelled the cited confessor to admit under oath the charges that had been brought against him, *reus in iudicium adducitur. . . et. . . iuramento dicendae veritatis obstrictus respondere debet. . .* Canon 1744 forbids the judge to demand such a confession of guilt. N. 12 in the Instruction of 1866 called for the issuing of the sentence by the bishop himself. In the revised Instruction a delegated judge may pronounce the sentence. Cf. Coronata, *Institutiones,* IV, 555; ibid., 554, footnote 5.

to be brought to the local Ordinary, to the officials of the Holy Office, or to the delegates of either if the sanctions of the laws were to become applicable, the revised norms of that same Office are to be the directive according to which, since the Code, false denunciations of the crime of solicitation will serve to open the judicial process.[136] As all previous Instructions of the Holy Office were to be observed strictly, *adamussim servare,*[137] . . . *Praeceptum. . . strictissimi iuris censendum est,*[138] so the *Pagella* of 1922 is equally peremptory. Its prescriptions are to be observed to the very finger tips, *ad unguem servent et servare faciant.*

C. Refutation Of The Simple Denunciation Theory.

Cerato and Blat called canon 2363 a new law: *"In canone* [2363] *ius prorsus novum habetur,*[139] and *"Mater Ecclesia condidit novum canonem."*[140] With such an assumption the principle of canon 6, 3°, which declares that the new law is to be interpreted in the light of the words that it employs, is to control the interpretation. As a consequence, the logical conclusion results that since the Code has its own regulations in canon 1936 for reporting crimes, the norms of that canon are to be invoked when the false denunciation of the crime of solicitation mentioned in canon 2363 is to be considered. Motry,[141] Tanquerey,[142] Michel[143] and Merkelbach[144] reach the same conclusion, though they do not call canon 2363 a new canon.

136. "Falso denuntiaverit — non utcunque, sed iuridice, seu ad formam iuris;. . ." — Cipollini, *De Censuris,* p. 128; Vermeersch-Creusen, *Epitome,* III, n. 565; Jone *Gesetzbuch,* III, 520; Augustine *Commentary,* VIII, 424.
137. S. C. S. Off., instr. 20 febr. 1866, n. 15 — *Fontes,* n. 990.
138. S. C. S. Off., instr. 6 aug. 1897, n. 3 — *Fontes,* n. 1190.
139. The original has ". . . in canone 904 ius prorsus novum habetur. . ." an apparent printing mistake. *De Delicto,* n. 129, adn. 2.
140. *Commentarium,* lib. V, n. 204.
141. *Diocesan Faculties,* p. 111.
142. *Synopsis,* I, n. 455, 1°.
143. *Noveau Code Canonique,* n. 490.
144. *Summa,* II, n. 643, C, b. Cf. also the anonymous writer of the article "Il Codice de Diritto Canonico: Riassunto e Dilucidazioni," —

Haring[145] and Blat[146] consider the crime complete when the calumniator employs the services of the officials specified in canon 1936 with the view that these bring the denunciation to the proper ecclesiastical judges who are empowered to draw up the legal accusation. If understood in the sense that the officials are the mandataries of the calumniator, it is conceivable that the simple denunciation will bring the latter under the penalties of the law, not because of the simple denunciation, but because he schemed that the officials make the report judicial for him: *Si quis... per alios... denuntiaverit.* It is not likely that the persons specified in canon 1936 will acquiesce so readily in accepting such a responsibility. They will be suspected of collusion if the trial eventually proves the incriminated confessor to have been innocent.[147] Iorio was not as sweeping as Blat and Cerato in calling canon 2363 a new canon. He stated that the Code transformed the false denunciation of an innocent *confessor* into a new law. The changed portion of the old law then is to be interpreted according to the evident meaning of its present words, while the rest of the canon is to be interpreted according to pre-Code norms of interpretation.[148]

The assumption of Cerato, Blat, Motry, Merkelbach, Tanquerey and Michel, who state that the false denunciation brought to judges or to persons designated in law as Superiors who review it *extrajudicially* will subject the calumniator to the excommunication of canon 2363, is hardly acceptable. The present writer opposes their doctrine for the following reasons:

1. The criminal process of the crime of solicitation is reserved to the tribunal of the Holy Office. The norms governing the prosecution of that crime are to be followed by inferior courts

Il Monitore Ecclesiastico, XXXI (1919), 149, and De Smet, *De Absolutione,* n. 123. De Smet however holds that while there is but one transgression there are two penalties.

145. *Grundzuege,* II, 993, footnote 3.
146. *Commentarium,* lib. III, Pars I, 260.
147. Cf. canon 2200, § 2.
148. "Falsam autem denuntiationem *confessarii* Codex in novam legem transtulit (can. 2363), quae ideo ad normam eiusdem can. 6, 3°, ex sua ipsius sententia est iudicanda." — *Compendium,* II, 417, footnote (3).

when such courts are specifically delegated in individual cases or where they are delegated by law.[149] The Instructions of the Holy Office, before as well as after the Code, indicate the manner of introducing a criminal trial by way of the judicial denunciation. The denunciation mentioned in canon 1936 does not correspond to the one demanded by the *Pagella* of 1922. The denunciation made in compliance with the rule of canon 1936 cannot serve as a basis for an inquest to be ordered by the judge or for an accusation to be prepared by the *promotor iustitiae.* The recipient of a simple denunciation cannot as a rule ascertain whether the deposition is true or false, and there is no way of determining it except by the inquest. This inquest, however, cannot be legally begun unless the formalities of law have been complied with, that is, unless the denunciation has been put *in forma.* The norms of the 1922 *Pagella* are to be observed to the very finger tips (*ad unguem*). This would not hold true if the kind of denunciation treated in canon 1936 were employed.

2. If there is any doubt whether the law which prescribes the mode of bringing false denunciations to ecclesiastical judges is changed, the principles of canon 6, 4°, direct that the earlier law is presumed to be still in force. Cerato's proof for his theory that canon 2363 is an entirely new law rests on the observation that the Gasparri edition of the Code has no *fontes* appended to it. The absence of *fontes* in the Gasparri edition is not always an indication that the law had no legal antecedent. In the preface to the Code Cardinal Gasparri stated that the *fontes* do not always correspond to the law in all its parts,[150] but that wherever possible the *Consultor* and his aides were commanded faithfully to give references to documents whence they took their material to formulate the new law.[151]

149. Cf. canons 247, § 2, and 1555, § 1.

150. ". . . Accedunt ad canones, in extrema quaque pagina, *notae,* quae varios indicant fontes unde ii eliciti sunt: qua in re vix animadvertere attinet, canones haud semper cum suis fontibus omni ex parte in sententia congruere. . ." — pp. XLII, XLIII. (Italics in original).

151. *Ibid.,* pp. XL, III.

As far as the penalty enacted in canon 2363 was concerned, there was no excommunication attached to the false denunciations of innocent confessors before the promulgation of the Gode. The only inhibitive sanction against that crime was the reservation to the Holy Father of the sin reserved *ratione sui.* The form of denunciation specified by the Constitution *"Sacramentum Poenitentiae"* was universally accepted as a judicial denunciation. There is no canonical reason warranting the conclusion that the method of making denunciations in the concept of canon 2363 has receded from that which obtained before the Code. According to canon 6, 3°, those canons which take over former laws only in part must be interpreted according to the earlier law in the part in which they agree; in those parts in which they disagree the meaning of the words employed by the canons is to be given attention. Canon 6, 4°, states that in cases of doubt whether the new law differs from the earlier one, it is presumed that the former law is restated. The assumption of Cerato, namely, that the Code has made provisions for the making of denunciations in canon 1936, and that these same provisions then are to be applied to canon 2363, is not clearly proved.

3. In misinterpreting the tenor of n. 7 of the Instruction of 1866, Cerato came to unsound conclusions not only in cases wherein denunciations of the factual crime of solicitation were to be made, but also in cases involving false denunciations. Number 7 of the Instruction reads:

> 7. Denunciationis onus est personale et ab ipsa persona sollicitata adimplendum. Verum si gravissimis difficultatibus impediatur, quominus hoc perficere ipsa possit, tunc vel per se, vel per epistolam, vel per aliam personam sibi benevisam suum adeat Ordinarium, vel sanctam Sedem per sacram Poenitentiariam, vel etiam per hanc supremam Inquisitionem, *expositis omnibus circumstantiis, et deinde se gerat iuxta instructionem quam erit acceptura.* Si vero necessitas urgeat, se gerat iuxta consilia et monita sui confessarii... Formulae autem hisce in casibus adhibendas tradunt probati auctores, quos inter Pignatelli consult. 104, Carena, Albitius, etc.[152]

152. *Fontes,* n. 990. (Italics inserted).

Using this document as a premise, Cerato concludes that the denunciation of the crime of solicitation can be made in a threefold manner, personally, by letter, or by an acceptable messenger.[153]

A careful reading of the Instruction leads to the conclusion that Cerato's interpretation of it is indefensible. Whenever a penitent is impeded from personally making a denunciation because of the presence of most grave hardships he is to have recourse to the local Ordinary or to the Holy Office to seek counsel regarding what he is to do in order that he may fulfill his duty to denounce the guilty confessor. That the letter to the local Ordinary or to the Holy Office is not to contain the denunciation is gathered from the substance of the formulas that the Instruction recommends for use. The formula of Pignatelli reads:

> A denuntiante fiat *Memoriale,* in quo declaret se aliquid habere exponendum, pertinens ad S. Officium, et ideo rogat Ill. ac Rev. Episcopum, ut personae prudenti ex clero saeculari, vel regulari committat, quae ad recipiendam suam personalem denuntiationem ad talem locum omni cautela et secreto se conferat, ut ita possit denuntians suae conscientiae providere. Deinde *memoriale* subscribitur nomine et cognomine exponentis. Potest porro dictum *memoriale* mediante confessario transmitti ad Praelatum, qui, noscens illud referri ad negotium spectans ad S. Officium, maximo secreto, id recipere debet; et duas assumit graves religiosas ac zelantes personas quarum alteram pro notario vel actuario adhibebit in *Acta* scribenda, alteram vero pro delegato speciali ad recipiendam denuntiationem.[154]

A circular letter from the Papal Secretary of State to all Ordinaries in 1919 expressed the desire of the Holy Father that local Ordinaries forbid under threat of grave penalties the private transmission of denunciations by mail to the Holy Office.[155]

153. *De Delicto,* n. 116, 1 ,2.

154. G. Pignatelli, *Consultationes Canonicas* (4 vols., Venetiis, 1716-1722), I, Consultatio 104; Cf. also Rota, *Enchiridion,* nn. 436-438, 445; Coronata, *Institutiones,* IV, 571; Aertnys-Damen, *Theologia Moralis,* II, 286.

155. Cf. Motry, *Diocesan Faculties,* p. 113; Cappello, *De Poenitentia,* n. 698, 7, footnote (104); Coronata, *op. cit.,* IV, 573, footnote (5).

From the misinterpretation of n. 7 of the 1866 Instruction it is evident that strange conclusions would result. Since Cerato maintains that the denunciation prescribed by canons 904 and 2368, § 2, can legally be made in a threefold manner: personally, by letter, or by messenger, he also concludes that the false denunciation spoken of in canon 2363 can be made similarly. As the report of a factual crime of solicitation made by letter or by a messenger is not made *in iudicio,* it is apparent that no valid canonical trial can be instituted. Correspondingly, a false denunciation that is not *in iudicio* likewise cannot fulfill the meaning of the word *denuntiaverit* as used in canon 2363.

4. The prescription of canon 2363 is that no calumniator can be absolved from the excommunication unless a formal retractation and reparation of the harm that might have ensued from the false denunciation has preceded. The local Ordinary is however restrained from punishing the reported confessor without following the due process of law. No harm could befall the innocent priest who is maliciously denounced of the false crime of solicitation unless the denunciation is judicially accepted.[156] The very purpose of the rigid formalities of the Instruction of the Holy Office is to prevent unjust penalties.

5. To hold that a *simple* false denunciation of the crime of solicitation would bring the censure of excommunication upon the calumniator, whereas a *judicial* false denunciation made under oath together with the accepted obligation of keeping secrecy would result only in a reserved sin for the incriminating person, leads to the absurd conclusion that the lighter crime is punished far more severely than the more serious one. As soon as the accused priest

156. "Falso denuntiaverit — non utcunque, sed iuridice, seu ad formam iuris; nam et haec denuntiatio sollicitatis praescribitur et nonnisi haec per se causa esse potest damnorum reparandorum, . . .siquidem ex denuntiatione tantum iuridica initium sumit processus iuris, quo confessarius, utut innocens, privari potest officiis, beneficiis, etc; ideoque grave damnum incurrere." — Cipollini, *De Censuris,* p. 128; Vermeersch-Creusen, *Epitome,* III, n. 565; Jone, *Gesetzbuch,* III, 520; Augustine, *Commentary,* VIII, 424; Cerato, *Censurae Vigentes,* n. 79, adn.

is denounced judicially, the inquest can be ordered, the *promotor iustitiae* can be given a command to formulate his indictment, and the local Ordinary, from the opening of the criminal trial till the end of the process, can suspend the confessor from exercising the sacred ministry or from hearing confessions.[157]

Such a suspension *ad interim* could never be imposed upon an innocent confessor, nor could the severer penalties mentioned in canon 2368, § 2, be inflicted upon him as a result of a *simple* false denunciation. No Superior has a legal right to punish a confessor reported guilty of the crime of solicitation without observing the process of law outlined in the *Pagella* of 1922. All these penalties however could be imposed as a result of a *judicial* denunciation.

Everyone will admit that an excommunication, even if reserved to no one, is a far more serious penalty than a sin *specialissime* reserved *ratione sui* to the person of the Holy Father.[158] An excommunication is a censure by which a person is excluded from the communion of the faithful and is subjected to all the effects enumerated in canons 2259-2267. Ayrinhac-Lydon paraphrase canon 2257, § 1, thus: "... a medicinal spiritual penalty that deprives the guilty Christian of all participation in the common blessings of ecclesiastical society."[159] Among other privations excommunication entails the privation of the right to assist at the divine offices,[160] the exclusion of the faithful from Christian fellowship,[161] loss of

157. "Si *reus citatus* comparens . . .*non confitetur* delictum, . . .acta inquisitionis tradantur *promotori iustitiae* qui *accusationis libellum* conficiat (can. 1954 et 1956) : interim jam poterit a sacro ministerio vel a confessionibus audiendis usque ad exitum judicii suspendi. . ." — Aertnys-Damen, *Theologia Moralis,* II, 289, III. (Italics in original) ; Wouters, *Manuale,* II, n. 426, Scholion I. ". . .Appelatio [a condemnatoria sententia] est in suspensivo, firma tamen rei suspensione forte jam ante sententiam definitivam lata. . ." — Aertnys-Damen, *op. cit.,* II, 289, IV. Cf. also canons 1956-58. Both cited authors paraphrase n. 51° of the 1922 *Pagella* in the quotations referred to.

158. The sin of canon 894 is no longer reserved that strictly. The hypothesis is posited only for contrasting emphasis.

159. *Penal Legislation,* p. 86.

160. Canon 2259, § 1.

161. Canon 2257, § 1.

the right to receive the sacraments,[162] the deprivation of the right to the suffrages of the Church,[163] the disbarment from the exercise of the legally accredited acts, among which are the right to act as sponsor at baptism and at confirmation.[164] Any of these penalties implies a greater deprivation and disqualification than the reservation of a sin reserved *ratione sui* to the Holy See. Only the loss of the right to the reception of the sacraments is common to both.

D. Summary And Conclusion.

Ever since the crime of solicitation has been accorded legislative attention in pontifical law its punishment has been placed under the jurisdiction of the Holy Office. The Instructions of that Office regulating the manner of introducing the criminal process as well as the prosecution itself bound all inferior courts most strictly. The revised Instruction, brought up to date, harmonized with the Code, and released on June 8-9, 1922, is just as rigorously to be adhered to.

Pre-Code canonists interpreted the phrases of the Constitution "*Sacramentum Poenitentiae*," namely, "*innoxios sacerdotes falso insimulare*" and "*innocentes confessarios impie calumniando*," as denoting a judicial denunciation made to the officials of the Holy Office, to the local Ordinary, or to the delegate of either. Because of the strictness of the Instruction of 1922 only judicial denunciations can serve as a basis for an inquest by the local Ordinary and for a subsequent accusation by the *promotor iustitiae* in cases involving the crime of solicitation.

It is certain doctrine today that no local Ordinary may lawfully resort to the use of the *suspensio ex informata conscientia,* and it is a probable opinion that he cannot even do so validly. As a consequence, no harm in the sense that canon 2363 treats it can come to an innocent confessor who is falsely incriminated by means of a simple, that is, a non judicial denunciation.

In all cases of penalties the doctrine of canons 19, 2219, 2228

162. Canon 2260, § 1.
163. Canon 2262, § 1, 3°.
164. Canons 2263, 766, 2°; 796, 3°.

is to govern. These canons respectively decree that a strict interpretation is to be given to the penal law; the milder interpretation of a penal law is to favor the transgressor; no penalty prescribed in law can be incurred unless the crime is consummated according to the evident meaning of the words of the law. Canon 2363 treats of a *res odiosa.* Hence the term *denuntiaverit,* as well as the phrase *apud Superiores,* is to receive a strict interpretation. Though canon 2363 introduces a new penalty for a crime regarding which the law had its counterpart before the Code, there is no solid canonical reason to hold that the manner of bringing the false denunciation to the attention of the superiors is to be different from the manner that obtained before the Code.

As the Instructions of the Holy Office, though not directly concerned with false denunciations, served as a guide regarding the form in which before the Code the false denunciations had to be made if they were to give rise to the application of the sanctions of the law, the *Pagella* of 1922 is to be the norm since the promulgation of the Code. Furthermore, the provisions of canon 6, 3°, specify that the portion of the new law which is in harmony with its pre-Code counterpart is not to receive an interpretation that is at variance with the interpretation of the earlier law. The conclusion then stands that the accusation referred to in canon 894 is not the legal accusation spoken of in canon 1934, but a judicial denunciation made in accordance with the *Pagella* of 1922.

The word *denuntiaverit* in canon 2363 is to receive a strict interpretation. Hence the simple denunciation, or any other denunciation that is not in harmony with the judicial denunciation specified by the *Pagella* of 1922, is not sufficient to give rise to the penalty of excommunication for the calumniator, or to the reservation of the sin as mentioned in canon 894. The *Superiores,* as recipients of judicial denunciations of the crime of solicitation, can be none other than the *iudices ecclesiastici* mentioned in canon 894, or the local Ordinaries designated in canon 904, exclusive of the vicar general, unless the latter has special delegation.

CHAPTER V

THE LIBELANT

Article 1. The Libelant Acting in His Own Name

A. The Libelant Of Canon 894.

The persons subject to the contraction of the reserved sin mentioned in canon 894 are all those capable of committing the transgression outlined in that canon. There are no exemptions from the reservation of sins accorded by law as there are from the incurring of censures. Thus cardinals as well as the *impuberes* are affected by the reservation of sins. Any person who has the use of reason can become a subject of the reserved sin listed in canon 894.

As soon as a person has fulfilled the conditions postulated in canon 894 his sin is reserved. It is necessary therefore that the calumniator with knowledge and ill will judicially denounce a priest (*sacerdos*) or a confessor (*confessarius improprie dictus*)[1] by falsely attributing to him the crime of solicitation as having been committed by him *qua confessarius*. Whether the competent officials institute a process to inquire into the truth of the allegation, or whether after the inquest they do not find sufficient indications of guilt and accordingly decline to prosecute the case, does not affect the reservation of the sin. The sin is reserved even if the accused priest's death in the meanwhile forestalls criminal action, or also if the calumniator refuses to co-operate with the *promotor iustitiae* and withholds proofs of probable guilt.[2] The transgression is complete and the reservation is in force as soon as the false deposition has been signed.[3]

Augustine implies that the reservation is not in force until the criminal trial has been inaugurated, that is, until a summons

1. Cf. *supra*, CHAPTER III, ARTICLE IV, for an explanation of this distinction.
2. Cf. canon 1937; Blat, *Commentarium*, III, Pars I, 260.
3. Cf. Wernz-Vidal, *Ius Canonicum*, VII, n. 500; Vermeersch-Creusen, *Epitome*, III, n. 565, 1, 2°, 2°; Sole, *De Delictis et Poenis*, n. 416; Chelodi, *Ius Poenale*, n. 88; Jone, *Gesetzbuch*, II, 126, e); *ibid.*, III, 520; Cappello, *De Poenitentia*, n. 607, 8°; Sipos, *Enchiridion*, p. 1012.

has been issued to witnesses or to the accused priest.[4] This opinion reflects an excessive leniency in favor of the delinquent. The latter would not always know when the trial is formally opened; moreover he might seek the forgiveness even before the summons is issued. There is no supporting proof to give this theory probability. On the contrary, judged from similar legislation affecting penalties, the reservation is in effect as soon as the libelant is conscious of his guilt.[5]

B. The Libelant Of Canon 2363.

With the exception of the persons excused or exempted by law from the incurring of censures,[6] the delinquent contemplated in canon 2363 is the same as the transgressor considered in canon 894 in all respects but one. Whereas the calumniator of canon 894 falsely incriminates an innocent priest (*sacerdos*) or *confessarius improprie dictus*[7] of the crime of solicitation the delinquent of canon 2363 falsely imputes the same crime to an innocent confessor (*confessarius proprie dictus*). The censure is incurred as soon as the delict referred to in canon 2363 is consummated.[8]

Article 2. The Libelant and his Agents

A. The *Mandans* And His Formal Agents.

By inducing another person to libel a priest or a confessor with the guilt of solicitation the executor of the command raises the question of formal and material co-operation. Though canon 894 does not specifically speak of co-operators, they are implied because of the impersonal wording of the canon.[9] In so far as this canon

4. *Commentary,* VIII, 424.
5. Cf. canon 2232, § 1.
6. Cf. canon 2227, § 2, for cardinals; canon 2230 for the *impuberes;* canon 2229, §3, 1°, for those who are ignorant of the law or of the penalty; canon 2205, § 2, for those who were under grave fear.
7. Cf. *supra,* CHAPTER III, ARTICLE IV for an explanation of this distinction.
8. Canon 2232, § 1.
9. Cf. Iorio, *Compendium,* II, n. 582 bis, *Quaer.* 30°.

is taken over *ex integro*[10] from the pre-Code law, the pre-Code interpretation of the law stands. The words of the Constitution "*Sacramentum Poenitentiae*" were clear and explicit when treating of co-operators: "*. . . quaecumque persona, quae. . . se inquinaverit, vel per se ipsam innocentes confessarios impie calumniando, vel sceleste procurando ut id ab aliis [aliorum impiis suasionibus, aut promissis, aut blanditiis, aut minis, aut quovis modo incitati(s)] fiat. . .*"[11]

Canon 2363 refers to the co-operators in the words: *Si quis per seipsum vel per alios confessarium denuntiaverit.* In the formal or voluntary co-operation where two or more persons conspire by common criminal design and agreement and co-operative effort to bring about a false incrimination, all persons who form the co-operative union are affected by the inhibitive sanctions of canon 894 and the penalty of canon 2363.[12] Since canon 2363 in its general terms, *Si quis per seipsum vel per alios,* does not exclude the formal co-operators in the execution of the crime of false denunciation, the general principles of canon 2209 are to govern. Through the applicability of the norms of canon 2231 the censure of excommunication is not incurred by those persons who serve merely as facilitating co-operators in the crime of false denunciation,[13] or by those who co-operate only negatively, that is, by those who are able to but do not prevent the commission of the crime.[14]

Every person who in conjunction with the principal agent criminally schemes to bring a false denunciation to ecclesiastical judges is under the penalty of the law. If the local Ordinary, his delegate, or the notary conspire with the libelant they cannot escape the censure or the reserved sin. By their common counsel and physical

10. There are a few exceptions, e.g. the milder discipline introduced in absolving from this reserved sin (Chapter VII) and the probability that only one who is a priest (*sacerdos*) can become the subject of a false accusation (Chapter III, Article III).
11. § 3 Document V in the Code.
12. Cf. canons 2209 §§ 1, 3; ". . .non solum procurator, sed et qui eius cura seu mandato seu influxu denuntiat, obnoxius est censurae." — Cerato, *Censurae Vigentes,* n. 79, b.
13. Cf. canon 2209, § 4 collated with canon 2231.
14. Canon 2209, § 6.

concurrence with the calumniator they become accomplices in the crime. Without their help the incrimination could not have occurred.[15]

Whenever a *mandans* issues a command to his participant in the crime of false denunciation of a confessor of the crime of solicitation it is necessary that the denunciation result directly from the influence exerted upon the formal co-operator. As soon as the executor of the false denunciation becomes a voluntary co-operator the norms of canon 2209, § 1, and § 3, are in operation. The *mandans* is the principal author of the crime. His formal participant is his effective co-operator. The latter's execution of the false denunciation must be considered an indispensable and necessary adjunct of the crime.

Canonists speak of three classes of counsel which the *mandans* can offer his co-agent. They are the doctrinal counsel, the hortative counsel, and the co-operative counsel.[16] The doctrinal counsel gives information or technical advice which facilitates the placing of the false accusation. It does not determine the will of another to proceed to or to refrain from placing the action. The hortative counsel evokes motives that are calculated to influence the will of another who is otherwise unwilling or undetermined.[17] The co-operative counsel is an embodiment of both. It offers instructions on procedure and at the same time lends encouragement to the criminal execution of the agreed incrimination of the innocent priest. Whenever the counsel is merely doctrinal, the element of mutual agreement is missing. He who offers it will not be considered guilty of the resultant crime, and hence will not be subject to the sanctions attached to the violation of that law.[18] Hortative as well as co-operative counsel however satisfy the canonical concept of counsel, and will subject the *consulens* to the penalty.[19]

15. Cf. Cerato, *Censurae Vigentes,* n. 79, 3; Cerato, *De Delicto,* n. 134; canon 2209, § 2; Louis Anthony Eltz, *Cooperation in Crime,* The Catholic University of America Canon Law Studies, n. 156 (Washington, D.C.: The Catholic University of America Press, 1942), p. 1.
16. Eltz, *op. cit.,* p. 109; Wernz-Vidal, *Ius Canonicum,* VII, 138.
17. Cf. Rota, *Enchiridion,* n. 106.
18. Cf. Eltz, *loc. cit.*
19. Eltz, *loc. cit.;* Berardi, *De Sollicitatione,* n. 360; Rota, *loc. cit.;* Cerato, *De Delicto,* n. 134.

Only when the formal co-operator is determined by motives of his own to defame the confessor, so that the hortative or co-operative counsel, or the physical help accorded to the co-operator by the *mandans* will be not a contributory but merely a facilitating cause for the crime, does the *procurans* escape the penalty. When the hortative counsel of the *mandans* fails to influence his agent, and his physical assistance is only of a facilitating character, then the element of an effective co-operator is no longer true of the *mandans*. In such an instance the *mandans* escapes guilt, and consequently also the penalty for the resulting false denunciation.[20]

B. The *Mandans* And His Material Agents.

The Code in canon 2209 is concerned with formal participants in crime, for it presupposes *dolus*, the deliberate will to violate the law on the part of all co-operators who are inspired to act by agreement towards a common end.[21] The phrase, *Si quis per seipsum vel per alios*, of canon 2363 includes material or external co-operation in crime, that is, the execution of an external action by two or more persons without common criminal intent or common delictual agreement.[22]

In any event, whether the *mandans* has a formal or a voluntary participant, or whether he has a material or an external participant, the full responsibility of the false denunciation will be ascribed to him in each instance, and the juridical sanctions of canon 894 or of canon 2363 will be visited upon him. The emergence of a penalty for the participant will be determined by the fact whether he is a formal or a material co-operator. Without the mandate the false accusation would never have been placed by the material agent. No penalties can be inflicted upon him, though the external violation of the law is verified. In his action there was no moral imputability.[23]

Thus a confessor or any other person who assumes the burden in the name of the penitent to report what he in good faith supposes

20. Rota, *Enchiridion*, n. 106; Berardi, *De Sollicitatione*, n. 355, VI.
21. Cf. Eltz, *Cooperation in Crime*, pp. 2, 3; Coronata, *Institutiones*, IV, 45.
22. Cf. Eltz, *op. cit.*, p. 1; Coronata, *loc. cit.;* Chelodi, *Ius Poenale*, p. 16.
23. Cf. canons 2199, 2200, 2218, §2; 2195, §1; 2242, §1. Cf. also Coronata, *Institutiones*, IV, 45; Chelodi, *Ius Poenale*, p. 16.

to be a factual crime of solicitation escapes all guilt as well as the penalty.[24] Physical violence, grave fear, and total ignorance of the evil for the execution of which the external actions are designed will also free the involuntary or external agent from the excommunication of canon 2363 and the reserved sin of canon 894.[25]

The phrase, *vel sceleste procurando ut id ab aliis fiat,* of the Constitution "*Sacramentum Poenitentiae*" was accepted so broadly that it was acknowledged as including not only the false denunciations made in the name of the *procurans,* but also those that the executor was prevailed upon to make in his own name.[26]

The phrase of canon 2363, *quis per seipsum vel per alios,* does not necessarily imply that the mandatary act in the name of the *mandans.* It can also mean that he is persuaded to commit the evil in good or bad faith in his own name. The sin and penalty in either case will redound to the *mandans.* In the notions of *mandans* is comprised not only a superior who has influence over the will of his subjects,[27] but also a confessor who refuses or threatens to refuse absolution to his penitent who demurs about making the denunciation,[28] and all other persons who persuade, beseech, threaten, offer money, or suggest in any manner whatever that the false accusation take place.[29] That the *procurantes* are under the penalties follows from the accepted rule of law: *qui facit per alium, est perinde ac si facit per seipsum.*[30]

The *mandans* is responsible only for the mandate he issued. If the material participant in the crime mistakenly defames a

24. Cf. canons 2218, § 2; 2242, § 1. Schuech, *Handbuch,* p. 685; Cipollini, *De Censuris,* p. 128; Cavigioli, *De Censuris,* p. 93.
25. Canon 2205, §§ 1, 2.
26. Cf. Rota, *Enchiridion,* n. 106; Berardi, *De Sollicitatione,* n. 355, VI.
27. Cerato, *De Delicto,* n. 134; D'Annibale, *Summula,* I, 178; Eltz, *Cooperation in Crime,* p. 105.
28. Rota, *loc. cit.;* Berardi, *op. cit.,* n. 360.
29. Cf. Const. "*Sacramentum Poenitentiae,*" 3 — Document V in the Code; Rota, Berardi, *locc. citt.;* Pruemmer, *Manuale Theologiae Moralis,* III, 468, Scholion II; Wernz-Vidal, *Ius Canonicum,* VII, n. 500; De Meester, *Compendium,* lib. III, Pars II, 268; Wouters, *Manuale,* II, n. 427, I, 1; Sole, *De Delictis et Poenis,* n. 416, 1°.
30. *Reg.* 72, R. J., in VI°.

different priest or confessor, neither will be under the penalties. The unintentional substitution of a different name was not imputable to the material executor of the crime. It will consequently free him from the sin as well as from the penalty. The *mandans* too will escape the penalty, for he had no intention to calumniate any priest or confessor in general, but a specific one. It is postulated that the specific cleric whom he designated be libeled, before he would fall under the penalty.[31]

If the participant in the crime became a formal participant by criminally substituting a different name, he exceeds the limit of the mandate and is personally responsible for the false denunciation, and liable for the effects that follow therefrom. His action is imputable and the penalties of the law would fall upon him. The *mandans* however escapes the penalties since the specific crime which he contemplated was not consummated.[32] Though the crime of false denunciation is not perfected according to the detailed specifications postulated in the law, the sin of calumny was committed. Upon realizing that an innocent priest has been defamed, all persons responsible for that calumny are obliged by the natural law and the principles of moral theology to retract the calumny.[33]

Before the sin is reserved or the excommunication incurred on the part of the *procurans*, it is necessary that his mandate be executed judicially. If the material participant in the crime brings the false charge to incompetent officials, makes a simple denunciation by letter or by messenger,[34] the denunciation was not

31. Cf. canons 19; 2219; 2228; 2242, § 1.
32. Cf. canon 2242, § 1.
33. Cf. Berardi, *De Sollicitatione*, nn. 353, IV, 396; Cerato, *De Delicto*, n. 136; Iorio, *Compendium*, II, n. 582 bis. Resolves, 4.
34. Woywod ("False Accusation of Solicitation," — *HPR*, XXXVIII [1938], 721) considers the simple denunciation to be sufficient to occasion the excommunication and the reservation of sin for the *procurans*. On page 719 of the article here cited he insists that the false denunciation must be made in judicial form. The reason for his exception whereby he puts the *procurans* under the penalties upon the simple denunciation by his agent, is based on the prescription of canon 1746, which declares that parties in a contentious trial must take the oath personally. Since the agent who makes a false denunciation for another cannot take an oath in the name of his

accepted judicially by the superior, the delict is not to be considered as consummated. An unfulfilled mandate of this kind is not penalized in the law either as an attempted or as a frustrated crime.[35] As the crime of false denunciation was not fully executed according to the meaning of the words *vel per alios falso denuntiaverit*,[36] the milder opinion is to favor the *mandans*, and no penalty can be visited upon him.[37]

C. The Libelant And False Rumors.

Chelodi extended the meaning of the phrase, *si quis per alios falso denuntiaverit* to comprise the calumniator who maliciously broadcasted false reports calculated to inspire some misguided person to bring the falsehood judicially to competent officials.[38] A number of canonists concur with him in this broad interpretation.[39] But it is hardly conceivable that the original calumniator could be branded with the crime of false denunciation, for his influence upon the will of the material or formal executor of the crime of false accusation is at best very remote, if it can be classified as an influence at all. Not even the words of the Constitution "*Sacra-*

procurans, the latter would never be under the penalties of the law unless a simple denunciation were made for him. The judicial denunciation however, can still be safeguarded by examining the meaning of canon 1316, § 2. This canon does not forbid the taking of an oath in the name of another except when the *canons* demand an oath. *Iusiurandum quod canones exigunt vel admittunt, per procuratorem praestari valide nequit.* In canon 1622 (collated with canon 1834) the proxy for a litigant can take a *iusiurandum decisorium*. This oath is permitted to the proxy, for it is not demanded by the *canons* of the Code but is asked for by the judge. In cases of false denunciation the oath that is called for to make the deposition judicial is prescribed not by the *canons* of the Code, but by the *Pagella* of the Holy Office, issued on June 8-9, 1922. It is an inconsistency on the part of Woywod that in one instance he insists on the judicial denunciation and in the other he waives it.

35. Cf. canon 2212, §§ 1, 4, collated with canon 2242, § 1.
36. Cf. canons, 2363; 2228.
37. Canons 19; 2219.
38. *Ius Poenale*, n. 88.
39. Wernz-Vidal, *Ius Canonicum*, VII, n. 500; Cavigioli, *De Censuris*, p. 93; Coronata, *Institutiones*, IV, 504; Jone, *Gesetzbuch*, III, 520, 521.

mentum Poenitentiae," "*. . . qui. . . aliorum impiis suasionibus, aut promissis, aut blanditiis, aut minis, aut quovis modo incitati. . .*" were ever accepted in such a wide sense.[40]

The executor of the judicial denunciation had to be influenced by another. In the terms of canonists the false rumors can be classified as doctrinal counsel, albeit false counsel, in so far as they suggest the advisability of bringing such a false denunciation to the proper judges for legal action. Inasmuch as doctrinal counsel in this case simply enlightens the intellect of another by means of false information, but does not affect his will by inducing him to proceed with the calumnious accusation,[41] the person who passes on the false information cannot be properly classed as a co-operator. Since the calumniator who started the false rumor does not directly influence the will of him who eventually makes the false denunciation, he does not fall under the penalty of canon 2363, nor under the reservation of the sin treated in canon 894. No one doubts about the gravity of the guilt inherent in his *sin* of calumny, but likewise no one can grant that the *crime* of calumny is present.[42]

D. Revocation Of The Mandate.

The *mandans* is freed from the penalty as soon as his command to malign the priest is effectively revoked. The command is considered effectively revoked when contrary hortative counsel is proffered or when the physical co-operation which would be a

40 .Berardi, *De Sollicitatione,* n. 360; Rota, *Enchiridion,* n. 106; Hollweck, *Die kirchliche Strafgesetze,* p. 280; Benedictus Ojetti, *Synopsis Rerum Moralium et Iuris Pontifici* (2. ed., 2 vols. in 1, Romae, 1904) II, 569 (hereafter cited *Synopsis*); Gury, *Compendium,* II, n. 569, footnote b; Many, "De Peccato Sollicitationis," — *Le Canoniste,* XVIII (1895), 721.

41. Cf. Wernz-Vidal, *Ius Canonicum,* VII, 138; Eltz, *Cooperation in Crime,* p. 109.

42. ". . .Reus peccati utique: at non videtur, quomodo possit reus dici *de delicto,* quod sin obnoxius censurae aut reservationis de iure." — Cerato, *De Delicto,* n. 133, 2, Adnotatio, (Italics in original); cf. also Cappello, *De Poenitentia,* n. 605, 2°; Cocchi, *De Delictis et Poenis,* n. 223, b); Salucci, *Il Diritto Penali,* II, n. 311.

causative element of the crime is withheld.[43] There is no question that a complete and effective withdrawal of the mandate will excuse the *mandans* from the penalty, for it will liberate him from guilt.[44] This is true as long as the false denunciation is not attempted. To revoke the mandate after the false incrimination is an accomplished fact will avail the *mandans* nothing. He is then under the penalties.[45] This holds true whether the mandatary implicated the innocent priest or confessor in good faith or in bad faith. The *mandans* was the principal author of the crime. The revocation of the mandate is possible up to the very minute the delator brings the false information to the judge.

When the revocation of the mandate has not succeeded, canonists are not in agreement whether the penalty of the law is in force. In a formal co-operation on the part of the *mandans* and his executor any earnest effort to neutralize the antecedent co-operation will excuse from the penalty.[46] As long as the effort to withdraw the initial co-operation is earnest but the attempt is only partially successful, then other circumstances rather than the erstwhile command of the *mandans* are responsible for the subsequent execution of the crime. The revocation sincerely made will remove contumacy. This is true even in the presence of a physical or moral impossibility to reach the mandatary to halt the false accusation. In the internal forum the *mandans* is free from the sin of co-operation. Because of the doctrine of canons 2218, § 2, and 2242, § 1,[47] it is probable that the *mandans* will escape the

43. Cf. Berardi, *De Sollicitatione,* n. 360; Rota, *Enchiridion,* n. 108; Bucceroni, *C. "Sac. Poenit.",* n. 58; Ojetti, *Synopsis,* II, 569; Many "De Peccato Sollicitationis," — *Le Canoniste,* XVIII (1895), 721; Ballerini-Palmieri, *Opus Theologicum,* V, n. 1155.
44. Cf. canon 2209 § 5; Salucci, *Il Diritto Penali,* I, 38; Eltz, *Cooperation in Crime,* pp. 134, 141.
45. Giraldi, *Expositio,* II, 560; Rota, *Enchiridion,* n. 108; Santi, *Praelectiones,* lib. V, tit. 2, n. 4.
46. Eltz, *Cooperation in Crime,* pp. 141, 145.
47. Non solum quae ab omni imputabilitate excusant, sed etiam quae a gravi, excusant pariter a qualibet poena tum latae tum ferendae sententiae etiam in foro externo, si pro foro externo excusatio evincatur. — Canon 2218, § 2; Censura punitur tantummodo delictum

censure of excommunication. In all cases of a sincerely withdrawn co-operation, even though ineffective, contumacy ceases. In the absence of contumacy no excommunication can be incurred.

Authors, however, speculate about the reasons favoring the stricter view. In practice the Code itself has issued guiding norms that are favorable to the release from rather than the subjection to the penalty. Unless a crime is committed according to the meaning of the law and has conjoined with it the element of contumacy, no censure can be incurred.[48] In penal legislation the strict interpretation, from the viewpoint of what the law demands, is to govern; the milder interpretation in penalties, from the viewpoint of the culprit, is to be accorded the delinquent.[49]

The issuance of the mandate to defame an innocent priest will not bring excommunication to the *procurans* until the false denunciation has been made. Between the time the mandate is issued and its provisions fulfilled no excommunication can be incurred because of the non-consummation of the mandate. If the *procurans* repents of his attempt to effect the calumniation of an innocent priest and purges himself of the contumacy by an earnest regret conjoined with an effort to stop the crime it is a safe opinion that no censure will be visited upon him.

The reason favoring this view is taken from canon 2242, § 1, which declares that a censure is in force only when an external, grave, and consummated delict is conjoined with contumacy. The case under consideration is no longer conjoined with contumacy. The contumacy ceased with the repentance coupled with serious though ineffectual efforts to prevent the crime. This mild opinion is defended by Jone,[50] Coronata,[51] Arregui,[52] Cer-

externum grave, consummatum, cum contumacia coniunctum — — Canon 2242, § 1.

48. Canons 2228; 2242, § 1.
49. Canons 19; 2219.
50. *Moral Theology,* n. 430, 7.
51. *Institutiones,* IV, 461. In footnote 12 Coronata cites twelve canonists who favor this view.
52. *Summarium,* n. 938, 3°.

ato,[53] Cavigioli,[54] and many others. Speculatively considered it is a probable opinion. Practically considered it is certain doctrine because of canons 19 and 2219 which prescribe that the milder interpretation is to favor the culprit.[55] This doctrine is applicable whether the executor of the false denunciation is a material or a formal co-operator.

Before closing the treatise on the libelant one may call attention to the Instruction of the Holy Office of July 20, 1890, which pointed out to local Ordinaries that frequently solicited penitents revealed the names of other penitents as having been solicited by the same confessor, but who have not fulfilled their obligation to denounce him.[56] These penitents are to be sought by edict of the local Ordinary and their denunciations elicited so that legal action can be taken against the denounced priest. The same penitents are to be examined most circumspectly, and put under secrecy about the solicitation. If a calumniator names other persons in his deposition, and the latter upon examination by the investigator judicially confirm the false report, the crime of false denunciation is considered complete and the penalties are *ipso facto* in force in relation to the persons who confirmed the calumniator's charge.

53. *Censurae Vigentes,* pp. 100, 101. Cerato restricts the opinion to cases covered by canon 2209, § 2.
54. *De Censuris,* p. 133.
55. Cappello, *De Censuris,* pp. 336, 337, 32, 33; Coochi, *De Delictis et Poenis,* 305, footnote (1); Eltz, *Cooperation in Crime,* p. 145; Ayrinhac-Lydon, *Penal Legislation,* p. 242.
56. *Fontes,* n. 1123.

CHAPTER VI

IGNORANCE IN RELATION TO THE CENSURE AND THE SIN

Article 1. The Meaning of Reservation

The notion of reservation regarding sin or censure implies in canon law the restricting or the withholding of jurisdiction from confessors, so that absolution from a designated sin or censure can be imparted only by those confessors whom the legislator specifies. Though a priest has the radical power through ordination to absolve from every sin submitted to his judgment, jurisdiction is required to exercise that power. In the reservation of a sin or of a censure this jurisdiction of the priest is limited.

The crime of false denunciation of an innocent priest or confessor is an abuse (*detestabile facinus, nefaria audacia*) that disturbs the Christian commonweal. To check this great evil and to undo the injury that has befallen a defamed priest the Holy See does not want zealous but unskilled confessors to judge the merits of such a case. It reserves the absolution of that transgression to itself. The trained officials of the *Sacra Poenitentiaria* are best equipped in law to judge whether the absolution is to be conceded immediately, or to be deferred to some later date; to decide what remedies can heal the wounded Christian social order; to provide suitable safeguards against a renewed manifestation of this abuse; to issue penalties that will adequately satisfy the offense.[1]

Article 2. The Kinds of Reservation

The Code speaks of three distinct types of reservations. The first affects the sin itself. It is the reservation of the sin which is reserved *ratione sui*.[2] The jurisdiction of the ordinary confessor

1. Cf. P. Maroto, "De ignorantia quoad falsam delationem, qua sacerdos innocens accusatur de crimine sollicitationis," *Apollinaris*, V (1932), 100, 6, A; M. Darmanin, "De Reservatione Peccatorum Iure Codicis Piano-Benedictini," — *Angelicum*, Romae, 1924, V (1928), 213-231, *passim*; Woywod, *Commentary*, I, n. 805; Cerato, *De Delicto*, n. 131, 5, 2.
2. Canons 894, §§ 1, 2; 894-900.

is partially limited, so that the absolution of a sin reserved *ratione sui* cannot be validly or licitly granted by him. The case must be submitted to the superiors who are competent in law to absolve the sin or to grant the needed delegation for its remission. The second type of reservation implies a limitation of the jurisdiction of inferior confessors in general by reserving to a superior the absolution from the incurred censures. A twofold division is possible here, the *reservatio solius censurae,* and the *reservatio peccati ratione censurae.*[3]

The reservation of a censure which does not impede the reception of the sacraments will not reserve also the absolution of the sin which gave rise to the censure. This is true of all suspensions. As soon as the penitent's contumacy ceases, any confessor may grant absolution from the sin. The censure, however, remains.[4] If the censure is not reserved the confessor may absolve from both the censure and the sin.[5] Whenever the censure impedes the reception of the sacraments, as is true in all cases of excommunication[6] and personal interdict,[7] the reservation of the censure carries with it the reservation of the sin reserved *ratione censurae.*[8] A connecting bond is formed between the reservation of the sin reserved *ratione censurae* and the reservation of the censure. The sin is reserved simultaneously with the reserved censure, so that whatever affects the reservation of the censure affects also the reservation of the sin. If such factors as diminished imputability, exemption, or excuse as recognized by the law suffices to preclude

3. Cf. Innocent Robert Swoboda, *Ignorance in Relation to the Imputability of Delicts,* The Catholic University of America Canon Law Studies, n. 143 (Washington, D.C.: The Catholic University of America Press, 1941), p. 227 (hereafter cited *Ignorance*); De Smet, *De Absolutione,* n. 121; b; Casimir Stadalnikas, *Reservation of Censures,* The Catholic University of America Canon Law Studies, n. 208 (Washington, D.C.: The Catholic University of America Press, 1944), p. 30-32 (hereafter cited *Reservation;*) Dargin, *Reserved Cases,* pp. 4-6.
4. Canon 2250, § 1.
5. Canon 2253, 1°.
6. Canon 2262, § 1.
7. Canon 2275, 2°.
8. Canon 2246, § 3.

the incurring of the censure on the part of anyone, then the sin of such a person likewise will no longer continue in the nature of a reserved sin.[9] When there is no reservation of a censure there can be no reservation of a sin reserved *ratione censurae.*[10] The same principle obtains with the cessation of the reserved censure through absolution. The cessation of the censure will mean the cessation of the reservation of the sin.[11]

ARTICLE 3. IGNORANCE IN RELATION TO THE RESERVED CENSURE OF CANON 2363

There is no difficulty in applying the norms of canon 2229 § 1, and § 3, 1°, on ignorance to canon 2363. Affecting ignorance will not excuse the transgressor from incurring the excommunication enacted in canon 2363. This holds true whether the delinquent personally defamed the priest, or whether he instigated another to do so. Since canon 2363 reveals no phrase which demands full measure of *dolus,* that is, a conscious design and intent amid complete knowledge and deliberation (*scienter, ausus fuerit, praesumpserit, etc.*) a crass or supine ignorance of the law or of its penalty will not excuse the delinquent from the incurring of the censure enacted in canon 2363. All other forms of ignorance will excuse him. The opinion that ignorance regarding the reservation of the censure would similarly excuse one from falling prey to its reservation had at best only a weak support in the past. It is not tenable today.[12]

9. Cf. canons 2229; 2205; 2227, § 2; 2230; 2218, § 2.
10. Canon 2246, § 3.
11. Canon 2246, § 3.
12. Wouters, *Manuale,* II, n. 427, II, 1; Swoboda, *Ignorance,* pp. 228, 229; Post- Code authors who defend the opinion which favors exemption even in this latter supposition are Farrugia (*De Casuum Conscientiae Reservatione, pp.* 29-43) and Arregui (*Summarium,* n. 608, b, footnote 1). Coronata (*Institutiones,* IV, 260, footnote 1) and Vermeersch-Creusen (*Epitome,* II, n. 174) acknowledge that the intrinsic reasons are very weak. They however do not dare to deny to this opinion any and all enjoyment of even an extrinsic probability.

Article 4. Ignorance in Relation to the Papal Reservation of a Sin

A. The Pre-Code Controversy.

Aside from the almost incontrovertibly certain opinion that ignorance of the reservation of a censure will not excuse the delinquent from the reservation attached to it, special consideration must be given to the question whether ignorance of the reservation inherent in the papally reserved sin considered in canon 894 will excuse the sinner from being subjected to the enacted reservation. It was a mooted question before the Code. Though it was a *"sententia probabilissima"* at the time of St. Alphonsus,[13] and a *"sententia verissima"* at the end of the nineteenth century,[14] that ignorance of the reservation was not an excusing cause for escaping the reservations of sins reserved *ratione sui,* there were many canonists and moral theologians who made an exception for the sin of the false accusation of an innocent confessor of the crime of solicitation.[15]

Inasmuch as the words of the Constitution *"Sacramentum Poenitentiae," "ut tam nefaria audacia et tam detestabile facinus metu magnitudinis poenae coerceatur,"* suggested that the reservation of of the sin took on the nature of a penalty, many authors considered ignorance of the reservation as a factor which forestalled the operativeness of the reservation. As such it merited the same consideration as any other penal law. The number of authors, however, who denied its penal character was so great that it was the more common and the more probable opinion in the late decades of the past century. The arguments were based on the observation that the reservation of a sin denotes simply a restriction

13. *Theologia Moralis,* lib. VI, n. 581.
14. D'Annibale, *Summula,* I, nn. 340-344; Petrus Cecchi, "De casuum reservatione et de conditionibus ad eam incurrendam requisitis," — *Analecta Ecclesiastica,* VI (1898), 314.
15. Hollweck, *Die kirchlichen Strafgesetze,* p. 280; *ibid.,* 107, footnote 7; Ojetti, *Synopsis,* II, 453; Many, "De Peccato Sollicitationis," — *Le Canoniste,* XVIII (1895), 723; Lehmkuhl, *Theologia Moralis,* II, n. 526; Bucceroni, *C "Sac. Poenit.",* n. 58; Bucceroni, *Institutiones,* II, n. 1279; Craisson, *Manuale,* II, nn. 1602, 1603.

of the confessor's power to absolve, and not a canonical penalty for the penitent.[16]

Berardi observed that Benedict XIV purposely refrained from attaching the penalty of a censure since ignorance of the censure could so readily excuse from the incurring of the censure. On the other hand, ignorance of the fact of reservation attaching to the sin could not excuse.[17] Berardi, however, was not unduly concerned with the speculation of the authors. *In praxi,* he averred, the confessors usually warned their penitents of the reservation that was attached to a false denunciation. If it happened that a penitent, while ignorant of the reservation, maliciously made a false denunciation,the extrinsic probability which denied that the reservation was in effect proved sufficiently strong to justify the absolution of of the contrite penitent. The Church supplied all needed jurisdiction. *Notissimum est autem quod in opinionum probabilitate iurisdictionem supplet Ecclesia.*[18] The controversy was never authentically settled by the Holy See. Inasmuch as the Constitution *"Sacramentum Poenitentiae"* appears with the force of law in the Code the controversy continues.

B. The Post-Code Controversy.

Prefacing their brief treatment of this controversy, modern authors state that the speculation concerning the question of ignorance as a factor excusing from the reservation is of mere academic interest. Invariably the officials who accept denunciations of the crime of solicitation will instruct the deponent not only regarding the excommunication enacted in canon 2363, but also regarding the reservation of the sin as defined in canon 894.[19] Following the lead of Rota, who made the recommendation before

16. *Vindiciae Alphonsianae* (2. ed., 2 vols., Tornaci, 1874), II, Part V, q. 12; Rota, *Enchiridion,* n. 114; D'Annibale, *Summula,* nn. 340-344; Craisson, *Manuale,* n. 1603; Maurus Kaiser, "De absolutione a reservatis Romano Pontifici," — *Analecta Ecclesiastica,* VI (1898), 374; Berardi, *De Sollicitatione,* n. 362.
17. *Loc. cit.*
18. *Loc. cit.*
19. Cf. Cappello, *De Poenitentia,* n. 538, 3; Cerato, *De Delicto,* n. 131, 4.

the Code,[20] many canonists declare that the judges have an obligation to inform all prospective denunciators of the existence of the inhibitive sanctions enacted in the law.[21] Neither the pre-Code Instruction which the Holy Office issued on February 20, 1866, nor the *Pagella* of the same Office released on June 9, 1922, placed any such obligation upon the judges to caution the informers. The earlier Instruction did however subject the deponent to an oath to tell the truth.[22]

Guided by the conviction that the delict treated in canon 2363 is the same as the sin specified in canon 894, most of the commentators in their reflections on the relation of ignorance to the reservation of the sin, can accordingly be expected to take an attitude which they might just as certainly disavow if they favored the view that these two canons point to two separate transgressions. Thus Cocchi,[23] Aertnys-Damen,[24] Coronata,[25] and Badii[26] teach that, since the Code has annexed a censure to the sin specified in canon 894, the clause *"ut igitur tam nefaria audacia et tam detestabile facinus metu magnitudinis poenae coerceatur"* of the Constitution *"Sacramentum Poenitentiae"* points no longer to the necessary existence of a penalty. The penal element in the reservation of the sin is secondary. The sin delineated in canon 894 is therefore to be treated as all other reserved sins. It is the opinion of Slater (1855-1928)[27] and of Woywood[28] that the legislator retained the reservation of the sin in the law of canon 894 despite the added censure enacted in canon 2363, since he was aware of the many excuses that could free the delinquent from incurring the censure

20. *Enchiridion,* n. 114.
21. Regatillo, *Institutiones,* II, n. 1111; Wouters, *Manuale,* II, n. 426, Scholion I, n. II; Vermeersch-Creusen, *Epitome,* III, n. 565; Cappello, *De Poenitentia,* n. 538, 3, 1°; Woywod, "False Accusation of Solicitation," — *HPR,* XXXVIII (1938), 720.
22. Nn. 6, 14 — *Fontes,* n. 990; Cf. canons 1744; 1780.
23. *De Delictis et Poenis,* n. 225, d).
24. *Theologia Moralis,* II, n. 389, 2°.
25. *Institutiones,* IV, 507, footnote 3; *ibid.,* IV, 166.
26. *Institutiones Iuris Canonici,* II, n. 368, d, footnote (3).
27. "False Accusation of Solicitation and the New Code," — *AER,* LIX (1918), 463.
28. "False Accusation of Solicitation," — *HPR,* XXXVIII (1938), 718.

if that were the only sanction invoked against the transgression. Since the principles which control the interpretation of the reservation of sins do not acknowledge ignorance of the legal fact of the reservation as a factor that excuses from the legal effect of the reservation, the need of applying to a higher authority for the necessary faculties for absolution will always have to be resorted to. The reason frequently alleged for the presence of both the censure and also of the reservation of the sin is this: the presence of the double sanction forestalls the frustration of purpose inherent in the penal law. If ignorance would excuse not only from the incurring of the censure, but at the same time would nullify the legal effect of the reservation of the sin, there would be little reason left for having the dual sanction to the law.[29]

That the reservation of sins is not a penalty for the penitent, but rather an administrative limitation of the confessor's faculties, is a doctrine which today is all but incontrovertably certain.[30] There are very few canonists today who defend the probability of the theory that ignorance of the reservation will excuse the sinner from the effect of the sin's reservation. Yet, as before the Code there were authors who made allowance for an exception relative to the papally reserved sin of the false accusation of an innocent confessor, so today there are commentators who consider the specified reservation which is mentioned in canon 894 to be still penal in character. The authors supporting this view are: De Smet,[31] Chelodi,[32] Cipollini,[33] Iorio,[34] and Colli-Lanzi.[35] Arregui implies that in the present consideration the factor of ignorance excuses

29. Coronata, *Institutiones,* IV, 507; Cerato, *De Delicto,* n. 129, adn. 5; Cerato, *Censurae Vigentes,* n. 79, Adn.
30. Cf. Maroto, "De ignorantia quoad falsam delationem, qua sacerdos innocens accusatur de crimine sollicitationis," — *Apollinaris,* V (1932), 99; Ferreres, *Compendium,* II, n. 672; Dargin, *Reserved Cases,* p. 16; Swoboda, *Ignorance,* p. 229; Stadalnikas, *Reservation,* pp. 21-25.
31. *De Absolutione,* nn. 122, 124, I, 5. De Smet applies the principle of canon 2229, § 3, 1°, to the reservation of the sin referred to in canon 894.
32. *Ius Poenale,* n. 88.
33. *De Censuris,* p. 129.
34. *Compendium,* II, n. 582 bis, *Quaer,* 30°; *ibid.,* n. 558, footnote (1).
35. *Theologia Moralis Universa,* III, 328.

"saltem probabilius."[36] Opposed, however, to this opinion are many more authors.[37] Canon 2230 excuses the *impuberes* from incurring the censure, even when the crime is committed with full knowledge of the penalty; yet *impuberes* are not excused from the reserved sin when they are ignorant of the reservation.[38]

The arguments supporting the view that ignorance of the reservation of the papally reserved sin will not excuse the transgressor from being subjected to the reservation can be reduced to the following:

1. The reservation of sins implies a restriction of the faculties of confessors, and not a penalty for the penitent. The law does not reward the ignorance of the delinquent by favoring him. The ignorance of the penitent cannot supply faculties to the confessor who is deprived of them by a higher superior.

2. The purpose of reserving a sin *ratione sui* according to canon 897 is disciplinary. It is medicinal in purpose only incidentally. Canon 897 declares that the reservation of a sin should serve to extirpate inveterate vice that is prevalent in a community (*ad inolitum vitium extirpandum*), and to restore a decadent Christian discipline to a status of healthful vigor and well being (*ad collapsam christianam disciplinam instaurandam*). Both of these purposes are disciplinary in character. The desire of breaking contumacy in the sinner or of securing his private good is only of secondary

36. *Summarium,* n. 608, 2°.

37. Cappello, *De Poenitentia,* n. 538, 1°; Coronata, *Institutiones,* IV, 507; Vermeersch-Creusen, *Epitome,* III, n. 565; *ibid.,* II, n. 174; Badii, *Institutiones, Iusis Canonici,* II, n. 368, d, footnote (3); Wouters, *Manuale,* II, n. 427, I, 3; *ibid.,* II, n. 384, VI, 4, *Quaer.* 1; Merkelbach, *Summa,* III, n. 643, C, a, 3; Ferreres, *Compendium,* II, n. 672, *Quaer.* 5, R. 2; De Meester, *Compendium,* III, Pars II, 268; Cocchi, *De Delictis et Poenis,* n. 225, d; Dargin, *Reserved Cases,* pp. 13-18; Sipos, *Enchiridion,* p. 1012; Pruemmer, *Manuale Theologiae Moralis,* III, n. 423, b; Aertnys-Damen, *Theologia Moralis,* II, n. 267; *ibid.,* n. 389, 2°; Genicot-Salsmans, *Institutiones,* II, nn. 345, 400; Cerato, *De Delicto,* n. 129, adn. 5; Cerato, *Censurae Vigentes,* n. 75, Adn.; Augustine, *Commentary,* IV, 318.

38. De Smet (*De Absolutione,* n. 124, I, 6°) denies this.

import. Though ignorance of the reservation of the sin will cause a deferment of absolution for the penitent, it is only an accessory inconvenience that accompanies the realization of the disciplinary intent of the reservation. The latter is sought and usually achieved by means of the reservation. The full purpose of the papal reservation before the Code was primarily disciplinary (*ut tam detestabile facinus, metu magnitudinis poenae coerceatur.*) Regarding the reservation which is specified in canon 894 the Code today does not refer to it as a penal sanction, nor does it enumerate the juridical sanction among the medicinal penalties listed in canons 2215 and 2216, 1°, nor among the vindicative penalties catalogued in canons 2298 and 2291.[39]

3. As ignorance of the irregularities *ex delicto*[40] and of the impediment of crime[41] does not excuse the candidate for major orders or the spouses who contemplate marriage from being subjected to the irregularity or the impediment, so likewise the ignorance of the reservation attached to the sin of the false accusation of an innocent priest cannot excuse.[42]

4. Thc very words of the Constitution "*Sacramentum Poenitentiae,*" "*ut tam detestabile facinus metu magnitudinis poenae coerceatur,*" are not within the dispositive portion of the law; they simply point to the motivating cause that prompted Benedict XIV to enact this disciplinary measure. But even granted that the penal character of the law were embodied in the dispositive part of the Constitution which reserves the sin, it would not follow that the penalty is of a medicinal character. The words "*ut... coerceatur*" still would point to a sanction purely disciplinary in character, one namely, which seeks to protect the Christian social order. These words are similar to those embodied in canon 897:

39. Cf. Cappello, *De Poenitentia,* n. 507, 3°; T. Slater, "False Accusation of Solicitation and the New Code," — *AER,* LIX (1918), 462; M. A. Gearin, "The Crime of False Accusation — Again," — *AER,* LX (1919), 64.
40. Cf. canon 988.
41. Cf. canon 1075, collated with canon 16, § 1.
42. Cf. Merkelbach, *Summa,* III, n. 643, C, a, 3.

"ad publicum aliquod inolitum vitium extirpandum." The latter canon deals entirely with the reservation of sins.

5. Although the Constitution is reconfirmed by the Code as a new law, its words must be measured by and brought in harmony with the general principles of interpretation decreed by the Code for the interpretation of the Code law.[43] The reserved sin of the false accusation of an innocent priest is placed under the Chapter *De reservatione peccatorum.* It is therefore to follow the norms of that chapter.[44] Canons 899 and 900 regulate the procedure on the absolution from and cessation of reserved sins. The element of ignorance as a potential factor excusing from the reservation is not alluded to at all. This silence of the lawgiver mutely furnishes proof that he did not intend to release the ignorant from the reservation.[45] Canon 894 nowhere indicates that the papal reservation is to be accorded an interpretation contrary to the principles expressed in canons 893-900. Its words, unlike those of the Constitution, do not refer to any penal nature as inherent in the invoked sanction of reservation in order to imply that its primary purpose is to punish the transgressor. Since only a delict is punishable with a penalty, accordingly, in so far namely, as the Code calls this a sin (*Unicum peccatum reservatum Sanctae Sedi*), the reservation cannot be classified as a penalty.[46] That the cessation of the papal reservation of a sin is also subject to the conditions outlined in canon 900 is now certain. On November 10, 1925, the Pontifical Commission for the authentic interpretation of the Code replied in the negative to the doubt whether the application of canon 900 is to be restricted to the reservations of cases established by the Ordinary, and in the affirmative to the

43. Cf. canons 18; 19; 6, 2°, 3°, 4°.
44. Aertnys-Damen, *Theologia Moralis,* II, 389, 2°; Darmanin, "De Reservatione Peccatorum Iure Piano-Benedictini," — *Angelicum,* V (1928), 240, 241; Maroto, "De ignorantia quoad falsam delationem, qua sacerdos innocens accusatur de crimine sollicitationis," — *Apollinaris,* V (1932), 103, n. 15.
45. Gearin, "The Crime of False Accusation — Again," — *AER,* LX (1919), 67.
46. Cf. canons 894, 2195, § 1; Cappello, *De Poenitentia,* 507, 4°.

question whether canon 900 applies also to the reservations of cases established by the Holy See.[47]

6. A confirmatory argument, that ignorance of the reservation of the sin reserved *ratione sui* does not excuse its transgressor from falling under the effects of the reservation, can be deduced from the declaration of the Pontifical Commission for the authentic interpretation of the Code when it declared that a *peregrinus* is bound by the reservation of the sins which is in force in a diocese in which he goes to confession.[48]

Coupled with the extrinsic authority that upholds the opinion that ignorance of the reservation does not excuse from the reservation, these intrinsic reasons help to build it up as the more probable opinion. The assertion of Arregui, namely that ignorance of the reservation will free the penitent, "*saltem probabilius*" from the effect otherwise inherent in the reservation, is much exaggerated. That his opinion however has probability is not denied by the writer.

As a true *dubium iuris* existed before the Code, so a *dubium iuris* still exists today. Without favoring either side, Regatillo calls the minority view probable.[49] Given an instance in which the confessor is in a quandary, canon 209 will relieve him of anxiety and supply the needed faculty for an assured remission of the sin. That the confessor will ever be disturbed by such anxiety is improbable in view of the potential ease with which the application of canon 900 will cause the reservation to cease entirely.

47. *AAS,* XVII (1925), 583, n. vii.
48. Nov. 24, 1920 — *AAS,* XII (1920), 575.
49. *Institutiones,* II, n. 1111.

CHAPTER VII

ABSOLUTION FROM THE RESERVED SIN AND CENSURE

ARTICLE 1. ABSOLUTION FROM THE RESERVED SIN

A. The Privileged Confessor.

1. Pre-Code Discipline.

Canon 894 reserves the sin of the false accusation of an innocent priest (*sacerdos*) to the Holy See. The manner of obtaining absolution therefrom is not as difficult as it was before the Code. Prior to the promulgation of the Code the sin was reserved *specialissime* to the person of the Holy Father.[1] Even the *Maior Poenitentiarius* was excluded from granting absolution or from delegating faculties for its absolution.[2]

2. Present Discipline.

The Code reserves the absolution from the sin specified in canon 894 to the Holy See. The *Sacra Poenitentiaria* now has competence.[3] Besides the *Maior Poenitentiarius*, all cardinals, from

1. Const. *"Sacramentum Poenitentiae,"* 1 iun. 1741, 3 — Document V in the Code; Cf. Rota, *Enchiridion*, n. 121; Berardi, *De Sollicitatione*, n. 359; Berardi, *Theologia Moralis*, V, n. 678; Lehmkuhl, *Theologia Moralis*, II, n. 526, 6°; Santi, *Praelectiones*, lib. V, tit. 2, n. 4; *ibid.*, Appendix, p. 232, n. 2; Many, "De Peccato Sollicitationis," — *Le Canoniste*, XVIII (1895), 722; Noldin, *De Sacramentis* (5. ed., 1904), n. 393, 5. Most of the modern authors speak of it as being reserved *speciali modo*, since the censure is reserved *speciali modo*. Cf. Cappello, *De Poenitentia*, n. 604, 4°; Ferreres, *Compendium*, II, n. 672, *Quaer.* 5, R. 2.
2. Cf. Pius IX, Litt Encycl., *"Gravibus Ecclesia,"* 24 dec. 1874 — *ASS*, VIII (1874), 187. Cf. also S. C. S. Off., decr. 27 iun. 1866 — *Fontes*, n. 995; *Collectanea*, n. 1294; S. C. S. Off., instr., 20 febr. 1866 — *Fontes*, n. 990; *Collectanea*, n. 1282; Franz Adam Goepfert, *Moraltheologie* (dritter Band, Paderborn: Ferdinand Schoeningh, 1902), p. 216; Lehmkuhl, *op. cit.*, II, n. 690, c, and n. 1120; Berardi, *De Sollicitatione*, nn. 358, 363; Gury, *Compendium*, II, n. 1075; Benger, *Compendium Der Pastoraltheologie* (2. ed., Regensburg, 1872), p. 271; Schuech, *Handbuch*, p. 685; Cavigioli, *De Censuris*, n. 115.
3. Cf. canons 258, § 1; 7; Iorio, *Compendium*, II, 417, footnote (3);

the moment of their promotion, have *ipso iure* faculties to absolve from this sin.[4] The same grant is extended by law to those confessors who are designated by the cardinals and by residential and titular bishops to hear their confessions or the confessions of members of their household.[5]

The bishops themselves do not possess jurisdiction over this sin, except through the concessions of canons 882 and 900. The extensive quinquennial faculties do not list this reservation of sin reserved *ratione sui* which residential bishops can remit. Neither do nuncios, internuncios, or Apostolic Delegates enjoy this power in virtue of the usual faculties granted by the *Sacra Poenitentiaria.* They do however have delegated jurisdiction to absolve from censures reserved *speciali modo,* among which canon 2363 is classified.[6]

B. The Ordinary Confessor.

1. In Danger Of Death.

Except for the individual delegation by the *Sacra Poenitentiaria* for individual cases, the ordinary confessor has, in ordinary circumstances, no jurisdiction over this sin. The Code however grants him sweeping powers, so that there are but few occasions in which he will have to apply to the Holy See for faculties. The first concession is made through canon 882, which delegates any priest, even though he do not posses any jurisdiction, even in the presence of a confessor who has special faculties, to absolve from this papally reserved sin.

There was never any disagreement among canonists before the Code whether the reservation ceased when the penitent was in danger of death. The concession of the Council of Trent (1545-1563) allowed all priests to absolve penitents when they were face to face with the danger of death.

Motry, *Diocesan Faculties,* p. 109; Claeys Bouuaert-Simenon, *Manuale.* II, n. 142, 2.

4. Canon 239, § 1, 1°; Cf. Wouters, *Manuale,* II, n. 387, I; De Smet, *De Absolutione,* n. 136, A; Arregui, *Summarium,* n. 613, 1°, a.
5. Canon 349, § 1, 1°, collated with canon 239, § 1, 1°.
6. Cf. Arregui, *Summarium,* Appendix, I, 603, n. 4.

> Verumtamen pie admodum, ne hac ipsa occasione aliquis pereat, in eadem Ecclesia Dei custoditum semper fuit, ut nulla sit reservatio in articulo mortis: atque ideo omnes sacerdotes quoslibet poenitentes a quibusvis peccatis, et censuris absolvere possunt.[7]

The very clear words of the Constitution "*Sacramentum Poenitentiae*" ruled out any contrary view:

> ... quaecumque persona, quae exsecrabile flagitio se inquinaverit... a quocumque sacerdote,... praeterquam a Nobis... excepto mortis articulo, spe absolutionis obtinendae,... perpetuo careat.[8]

Contrasted with the words "*excepto mortis articulo*" of the Constitution, canon 882 employs the phrase "*in periculo mortis.*" Even though there is a difference between the two phrases, canonists accepted the phrase "*excepto mortis articulo*" in the generous extension of "*in periculo mortis.*" Any precarious condition of the penitent that engendered a fear in the mind of the confessor that death might probably ensue was the common interpretation given the phrase "*excepto mortis articulo*" by pre-Code canonists. No distinction was made whether the danger of death arose from intrinsic or extrinsic causes. The danger that attended soldiers who were preparing for battle or who were actually engaged in battle, the perils incident to a dangerous sea voyage, and the imminence of execution or of capital punishment were the common examples listed as extrinsic causes. A difficult labor at childbirth, the critical stage of a major illness, serious wounds, and advanced age were the examples of intrinsic causes of death. Persons who were in danger of losing their minds perpetually, or of coming into circumstances where opportunity for confession would be lacking, were also classified among those who were considered to be in danger of death.[9]

7. *Canones et Decreta Sacrosancti Oecumenici Concilii Tridentini* (Editio Stereotypa, Ratisbonae, 1884), Sess. XIV, de poenitentia, c. 7.
8. § 3 — Document V in the Code; Cf. also Rota, *Enchiridion*, n. 113; Berardi, *De Sollicitatione*, n. 364; Many, "De Peccato Sollicitationis," — *Le Canoniste*, XVIII (1895), 723; D'Annibale, *Summula*, III, n. 323.
9. Cf. D'Annibale, *Summula*, I, n. 38; Rota, *Enchiridion*, n. 119; Moriarty, *Extraordinary Absolution*, p. 70; Berardi, *De Sollicitatione*, n. 364; Leo Iacobus Linahen, *De Absolutione Complicis in Peccato Turpi*,

Modern canonists are very liberal in interpreting the phrase "*in periculo mortis.*" Whenever there is a truly probable danger of death any priest may invoke the grant of canon 882. In the formation of his judgment whether there is a probable danger of death the priest can rely on professional counsel, on the advice of those present, and certainly on his own opinion. If in the experience of medical men or from the observation of the confessor death follows frequently from the danger in which the penitent is presently to be found, absolution can be granted.[10] Certain danger, most probable danger, or imminent danger is not required before canon 882 can be applied.[11] If a positive and probable doubt is had in discerning whether the danger of death is real or only apparent, the Church will grant jurisdiction.[12] Genicot-Salsmans say that if a person is in a probable danger of death, even though there is greater likelihood that recovery from the danger will ensue, the penitent can still be absolved.[13]

Besides the examples listed by the older canonists, the dangers of death occasioned by a person's submitting to grave and serious operations, or by his living in air raid zones, or in regions infested with contagious pestilence, by his taking a perilous air journey, are referred to by modern authors.[14] The priest's judgment of what constitutes a danger of death is not solely to be governed by the examples generally found in text books of canon law or of moral theology, but by the dangers where they actually exist. The occupations therefore which insurance companies decline to

The Catholic University of America Canon Law Studies, n. 164 Washington, D.C.: The Catholic University of America Press, 1942), p. 45.

10. Cf. Moriarty, *Extraordinary Absolution,* p. 70; Cipollini, *De Censuris,* p. 51; Joseph F. Connolly, "The Emergency Powers of Canons 1043, 1044, and 1045, and Some War Time Considerations," — *The Jurist* (Washington, 1941-), V (1945), 30-33.
11. Cappello, *De Poenitentia,* n. 408.
12. Canon 209; Cf. Moriarty, *op. cit.,* p. 72.
13. *Institutiones,* II, n. 422.
14. Jone, *Moral Theology,* n. 579; Cappello, *De Poenitentia,* n. 408; Coronata, *Institutiones,* IV, 174; Linahen, *De Absolutione Complicis in Peccato Turpi,* pp. 44, 45; Moriarty, *loc. cit.;* Connolly, *art. cit.,* — *The Jurist,* V (1945), 30, 32, 33.

accept as insurance risks could well be considered as dangers of death.[15]

Any priest can validly and lawfully remit this papally reserved sin when he has formed the judgment that his penitent is in probable danger of death. The canonical status of the priest is no consideration when the good of souls is at stake. Whether the priest is approved, is subjected to ecclesiastical penalties, is irregular, or has defected from the faith, he is none the less capable of administering a valid absolution to a dying penitent, even in the presence of an approved priest who has this special faculty to absolve.[16]

Moriarty[17] and Cappello[18] affirm that a priest of an Oriental rite may use the privilege of canon 882. In cases of death no distinction between Catholics of the Latin or of the Oriental rite holds.

2. In Extraordinary Cases.

a. Pre-Code Discipline.

1) In Occult Cases.

The Council of Trent permitted bishops to absolve from all occult cases that were reserved to the Holy See.[19] Post-Tridentine

15. Persons who, when engaged in the more dangerous occupations, are denied insurance policies are: glider and test pilots, sykwriters, automobile racers and speed testers, divers, submarine crews, shot firers in the mining industry, drillers and shooters using explosives in oil wells, steeple-jacks, manufacturers and handlers of explosives, electric linemen, cable splicers, trouble shooters, deep sea fishermen, iron workers, miners, roofers, and many others. — Cf. Connolly, "The Emergency Powers of Canons 1043, 1044, and 1045, and some War Time Considerations," — *The Jurist, loc. cit.*
16. Cf. Claeys Bouuaert-Simenon, *Manuale,* II, n. 130; Augustine, *Commentary,* IV, 287, 288; Cappello, *De Poenitentia,* nn. 408, 3, 409, 9; James Patrick Kelly, *The Jurisdiction of the Simple Confessor,* The Catholic University of America Canon Law Studies, n. 43 (Washington, D.C.: The Catholic University of America, 1927), pp. 92, 93; Moriarty, *Extraordinary Absolution,* p. 73; Vermeersch-Creusen, *Epitome,* II, n. 152, footnote 1.
17. *Op. cit.,* p. 77.
18. *De Censuris,* n. 132, 1.
19. Sess. XXIV, *de ref.* c. 6.

authors disputed whether this grant was operative only in those cases which were reserved to the Holy See prior to the Council of Trent, or whether it applied also to cases which were to be reserved to the Holy See after the Tridentine council. St. Alphonsus, citing ten authors, taught that *valde probabilius* the concession extended also to those cases that were to be reserved after the time of the Council. He however allowed for an exception.[20] Since the Bulla Coenae *"Consueverunt"* of Gregory XIII (1572-1585)[21] and the Constitution *"Decori"* of Pius V (1566-1572)[22] employed the words *"nisi in mortis articulo constitutus"* and *"nisi in mortis articulo, absolvi possit,"* the absolution from the sins and censures listed in these respective documents was definitely reserved to the Holy See, and no simple confessor could validly remit them except in danger of death. St. Alphonsus concluded that every Bull or Constitution that appeared after the Council of Trent with similar derogating clauses denied to bishops the right to use the general faculty bespoken for them by the Council of Trent. The Constitutions and Bulls which did not have such derogating clauses left it possible for them to grant absolution in occult cases.[23]

St. Alphonsus knew of the papally reserved sin specified in the Constitution *"Sacramentum Poenitentiae,"* but he did not comment on it. Berardi[24] and Many[25] applied the principle formulated

20. *Theologia Moralis,* lib. VI, n. 594, *dub. 7.*
21. 4 apr. 1583, § 23, ". . .Ceterum a praedictis sententiis nullus per alium quam per Romanum Pontificem, nisi in mortis articulo constitutus, nec etiam tunc nisi de stando Ecclesiae mandatis et satisfactione praestita, absolvi possit. . ." — *Bullarium,* VIII, 417, 419.
22. 1 febr. 1570, ". . .volumus, sancimus, et ordinamus ,nulli abbatissarum . . .a monasteriis . . . exire . . . Egredientes. . . excommunicationis maioris latae sententiae vinculo statim eo ipso, absque aliqua declaratione, subiacere, a quo, praeterquam a Romano Pontifice nisi in mortis articulo, absolvi nequeant." — *Fontes,* n. 133; *Bullarium,* VII, 809.
23. *Theologia Moralis,* lib. VI, n. 594, *dub.* 7; Cf. also Prospero Fagnani, (1598-1678), *Commentaria in Quinque Libros Decretalium* (4 vols., Romae, 1661), lib I, tit. 2, cap. 13, nn. 29, 30.
24. *De Sollicitatione,* n. 363.
25. "De Peccato Sollicitationis," — *Le Canoniste,* XVIII (1895), 723; Cf. also Bucceroni, *C. "Sac. Poenit.",* n. 60.

by St. Alphonsus, and taught that although the Constitution *"Sacramentum Poenitentiae"* did not *nominatim* set aside the concession of the Council of Trent, it did so implicitly by forbidding every priest and bishop *quantavis auctoritate et dignitate munitus praeter R. Pontificem* to absolve from the reserved sin, except in danger of death (*nisi in fine vitae, et excepto mortis articulo.*)[26]

2) In Extraordinary Cases.

The Council of Trent had decreed that no penitent could be absolved from a papal reservation outside the danger of death. The confessors were to persuade their penitents who were subjected to such reservations to go to their superiors for absolution.

> ... custoditum semper fuit, ut nulla sit reservatio in articulo mortis;... extra quem articulum sacerdotes quum nihil possint in casibus reservatis, id unum poenitentibus persuadere nitantur, ut ad superiores, et legitimos iudices pro beneficio absolutionis accedant.[27]

At the time Rota published his *Enchiridion* (1884) and Berardi his monograph *De Sollicitatione* (1886) it was the *sententia communissima* to acknowledge to bishops the power to absolve penitents who were perpetually impeded from going to Rome for absolution.[28] In such circumstances the papally reserved sin was given the same consideration as an episcopally reserved sin, from which the bishop could absolve even in the absence of urgency for immediate absolution.[29] All persons who were perpetually impeded from going to the Holy See were accorded the same privileges in this regard

26. Concurring with the views of Berardi and Many were Ojetti (*Synopsis,* II, 569,) Lehmkuhl (*Theologia Moralis,* II, 529, 2°) and Gury (*Compendium,* II, n. 574, II). Rota, however (*Enchiridion,* n. 116) and Craisson (*Manuale,* II, n. 1616) did not follow that opinion. They acknowledged to bishops the power to absolve from this papally reserved sin in occult cases.
27. Sess. XIV, *de poenitentia,* c. 7.
28. Rota, *op. cit.,* n. 116; Berardi, (*op. cit.,* n. 365) merely refers to the *sententia communissima.* He himself strongly opposed it. Cf. *ibid.,* n.389.
29. Cf. Bucceroni, *Institutiones,* II, n. 800; Rota, *Enchiridion,* n. 116; D'Annibale, *Summula,* I, n. 368, footnote 17; Craisson, *Manuale,* II, n. 1616; St. Alphonsus, *Theologia Moralis,* lib. VII, nn. 84-88.

as persons who were in *articulo mortis.* As a result any confessor could absolve them.[30]

Though this practice was the *doctrina magis communis,*[31] Berardi opposed it by pointing out that thus the very purpose of the papal reservation for the sin of the false accusation of an innocent confessor was defeated.[32]

Instead of demanding that the penitents go personally to the Holy See to receive absolution from reserved sins, Giraldi mentioned that the practice had become common in 1775 to write for faculties to remit the papally reserved cases.[33] St. Alphonsus however defended the opinion that the *obligation* to write for faculties was not binding, since nowhere in law was there mention of such an obligation.[34] The Holy See was asked whether this opinion of St. Alphonsus could be sustained. On July 18, 1860 the Holy Office answered the following query:

> 2. An impediti adire Roman in persona, teneantur adire saltem per epistolam, aut procuratorem ad absolutionem a casibus Sedi Apostolicae reservatis impetrandam.

The reply was:

> Resp. Ad 2. Consulat probatos auctores, inter quos Sanctum Alphonsum Mariam de Ligorio. . .[35]

After this response of the Holy Office the more probable opinion of St. Alphonsus became the *sententia communissima.* The interpretation given the teaching of St. Alphonsus in view of the reply of the Holy Office was short-lived. Six years later, on June 27, 1866, the same Holy Office published a decree which directly affected the reservation of the sin as enacted in the Constitution "*Sacramentum Poenitentiae.*"[36] It stated that the usual faculties which it was the

30. Ballerini-Palmieri, *Opus Theologicum,* V, n. 679; Rota, *Enchiridion,* n. 116.
31. Lehmkuhl, *Theologia Moralis,* II, 529, 2°; Berardi, *De Sollicitatione,* n. 365, II.
32. *Op. cit.,* nn. 365, II; 366; 389.
33. *Expositio,* II, 758.
34. *Theologia Moralis,* lib. VII, nn. 84, 89, 90.
35. Found quoted in Rota, *Enchiridion,* n. 116; also in *Vindiciae Alphonsianae,* II, Par, V. qu. xvi, footnote 1.
36. *Fontes,* n. 995.

custom to grant to bishops were never to contain the power to absolve from the cases which Benedict XIV reserved in his Constitution *"Sacramentum Poenitentiae."*

The Constitution *"Apostolicae Sedis"* of Pius IX, issued on October 12, 1869 reorganized the existing legislation on censures, and revolutionized the discipline affecting their absolution. It did not touch the papally reserved sin. Canonists were in doubt whether the former leniency accorded to bishops and priests for granting absolution from censures and cases reserved to the Holy See when the penitent could not approach the Holy See for absolution could still be followed. A reply was eventually issued by the Holy Office on June 23, 1886. This response abrogated the decision the same Office had issued on July 18, 1860. The new order introduced a much stricter discipline.

> 1. Utrum tuto teneri possit sententia docens ad Episcopum aut ad quemlibet sacerdotem approbatum devolvi absolutionem casuum et censurarum, etiam speciali modo Papae reservatorum, quando poenitens versatur in impossibilitate personaliter adeundi S. Sedem.
>
> 2. Quatenus negative: utrum recurrendum sit, saltem per litteras ad Emum Card. Poenitentiarium pro omnibus casibus Papae reservatis, nisi Episcopus habeat speciale indultum, praeterquam in articulo mortis, ad obtinendam absolvendi facultatem.
>
> Resp. ad 1. Attenta praxi S. Poenitentiariae, praesertim ab edita Constitutione Apostolica sac. mem. Pii PP. IX quae incipit *Apostolicae Sedis,* Negative.
>
> Ad. 2. Affirmative: at in casibus vere urgentioribus, in quibus absolutio differri nequeat absque periculo gravis scandali vel infamiae, super quo confessariorum conscientia oneratur, dari posse absolutionem, iniunctis de iure iniungendis, a censuris etiam speciali modo Summo Pontifici reservatis, sub poena tamen reincidentiae in easdem censuras, nisi saltem infra mensem per epistolam et per medium confessarii recurrat ad S. Sedem. Facto verbo cum SSmo. SSmus approbavit.[37]

In so far as the Constitution *"Apostolicae Sedis"* did not make mention of the papally reserved sin, and the decree of June 23,

37. S. C. S. Off., 23 iun. 1886 — *Fontes,* n. 1102.

1886 introduced a new discipline affecting absolution of reserved cases and censures (*absolutionem casuum et censurarum*) canonists were debating whether a relaxation regarding the papally reserved sin had been effected. Could the *sententia communissima* of the authors who acknowledged the power to any confessor to absolve from this papally reserved sin when the penitent was impeded from going to Rome to obtain faculties, be still followed? On November 7, 1888, the *Sacra Poenitentiaria* clearly showed that the lenient interpretation of authors, based on the July 18, 1860 decision of the Holy Office could no longer be adhered to.

> 1. Decreti 23 iunii 1886, ad 1., quae sic se habet: "*Attenta praxi S. Poenitentiariae, praesertim ab edita Constitutione Apostolica S. N. Pii IX, quae incipit*: APOSTOLICAE SEDIS, *Negative*," non videtur respicere casus specialiter reservatos Summo Pontifici sine censura; siquidem de his non agitur in Constitutione *Apostolicae Sedis*. Numquid ergo integra manet vetus doctrina Theologorum dicentium de his absolvere posse episcopos vel eorum delegatos, vel, ut vult Castropalao, simplicem sacerdotem, quando poenitens Romam nequit petere, quin scribere necesse sit?
>
> Sacra Poenitentiaria mature consideratis expositis ad proposita dubia respondet: ad 1um. negative.[38]

This decision meant a victory for the opinion which Berardi had so earnestly and consistently defended. For several years he stood in isolation in his defense of this view against a *sententia communissima* which had favored a more liberal doctrine and practice.[39]

Authors writing after 1888 were slow to adopt this new discipline. Ballerini-Palmieri[40] and Lehmkuhl[41] in their 1892 and 1910 editions respectively still contended that it was the *doctrina communis* and a *sententia communis* to permit penitents who could not go to the Holy See for absolution from this reserved sin, to be absolved by any confessor. Many of the pre-Code authors,

38. S. Poenit., 7 nov. 1888, ad 1 — *Fontes,* n. 6437; *Collectanea,* n. 1695.
39. Berardi expressed his delight when he heard this report from Rome. Cf. *De Sollicitatione,* "Monitum," pp. 195-196.
40. *Opus Theologicum,* V, n. 679.
41. *Theologia Moralis,* II, n. 529, II, 2°.

aware of the strict discipline, made allowance for urgent cases by means of indirect absolution from this papally reserved sin.[42]

b. Present Legislation.

The Code with reference to absolution in extraordinary cases made provisions that are far more liberal than those that obtained in the pre-Code discipline. Canon 900 does not grant faculties to the confessor for absolution in the manner that canon 882 grants them, but it declares under what conditions the papally reserved sin ceases to be reserved. If its provisions are verified, any confessor in virtue of the ordinary faculties which he possesses can absolve from this sin. By comparison with the pre-Code *praxis* it was unbelievable that such a sharp mitigation had been envisioned by the legislator. On that account the post-Code authors were reluctant to apply the provisions of canon 900 when considering the absolution from the papally reserved sin. Though canon 893, § 3, decreed that the chapter on the reservation of sins was not to be confused with the parallel norms on the reservation of censures, it was not so evident whether the analogous norms of canon 2254 could be employed for the absolution from the sin reserved to the Holy See *ratione sui.*

Farrugia, hesitant in permitting the use of canon 900, taught that the sin could be absolved under the circumstances that obtain in the extraordinary absolution from censure.[43] The obligation of recourse was not to be overlooked. De Smet tolerated the use of canon 900, but only when the conditions of canon 2254, § 3, were verified, that is, when the penitent found it impossible to return to the same confessor for absolution upon the latter's obtaining of faculties. The urgency outlined in canon 2254, § 1,

42. Cf. Ignaz Rieder, "Zur Absolutio a Censuris Papae Reservatis," — *Theologisch praktische Quartalschrift* (Linz, 1832-), LI (1898), 910, n. 5; Berardi, *De Sollicitatione,* n. 390; Many, "De Peccato Sollicitationis," — *Le Canoniste,* XVIII (1895), 723; Lehmkuhl, *op. cit.,* II, 539; Bucceroni, *Institutiones,* II, n. 802. Leitner (Santi-Leitner, *Praelectiones,* lib. V, tit. 2, n. 4) disregarded the response of the *Sacra Poenitentiaria* and permitted absolution in virtue of the decree of of the Holy Office of June 23, 1886.

43. Cf. *De casuum Reservatione,* pp. 61, 65.

was considered by De Smet to provide no sufficient ground for absolving from the papally reserved sin.[44]

Cerato,[45] Blat,[46] Augustine[47] and Pruemmer[48] did not even venture this far. They forbade the use of canon 900 as well as the use of canon 2254. Cerato[49] and De Smet[50] recommended the pre-Code practice of resorting to indirect absolution from the sin in extraordinary cases. This practice had not been reprobated by the Code. After the indirect absolution either the penitent or the confessor was obliged to apply for faculties for the direct absolution.

The reluctance of the authors cited in the preceding paragraphs to permit the use of canon 900 was based on the following arguments.

1. The words "*Quaevis reservatio omni vi caret*" of canon 900 were taken from an Instruction of the Holy Office issued on July 13, 1916.[51] The Instruction had the phrase *Quaevis* ORDINARARIORUM *reservatio.* Even though the word ORDINARIORUM was deleted when canon 900 was formulated, these authors maintained that the pre-Code legislation and interpretation remained in force. The chapter on the reservation of sins was in its application to be restricted to diocesan reserved sins, and to sins reserved in an exempt religious institute.[52]

2. The possibility of leaving the territory where the sin was reserved to seek absolution elsewhere where the sin was not reserved was absurd. The legislation of canon 894 constituted universal law, and the reservation bound everywhere.

3. It was inconceivable, so these canonists argued, that the *Sacra Poenitentiaria* would deny a rescript to a penitent or to his

44. *De Absolutione,* nn. 136; 137, B; 142.
45. *De Delicto,* n. 131, 4, 2; 131, 5, 2.
46. *Commentarium,* lib. III, Pars II, 260.
47. *Commentary,* IV, 335, 3°.
48. *Manuale Iuris Canonici,* n. 306, 2.
49. *Op. cit.,* n. 131, 4, 2.
50. *Op. cit.,* n. 136.
51. n. 7 — *AAS,* VIII (1916), 313; *Fontes,* n. 1302.
52. Augustine, *loc. cit.*

confessor who sought faculties for absolution from the papally reserved sin.

4. The possibility of violating the seal of the confessional by contacting the *Sacra Poenitentiaria* could be practically ignored. Sufficient safeguards could always be resorted to with the effect that this danger was obviated.

On the other hand, a number of canonists taught that canon 900 could be invoked for the sake of absolving from this papally reserved sin. Their basic argument also was taken from the same Instruction of the Holy Office. They contended that the legislator designedly deleted the word ORDINARIORUM from canon 900 in order that the conditions of canon 900 could be applied to the reserved sin specified in canon 894.[53]

This opinion was favored by the Pontifical Commission for the authentic interpretation of the Code. On November 10, 1925, it gave a response to the following questions:

> 1. Utrum *quaevis reservatio,* de qua can. 900, sit tantum ratione peccati an etiam ratione censurae.
>
> 2. Utrum canon 900 agat de reservatione casuum ab Ordinariis tantum an etiam a Sancta Sede statuta.
>
> Resp. ad 1um. Affirmative ad primam partem, negative ad secundam.
>
> R. ad 2um. Negative ad primam partem, affirmative ad secundam.[54]

This decision ended all controversy. The norms of canon 2254 can not be applied in the granting of absolution from the papally reserved sin. Canon 900 makes ample provisions for its remission in urgent cases. It is the conclusion of Moriarty in his study *The Extraordinary Absolution from Censures* that the urgent necessity which permits the use of canon 2254 will be sufficient for the cessation of the reservation according to canon 900.[55]

53. Cf. Cocchi, *De Delictis et Poenis,* n. 226, e), footnote (1); Ferreres, *Compendium,* II, n. 679; Gearin, "The Crime of False Accusation — Again," — *AER,* LX (1919), 67; Dargin, *Reserved Cases,* p. 28; Genicot-Salsmans, *Institutiones,* (10. ed., 1922), n. 348.

54. *AAS,* XVII (1925), 583, n. vii.

55. P. 193; cf. also Cappello, *De Poenitentia,* n. 604, 1, 5°; Wouters, *Manuale,* II, n. 385, 2, b; Genicot-Salsmans, *Institutiones,* II, n. 400;

Canon 900 outlines five conditions under which the reservation of sins loses all legal force and effect:

1. Whenever a sick person cannot leave his home. The inability is accepted in a wide sense to include a moral as well as a physical disability. Wherefore, the aged, the physically indisposed, persons with imaginary ailments, the paralyzed, and all persons confined to prisons and other institutions are included.[56]

2. When couples confess in preparation for their marriage. This privilege holds even for the marriage that is to be convalidated.[57] If the parties confess several weeks prior to their marriage, or confess a second time because of a previous sacrilegious confession, or because of a denied absolution, provided only that the condition *matrimonii ineundi causa* is verified, the reservation ceases.[58] The fact that the contemplated marriage did not eventuate will not affect the reservation of the sin that is already remitted, nor will it impose an obligation upon the penitent to have recourse to the superior.

3. Whenever the legitimate superior who has faculties to absolve from the sin or to delegate faculties for its remission denies jurisdiction. Only the Holy Father and the *Maior Poenitentiarius* can validly delegate faculties for absolution from this papally reserved sin. Cardinals and the confessors, they and the residential and titular bishops designate have the power to remit the sin, but they cannot delegate the faculty to others to lift the reservation. The purpose of the reservation has been fulfilled as soon as the superior is informed of the commission of the sin. The purpose of the reservation is purely disciplinary. Whether the superior grants jurisdiction or refuses it, the penitent upon his return to the confessor has a right to absolution.[59]

Dargin, *Reserved Cases,* pp. 86, 89; De Meester, *Compendium,* III, Pars II, 185, footnote 6.

56. De Smet, *De Absolutione,* n. 138, 1; Cappello, *De Poenitentia,* n. 552, 2; Claeys Bouuaert-Simenon, *Manuale,* II, n. 145, 1; Augustine, *Commentary,* IV, 335, I.
57. Augustine, *loc. cit.*
58. De Smet, *op. cit.,* n. 138, 2; Cappello, *op. cit.,* n. 552, 3.
59. Cf. Noldin-Schmitt, *De Sacramentis,* n. 365, c; Claeys Bouuaert-Simenon, *Manuale,* II, n. 145, 1.

4. The reservation ceases whenever the confessor foresees that great hardship is experienced by the penitent. This may be occasioned by a spiritual or moral, a physical or an economic cause. As long as it effects the hardship it will be adequate to effect the cessation of the reservation.[60]

The hardships commonly accepted by commentators are: the difficulty incident to returning a second time to the same confessor for absolution; loss of reputation or the menace of scandal if one refrains from Holy Communion when it is known that a sacramental confession was made; failure to celebrate mass in similar circumstances; the spiritual harm caused by remaining in mortal sin for the length of time required to obtain faculties. Even a day, and to some devout soul even a portion of a day, could be recognized as a true hardship. The fear of disheartening a penitent who in consequence of a non-absolution may become set in his determination not to return to the sacraments is also accepted as a *grave incommodum.*[61]

The use of the telephone, of the telegraph, and of travel by rail in order to reach the legitimate superior may be resorted to, but there is no obligation to do so. They are even today regarded as extraordinary means, for no one except the Holy Father and the *Maior Poenitentiarius* can grant delegation for the remission of this papally reserved sin.[62]

5. When in the estimation of the confessor there is danger of violating the seal of the confessional, a valid and a lawful absolution from the reserved sin may be imparted. It is not likely that this excuse can be alleged, for the danger of violating the

60. Cappello, *De Poenitentia,* n. 554, 3°.

61. Claeys Bouuaert-Simenon, *Manuale,* II, n. 145, 2; Cappello, *op. cit.,* n. 554, 4°; Vermeersch-Creusen, *Epitome,* II, n. 179; Augustine, *Commentary,* IV, 336; Noldin-Schmitt, *De Sacramentis,* n. 365, d; Genicot-Salsmans, *Institutiones,* II, n. 348; Dargin, *Reserved Cases,* p. 34.

62. *PCI,* 12 nov. 1922, ad V — *AAS,* XIV (1922), 662, 663; Cf. also Claeys Bouuaert-Simenon, *Manuale,* II, n. 145, 2; Cappello, *De Poenitentia,* n. 554, 4°.

seal is lessened in direct proportion to the distance that separates the delegating superior from the penitent. Since canon 894 binds the faithful the world over, Orientals as well as Latins, there is no need to discuss the territoriality of the law. No confessor need ever be disturbed whenever the conditions of canon 900 are verified. He can proceed with absolution.

3. Retractation, Reparation Of The Harm, And The Grave Penance.

Unlike canon 2363, canon 894 has no clauses which forbid absolution unless a formal retratation of the false accusation has been made, the resultant harm repaired, and a grave and protracted penance imposed. Is it to be assumed that the reserved sin specified in canon 894 can be remitted if these requirements are not met? The conditions mentioned in canon 2363 are regarded as nothing more than an articulate expression in positive legislation of the natural law, and a restatement of the principles of moral theology. It is apparent however that the element of *formal* retractation is canonical legislation and not demanded by the principles of moral theology.[63]

All pre-Code authors demanded retractation, though they did not insist that it be formal.[64] Berardi even demanded that this retractation be made after the demise of the calumniated priest. The scandal given to the faithful through their knowing that dishonor has been brought to the sacrament of penance, and disgrace to the clerical state, must be repaired.[65]

Since the promulgation of the Code the Church has at various times admitted the need of fulfilling the three conditions stated in canon 2363 when a confessor absolves from the reserved sin mentioned in canon 894. Pius XI in his Constitution "*Servatoris Iesu Christi*" in extending the jubilee year of 1925 to the entire world

63. Cf. Wernz-Vidal, *Ius Canonicum,* VII, n. 500; Blat, *Commentarium,* lib. V, 274; Iorio, *Compendium,* II, 420, footnote, (1); Cipollini, *De Censuris,* p. 129.
64. Noldin, *De Sacramentis* (5. ed., 1904), n. 393, 5; Schuech, *Handbuch,* p. 689; Berardi, *De Sollicitatione,* n. 353, IV; 396.
65. *Loc. cit;* Cerato (*De Delicto,* n. 136) is the only modern author to mention this obligation.

for 1926, made that obligatory when he permitted confessors to absolve from the papally reserved sin.

> Qui falsam sollicitationis denuntiationem admiserit, is ne absolvatur, nisi aut eam formaliter retractaverit, aut saltem ad eam quamprimum retractandam atque ad sarcienda calumniae damna serio paratum se praebeat.[66]

In the *Bulla Cruciata* of Pius XI (*Carissime in Christo*), dirrected to King Alphonsus of Spain, faculties were granted to all confessors to remit the reserved sin stated in canon 894, but only after the formal retractation had been made, the harm had been repaired, and a grave and protracted penance had been imposed upon the penitent.[67]

The same conditions were demanded by the *monita* of the *Sacra Poenitentiaria* when the jubilee year commemorating the 1900th anniversary of our Lord's death was extended to the entire world in 1934.

> Ad peccatum quod attinet, per canonem 894 reservatum ratione sui,. . . confessarii absolutionem ne impertiant, nisi paenitens falsam denuntiationem formaliter retractaverit, et damna si qua inde secuta sint, pro viribus reparaverit, imposita insuper gravi et diuturna paenitentia.[68]

66. 25 dec. 1925, pars de facultatibus, vii — *AAS,* XVII (1925), 616; It is to be noted that no distinction was made whether the absolution was granted for the sin as mentioned in canon 894 or the crime as specified in canon 2363. The reference is impersonally made to the false denunciation of the crime of solicitation.
67. 15 aug. 1928, n. 1 — *AAS,* XXI (1929), 17. Note that the Bull used the word *crimen* in referring to the reserved *sin* treated in canon 894: ". . .In hac concessione facultas quoque comprehenditur absolvendi a casu falsae denuntiationis de crimine sollicitationis, de quo in canone 894 iuris canonici Codicis; sed confessarius electus a tali crimine non absolvat, nisi ad normam canonis 2363 ipsius Codicis. . ."
68. S. Poenit., *monita,* 3 apr. 1934, vii — *AAS,* XXVI (1934), 151; Note here that reference is made to the sin stated in canon 894 with the word *peccatum* and not with the word *crimen* as in the *Bulla Cruciata* document to King Alphonsus. Cf. also Pius XI, const. "*Quod superiore anno,*" 2 apr. 1934, IX, n. 1 — *AAS,* XXVI (1934), 145; S. Poenit., *monita,* 28 febr. 1933, 2, n. vii — *AAS,* XXV (1933), 60; In the general *monita* of the *Sacra Poenitentiaria* of July 1924, the instruction regarding the condition under which the

In so far as a valid absolution is conditioned on the readiness of the penitent to make retribution for the injury he has brought by his calumny, it is apparent that retractation and reparation of the harm must be made and a suitable penance imposed as satisfaction. The question whether the retractation must be made formally, and whether a serious promise to do so will suffice before absolution is imparted and the harm repaired, will be given attention in the next article.

4. Recourse.

According to the more common opinion an indirect recourse to the Holy See is to be made even though the sin stated in canon 894 has been remitted in consequence of the operative application of canon 900. For the reason that most of the canonists identify the sin stated in canon 894 with the crime mentioned in canon 2363 it follows that whenever the prescriptions of canon 900 are utilized in conjunction with the emergency faculties granted in canon 2254, § 1, recourse for the mandates is always required in compliance with the norms of the latter canon. If the conditions of canon 900 are verified the confessor can proceed to remit the sin, but he may be prevented from using that power because of the presence of the censure of excommunication as specified by canon 2363. According to a safe opinion the *grave incommodum* mentioned in canon 900 is equivalent in its import to that which is implied in the phrase *"si durum sit poenitenti in statu gravis peccati permanere"* contained in canon 2254, § 1.[69]

The same urgency that permits the confessor to invoke the norms of canon 900 will also allow him to employ the supplied jurisdiction of canon 2254, § 1. In such an emergency the censure can be removed, and only after its removal may the reserved sin be forgiven. The obligation of commanding recourse for the man-

reserved sin stated in canon 894 can be forgiven is not referred to. Cf. *AAS,* XVI (1924), 338-339. The faculties granted on the occasion of the Holy Year commemorating Pius XI's fiftieth ordination anniversary did not set these conditions, though permission to absolve from the reserved sin was granted. — *AAS,* XXI (1929), 9.

69. Cf. references in footnotes 61 and 79-84 of this CHAPTER.

dates remains because of the law of canon 2254, § 1. In this manner, authors insist, indirect recourse is necessary even if the sin stated in canon 894 has been remitted in virtue of the operative application of canon 900.

It is the contention of the present writer however that there is no identity of transgressions referred to in canons 894 and 2363. Hence the penalties do not coalesce, and the confessor can absolve from the papally reserved sin without even indirectly imposing the obligation to make a recourse.[70]

5. Reincidence.

The norms that regulate the absolution from censures are not to be employed with reference to the absolving from reserved sins. The problem of a renewal of the reserved sin in consequence of the failure to fulfill the conditions specified in canon 2363 need not be discussed if the promise of their fulfillment has been elicited from the penitent. Cerato in his first edition of *Censurae Vigentes* (1918) held that the sin would be reserved again. In the revised edition he deleted that statement.[71]

Article 2. Absolution from the Censure of Excommunication

A. The Privileged Confessor.

When compared with the reservation of the sin reserved *ratione sui,* the excommunication and its reservation to the Holy See *speciali modo* must be regarded as the more serious disadvantage. The number of confessors who have special jurisdiction, delegated or ordinary, to remove the excommunication treated in canon 2363 is greater than the number of confessors who can absolve the reserved sin. Besides the Holy Father and the *Maior Poenitentiarius,* all cardinals, from the time of their elevation, can absolve this excommunication.[72] The same jurisdiction is enjoyed by their confessors as well as by the confessors of residential or titular bishops.[73] The bishops do not possess jurisdiction over this excommunication,

70. Genicot-Salsmans, *Institutiones,* II, n. 500.
71. P. 164, b.
72. Canon 239, § 1, 1°.
73. Canon 349, § 1, 1°, collated with canon 239, § 1, 1°.

neither in occult cases,[74] nor by virtue of their quinquennial faculties. Nuncios, internuncios, and Apostolic Delegates, by virtue of special delegation from the Holy See, can absolve from excommunications reserved *speciali modo* to the Holy See.[75] This same privilege is enjoyed by all Ordinaries in mission territories.[76]

B. The Ordinary Confessor.

1. In Danger Of Death.

The Code provides for the granting of most extensive powers to any validly ordained priest to absolve from all sins and censures in danger of death, no matter to whom and in what they are reserved. Canon 882 prescribes that the norms of canon 2252 concerning the recourse for the mandates after convalescence are to be observed for absolution from *specialissimo modo* and *ab homine* reserved censures. The excommunication annexed to the crime of the false denunciation of an innocent confessor being only a *speciali modo* reserved censure, the convalescent calumniator is relieved of the *onus recurrendi,* when absolved in danger of death. He is however bound in conscience to execute the three conditions specified in canon 2363, if he perchance was absolved on the strength of a promise to fulfill this duty as soon as the state of his health permits.

2. In Extraordinary Cases.

The Code also makes ample provision for the removal of this censure in extraordinary cases. Canon 2254 outlines the specifications that will constitute an urgent case. When these conditions are verified any confessor who is approached for absolution from this *speciali modo* reserved excommunication may absolve.[77]

74. Canon 2237.
75. Index facultatum quas, pro locis missionis suae, Nuntiis, Internuntiis, et Delegatis Apostolicis penes civitates seu Nationes post Codicis Iuris Canonici publicationem tribuere Ssmus Dominus Noster decrevit, ceteris abrogatis. — Arregui, *Summarium,* Appendix, I, 603, n. 4.
76. Formulae Facultatum quas S. Congregatio de Propaganda Fide concedere solet Ordinariis in terris Missionum. — Coronata, *Institutiones,* V, 292, n. 11.
77. For an exhaustive study of canon 2254 cf. Moriarty, *Extraordinary Absolution,* pp. 142-261; Coronata, *Institutiones,* IV, 178-185; Ayrin-

The specifications of canon 2254 are three in number:

1. the danger of scandal;
2. danger of infamy;
3. hardship of remaining in grave sin.

It is the duty of the confessor to judge whether a particular case is an extraordinary case. The confessor is given the same latitude in canon 2254 concerning the presence of a probable reason that renders the case extraordinary that is given to him in canon 882 regarding his judgment of the presence of the probable danger of death. As long as he has a positive and probable doubt relative to the presence of any of these conditions canon 209 will protect him. If the subjective judgment is such as to assure the conscience of the confessor that a true *casus urgentior* is present and he absolves, but subsequent facts reveal that he was in error, the absolution is valid. This is not true however if the *casus urgentior* was maliciously feigned by the penitent.[78]

Canonists have offered no objective norm whereby one may appraise the specification which is identified with the hardship of remaining in grave sin. The subjective disposition of every individual varies within wide ranges. Whatever constitutes a hardship for some given person cannot always be regarded as such for another. Any anxiety that will seriously disturb a penitent's peace of mind in consequence of his necessitated continuance in a state of mortal sin is sufficient to constitute an extraordinary case.[79] If the penitent does not show any reluctance to remain in mortal sin, the zealous confessor can, and Vermeersch-Creusen[80] and Beste[81] say that he has a duty, to arouse a state of concern and fear for the results of sin in order to dispose him for absolution.[82] The majority of canonists admits that absolution can be given if it is hard for

hac-Lydon, *Penal Legislation,* nn. 97-106; Coochi, *De Delictis et Poenis,* 119-127.

78. Moriarty, *op. cit.,* pp. 72, 144.
79. Claeys Bouuaert-Simenon, *Manuale,* III, 543, III; Cappello, *De Censuris,* n. 124, 4; Moriarty, *op. cit.,* p. 151.
80. *Epitome,* III, 454, 1, 2°.
81. *Introductio in Codicem,* p. 911.
82. Cf. Coronata, *Institutiones,* IV, 179; Moriarty, *Extraordinary Absolution,* p. 151.

a penitent to remain in mortal sin for one day.[83] Some allow even less than a day.[84]

Canon 2254 presupposes that the minister who makes use of this emergency concession is a confessor who has the ordinary faculties. This canon does not supply jurisdiction for the hearing of the confession, but only extends the confessor's jurisdiction to include the power to grant absolution from the censure which the confessor ordinarily could not absolve. Since the canon directly concerns the good of souls an Oriental confessor can use it and absolve from the censure enacted in canon 2363.[85]

Canon 2254, § 1, binds the confessor under pain of sin to demand that his penitent have recourse for the mandates within a month.[86] The penitent is granted the option to make the recourse to nuncios, to internuncios, or to Apostolic Delegates, or also to the Ordinaries in mission territories, since all these persons are privileged by the Holy See to absolve from the *speciali modo* reserved censures and are therefore qualified to issue the mandates.[87] The obligation of making recourse affects the penitent personally. It

83. Claeys Bouuaert-Simenon, *Manuale,* III, n. 543; Moriarty, *loc. cit.;* Ayrinhac-Lydon, *Penal Legislation,* n. 102; Coronata, *loc. cit.*
84. Coronata, *loc. cit.;* Beste, *Introductio in Codicem,* p. 911.
85. Cf. Moriarty, *Extraordinary Absolution,* p. 155; Cappello, *De Censuris,* n. 132, 1.
86. *Tempus utile* is understood here. Cf. Coronata, *Institutiones,* IV, 181; Cocchi, *De Delictis et Poenis,* n. 79, C, a; De Meester, *Compendium,* III, Pars I, 186; Kelly, *The Jurisdiction of the Simple Confessor,* p. 173; Blat, *Commentarium,* lib. V, 117; Moriarty, *op. cit.,* p. 207.
87. Coronata, *Institutiones,* V, 292; *ibid.,* IV, 176; Cappello, *De Censuris,* n. 115, 4; Moriarty, *Extraordinary Absolution,* pp. 113, 114, 202; De Meester, *op. cit.,* 182, footnote 1; Kelly, *op. cit.,* pp. 174, 175. Cerato (*Censurae Vigentes,* p. 41) denies that they have this right. The authors upholding the competence of these delegated individuals to issue mandates base their assertion on the authentic interpretation of the Pontifical Commission in answer to the question occasioned by the phrasing of canon 2252, *"recurrendi. . . ad S Poenitentiariam vel ad Episcopum aliumve facultate praeditum,"* namely whether a bishop who is delegated to absolve from the reserved censures can also issue the mandates. The answer affirmed that he could. *PCI,* 12 nov. 1922, ad viii — *AAS,* (1922), 663.

is definitely a grave injunction. If deliberately neglected it will result in the reincurrence of a censure of the same species, though materially distinct.[88]

Commentators are in dispute whether the obligation to observe the mandates binds under the penalty of reincidence. After a judicious weighing of the arguments, Moriarty concludes that a *dubium iuris* exists.[89] The milder view has sufficient probability to favor non-reincidence.

The alternative method of obtaining absolution through the application of the norm of canon 2254, § 2, needs hardly be discussed in view of the limited number of confessors privileged to absolve from the *speciali modo* reserved censure. When the penitent is impeded from making the recourse or of returning to the same confessor to receive the mandates, the confessor is free to invoke the grant of canon 2254, § 3. Instead of imposing the obligation of recourse, he enjoins a congruous penance and satisfaction for the censure. These are enjoined with the threat that in the event of their non-fulfillment on the part of the penitent within the time set by the confessor, the penitent will be subjected anew to the same kind of censure.

3. Absolution According To Canon 2247, § 3

The non-privileged confessor who is unaware that a censure is attached to the false denunciation of an innocent confessor of the crime of solicitation, or that the censure is reserved *speciali modo* to the Holy See, and absolves from such a censure, does so validly. Canon 2247, § 3, supplies the faculty. The degree of ignorance is not considered. Whether the ignorance is culpable, even crass or supine, the absolution is valid.[90]

Inadvertance, forgetfulness, distraction and error are rated as equivalent to ignorance according to canon 2202, § 3. If absolution is imparted under these disturbing influences it is valid and the

88. Moriarty, *Extraordinary Absolution,* pp. 195, 216; Cappello, *De Censuris,* nn. 127, 129.
89. *Op. cit.,* p. 218, footnote 272.
90. De Smet, *De Absolutione,* n. 133, 2; Stadalnikas, *Reservation,* p. 107; Coronata, *Institutiones,* IV, 167; Ayrinhac-Lydon, *Penal Legislation,* p. 67.

censure is removed directly. No further burden to have recourse is placed upon the penitent. Canon 2247, § 3, however, does not contemplate the question of ignorance on the part of the confessor regarding the reservation of the sin reserved *ratione sui.* It does not grant faculties to him who through ignorance or in any disturbed mental condition absolves from the reserved sin specified in canon 894.

Canon 2246, § 3, provides for the valid absolution of the sin that was reserved *ratione censurae* when the censure has been removed by means of the applied operation of canon 2247, § 3. As soon as the censure ceases the reservation of the sin ceases forthwith. Since most of the canonists hold that the transgression mentioned in canon 894 is the same as the crime stated in canon 2363, in their view, the cessation of the excommunication will not cause the cessation of the reservation of the sin outlined in canon 894. Special faculties are still needed for effecting the remission of the sin reserved *ratione sui.* If however the penalty of canon 2363 is removed by a forgetful confessor through the supplied power of canon 2247, § 3, the sacramental formula of absolution will then simultaneously, but indirectly, remit the sin reserved to the Holy See. It is accepted doctrine that as long as other sins are confessed in conjunction with the reserved sin the absolution of a reserved sin imparted through ignorance of the reservation on the part of the confessor is valid.[91] As Pre-Code canonists taught that an ordinary confessor could absolve indirectly from the papally reserved sin when an extraordinary need for absolution is present,[92] so analogously, when absolution is imparted by a confessor who is ignorant of the reservation attached to a sin, the absolution is valid.

91. Cf. Matthaeus A. Coronata, Conte, *Institutiones Iuris Canonici Ad Usum Utriusque Cleri et Scholarum, De Sacramentis Tractatus Canonicus* (2 vols., Taurini: Marietti, 1943), I, 431; Pruemmer, *Manuale Theologiae Moralis,* III, n. 428, 1; Cappello, *De Poenitentia,* n. 556. Checchi ("De casuum reservatione et de conditionibus ad eam incurrendam requisitis," — *Analecta Ecclesiastica,* VI [1898], 314) held that even when the confessor absentmindedly granted absolution from a reserved sin, the absolution would not be valid.
92. Cf. authors cited in footnote 42 of this CHAPTER. Cerato (*De Delicto,* n. 141, 4, 2) and De Smet (*De Absolutione,* n. 136) recom-

4. The Conditions Of Canon 2363.

a. The Formal Retractation.

The privileged confessor or the ordinary confessor who invokes the benign provisions of canons 2254, §§1, 3, or 882 cannot remove the excommunication determined in canon 2363 (*a qua nequit ullo in casu absolvi*), unless a formal retractation of the false charge has been made, the harm resulting therefrom has been repaired, and a grave and a protracted penance has been imposed. When viewed in the light of canons 2242, § 3, and 2248, § 2, these three conditions mentioned in canon 2363 present a perplexing problem. According to canon 2242, § 3, contumacy ceases when the penitent has sincerely repented, has made adequate reparation for the injury caused by his violation of the law and has rectified the scandal or at least has *seriously promised* to do so.

It is within the province of the superior from whom absolution is sought to pronounce on the sincerity of the repentance, the sufficiency of the reparation of the harm and scandal, or the earnestness of the promise. Canon 2248, § 2, rules that no absolution is to be denied to a penitent who has receded from his contumacy according to the norms of canon 2242, § 3. Does the law of canon 2363 present an exception to the law of these two canons?

It is ordinarily assumed that whenever a penitent appears for confession he has receded from his contumacy. Moreover, if he is ready to promise satisfaction for the harm done, to restore the good name of the calumniated confessor as well as to make a formal retractation, canon 2248, § 2, decrees that he is not to be denied absolution. The promise to fulfill these obligations is ordinarily not sufficient to merit absolution from the excommunication, since canon 2363 demands that the formal retractation and reparation of the harm be an accomplished fact, (*nisi formaliter retractaverit, et damna pro viribus reparaverit.*)[93]

mended indirect absolution in extraordinary cases. Both of these commentators indeed wrote after the promulgation of the Code, but before the *PCI* gave its authentic interpretation with reference to the application of the norms of canon 900 to the papally reserved sin.

93. Cf. Sole, *De Delictis et Poenis,* n. 416, 5°; Regatillo, *Institutiones,* II, n. 1111.

There is a wide divergence of opinions among canonists concerning the interpretation of the clause *"nisi formaliter retractaverit, et damna pro viribus reparaverit."* This diversity of views of the various authors depends on the occasions in which the absolutions are granted, that is, whether granted

a. in danger of death;

b. in extraordinary cases arising from the danger of *infamia* or of scandal;

c. in extraordinary cases arising from the hardship of remaining in grave sin for a period of time;

d. or in the ordinary cases in which no urgency for absolution is pressed by the penitent and the confessor cannot dispose him sufficiently to invoke the privilege granted by canon 2254.

The two extreme views expressed by the commentators relate to the question of the granting of absolution from the censure on the strength of a mere promise to retract, as canon 2242, § 3, directs, or of the denial of the absolution even in danger of death, unless the strict prescriptions enacted in canon 2363 are complied with. The only instance of unanimous agreement is in the ordinary case when neither the ruling of canon 882 nor that of canon 2254 is employed. In such an instance the delinquent is to appear personally before the local Ordinary, before an official of the Holy Office, or before a delegate of either, to make a judicial and formal retractation in writing.[94]

That the juridical retractation before these designated judges is the only form of retractation considered by canon 2363 is by no means certain. A less formal retractation before other persons, before witnesses, or in writing cannot be considered contrary to the notion of formal retractation. In emergency cases many canon-

94. Regatillo, *loc. cit.;* Davis, *Moral and Pastoral Theology,* III, 406; De Smet, *De Absolutione,* n. 128, 4; Cerato, *De Delicto,* n. 132, 3; Sole, *loc. cit.;* Genicot-Salsmans, *Institutiones, II,* n. 400; Pruemmer, *Manuale Theologiae Moralis,* III, 468, 2; Wernz-Vidal, *Ius Canonicum,* VII, n. 500; Sipos, *Enchiridion,* pp. 1012-1013; Chelodi, *Ius Poenale,* n. 88; Jone, *Gesetzbuch,* III, 521; Augustine *Commentary,* VIII, 425; Coronata, *Institutiones,* IV, 505, 506; Cappello, *De Censuris,* n. 290.

ists favor the less formal retractation. The axiom of law canonized by canon 2219 — *in poenis benignior est interpretatio facienda* — and the very wide range of the emergency provisions specified in canons 882 and 2254 will modify the apparently inflexible requirements determined in canon 2363. If this lenient interpretation would not be acceptable, the liberal grants made in canons 882 and 2254 would be totally nullified when applied to cases contemplated in canon 2363. Neither canon 882 nor canon 2254 contain clauses calling for exceptions when there is question of their application to canon 2363.

Many canonists will show consideration to a dying penitent and interpret canon 2363 in such a manner as to permit the granting of absolution before the formal retractation and reparation of harm has been made.[95] Yet there are some authors who take exception to this doctrine. Chelodi[96] and Wernz-Vidal[97] think that absolution would have to be withheld even in danger of death. To this one may answer that though the conditions set by canon 2363 are strict, they cannot be so severely accepted as to demand the impossible. When a person is at the very point of death, hardly able to speak, much less able to write, and the confessor is the only person present, no one would expect him to advise the penitent to make an act of perfect contrition and permit him to depart this life without absolution because of the letter of the law of canon 2363.[98] As long as the penitent has the proper dispositions and is willing to do his utmost to have a retractation made by another if he should die, or to make it personally if he should survive, it would be manifesting uncalled for legalism to deny absolution on the plea that the benign concession of canon 882 is made inoperative by the law of canon 2363. By applying the principle of law — *suprema lex est salus animarum* — the spiritual good of the dying penitent takes precedence over the temporal good of the calumniated priest. Fur-

95. De Smet, *De Absolutione,* n. 128, 4; Cavigioli, *De Censuris,* p. 92; Cerato, *De Delicto,* n. 130, 3; Coronata, *loc. cit.;* Augustine, *loc. cit.;* Sole, *loc. cit.*; Cocchi, *De Delictis et Poenis,* n. 226, e); Moriarty, *Extraordinary Absolutione,* p. 269.

96. *Ius Poenale,* n. 88.

97. *Ius Canonicum,* VII, n. 500.

98. Cf. Cipollini, *De Censuris,* p. 130.

thermore, the use of *epikeia* will certainly permit granting of the absolution. Otherwise the observance of the law would be too difficult and actually harmful, two reasons justifying the use of *epikeia*.[99]

The good name of the calumniated priest need not remain damaged because of the apparent rigor of the law enacted in canon 2363. The confessor can be urged to obtain the penitent's permission to use the confessional knowledge to bring the retractation to the competent officials. Consideration must also be shown to the innocent calumniated confessor, so that he does not suffer on account of the false accusation. In case death should intervene, or if the penitent should have a change of heart after his recovery and refuse to retract formally, the good name of the maligned priest will be restored.

In order that the confessor might not expose himself to the danger of violating the confessional seal, he could request that the retractation itself be in writing. If that is not possible, at least the permission for the use of the confessional matter pertaining to the false denunciation should be in writing.[100] If the penitent is in full possession of his faculties he can write the retractation himself or at least dictate it and sign the statement. An alternative method would be to call two witnesses who can be commissioned by the dying penitent to make the formal retractation in his name. This arrangement will excuse the confessor of all responsibility, and likewise safeguard the seal of confession as well. If necessary, the witnesses can be put under oath of secrecy to protect the penitent's reputation.[101]

When the penitent lapses into unconsciousness immediately after his confession before he has permitted the confessor to use

99. Arregui, *Summarium,* n. 75; Beste, *Introductio in Codicem,* p. 82; Jone, *Moral Theology,* n. 56; Noldin-Schmitt, *Summa Theologia Moralis,* I, n. 160.

100. Cf. Cipollini, *De Censuris,* p. 130; Augustine, *Commentary,* VIII, 425; Cerato, *De Delicto,* n. 130, 3; Sole, *De Delictis et Poenis,* n. 416, 5°; Cocchi, *De Delictis et Poenis,* n. 226, e).

101. Cf. De Smet, *De Absolutione,* n. 128, 4; Jone, *Gesetzbuch,* III, 521; Pruemmer, *Manuale Theologiae Moralis,* III, n. 468, Scholion 2; Davis, *Moral and Pastoral Theology,* III, 406; De Meester, *Com-*

the confessional knowledge, the confessor will be held to the seal, and the incriminated priest will correspondingly be exposed to the penalties mentioned in canon 2368, § 2. It is a misfortune that would have befallen him anyway if the penitent had never gone to confession.

In a conflict of laws, the principle that the spiritual welfare of a soul is to receive preference over the temporal good of another is to govern. Where the salvation of a soul is concerned, then the laws which are purely ecclesiastical laws cease to bind when they are in conflict with the ministration of the spiritual wants of that soul. *Epikeia* can be resorted to. In such extreme cases the legislator cannot reasonably wish to have the confessor be a legalist. After giving signs of repentance and expressing willingness to retract formally or to have the retractation made in his name if he should die, the penitent is entitled to the benefit of absolution.

When the extraordinary faculties mentioned in canon 2254 are invoked, many authors recommend the same procedure of the less formal retractation as outlined for the case in which the penitent is in danger of death.[102] Cerato[103] and Wouters[104] allow the confessor the use of the faculty granted in canon 2254, § 1, before the formal retractation has been made, but only when the absolution cannot be deferred without danger of infamy or scandal. These same authors will not permit the use of the faculty when the hardship of remaining in mortal sin for a length of time is alleged as a plea for its use. In the latter instance the letter of the law of canon 2363 is to be insisted upon, so these authors maintain, and a formal retractation must precede the absolution. But one may

pendium, III, Pars II, 268, footnote, 5; Salucci, *Il Diritto Penale,* II, 274; Vermeersch-Creusen, *Epitome,* III, 564; Beste, *Introductio in Codicem,* p. 961; Ayrinhac-Lydon, *Penal Legislation,* n. 325, c; Moriarty, *Extraordinary Absolution,* p. 269; Sole, *De Delictis et Poenis,* n. 416, 5°.

102. References found in footnotes 100-101. Cappello (*De Censuris,* n. 291) does not refer to the less formal manner of making retractation, but he permits the use of the faculty granted in canon 2254.

103. *De Delicto,* n. 130, 3.

104. *Manuale,* II, n. 895, XIII, footnote 1. Pistocchi (*I Canoni Penali,* p. 216) cites Cerato with approval.

well answer that, since these two cases of urgency have been paralleled in canon 2254, § 1, there is no reason for making such an arbitrary distinction.[105]

What however is to be done by the confessor when even the less formal retractation is impossible? It will be a rare occurrence that a healthy penitent cannot put his retractation into writing, or at least dictate it and then sign it when it is prepared by another, or to summon two witnesses in order to make an oral retractation in their presence and then commission them to carry the report to the competent judge. With such an eventuality assumed, could the confessor absolve the penitent on the strength of a sincere promise that he will retract as soon as possible? Few commentators are articulate in the consideration of such a contingency. Most authors simply state that a mere promise to retract the false denunciation will not entitle the penitent to receive the benefit of absolution.[106] Coronata does not favor the granting of absolution on the strength of a promise to retract. He does admit however that the absolution would be valid.[107]

Cerato,[108] De Smet,[109] Cipollini,[110] Moriarty,[111] Cocchi,[112] Ver-

105. *Moriarty, Extraordinary Absolution,* p. 270.
106. Chelodi, *Ius Poenale,* n. 88; Wernz-Vidal, *Ius Canonicum,* VII, n. 500; Augustine. *Commentary,* VIII, 425; Sipos, *Enchiridion,* pp. 1012, 1013; Cavigioli, *De Censuris,* p. 92 ;Ayrinhac-Lydon, *Penal Legislation,* p. 262, c; Blat, *Commentarium,* lib. V, 275. Woywod ("False Accusation of Solicitation," — *HPR,* XXXVIII [1938], 720), regards such a procedure inadvisable.
107. *Institutiones,* IV, 505.
108. ". . .Si id [formalis retractatio coram Superiore ante absolutionem] praestari non possit, seria promissio admittatur sufficiens. . ." — *De Delicto,* n. 130, 3. Cf. also *Censurae Vigentes,* n. 79, f.
109. *De Absolutione,* nn. 128, 4; 129.
110. *De Censuris,* p. 129. This author is not so articulate as either Cerato or De Smet. He asks a rhetorical question whether a serious promise to make a formal retractation is sufficient. By implication his question demands an affirmative answer.
111. *Extraordinary Absolution,* pp. 265-273; *Cf.* especially 268.
112. ". . .**nec** sufficit seria promissio retractationis . . . excipitur . . casus physicae impossibilitatis." — *De Delictis et Poenis,* n. 224, c (Bold faced type in original).

meersch-Creusen[113] and Jone[114] do affirm that a serious promise will suffice when the penitent is physically incapacitated for making the formal retractation. The latter opinion does appear to be the more satisfactory. The beneficial value of canon 2254 would be nullified if the formal retractation and reparation of harm would always have to precede the absolution. Seldom does a false denunciator confess to the local Ordinary, to an official of the Holy Office, or to a delegate of either, to whom alone he could make the formal retractation before receiving absolution.

A privileged confessor, in consequence of the requirements of canon 2363, would be restrained from using his faculty before he had exacted and actually effected the formal retractation and reparation of the harm. It can readily be seen that in the latter contingency the conditions of canon 2363 can, and are to be, strictly observed. The urgency for absolution as canon 2254 speaks of it is not necessarily present when a privileged confessor is approached.

To absolve a penitent who has promised formal retractation and reparation of the harm as soon as possible does not connote a violation of the strict demands of canon 2363, as it might at first appear. One of the conditions demanded by canon 2254, § 1, before absolution be imparted is the duty of the confessor to impose a recourse for the mandates. These are issued directly by the *Sacra Poenitentiaria,* or by the privileged confessors, and sent to the confessor to whom the penitent has to return. A failure to make this recourse will mean a relapse into the same kind of censure, and the penitent's status reverts to the condition in which he was before the absolution. In applying for the mandates the confessor should state that the absolution was granted after a promise to retract the false incrimination. The *Sacra Poenitentiaria* can be requested that in formulating and transmitting the mandates it demand that they be fulfilled *sub poena reincidentiae* for the sake of safeguarding the reputation of the maligned priest. This suggestion is offered with a view to preventing the penitent from using the probable opinion which would free him from reincurring

113. *Epitome,* III, n. 565, 2.
114. *Gesetzbuch,* III, 521.

the censure in spite of his non-observance of the mandates.[115]

Assurance that the good name of the calumniated confessor will be restored is had when the confessor uses the norms of canon 2254, § 3. Instead of imposing the obligation of recourse, he assigns the proportionate satisfaction and penance for the censure. Canon 2363 dictates the quantity as well as the quality of the penance and satisfaction. The penance is to be of an exacting and protracted character, the satisfaction is to consist of the formal retractation and the reparation of the harm and scandal. If the penitent fails to perform either the penance or the satisfaction within the time specified by the confessor, then a new censure of the same species is in force.[116]

The examination of the faculties granted during the Holy Year of 1925 will help to form a safe judgment regarding the mind of the Church whether a confessor can absolve a calumniator after receiving from him a serious promise that he will make the formal retractation after his absolution from the censure. In his Constitution *"Servatoris Iesu Christi"* Pius XI stated that confessors could absolve penitents guilty of the crime of false denunciation if the latter had formally retracted the accusation, or had manifested a readiness to do so as soon as possible and to repair the harm that had ensued from the calumny.

> ...Qui falsam sollicitationis denuntiationem admiserit, is ne absolvatur, nisi aut eam formaliter retractaverit, aut saltem ad eam quam primum retractandam, atque ad sarcienda calumniae damna serio paratum se praebeat.[117]

115. Cf. Moriarty, *Extraordinary Absolution,* pp. 134-141. Even if the *Sacra Poenitentiaria* or the privileged confessor who is approached for the mandates does not impose the observance of the mandates *sub poena reincidentiae,* the reputation of the calumniated confessor would still be safeguarded because of the teaching of moral theologians that *probabilism* cannot be used when the *certain* right of a third person is put into jeopardy. Cf. Woywod, *A Practical Commentary,* I, 11, (3); Jone, *Moral Theology,* n. 93, 1; Davis, *Moral and Pastoral Theology,* I, 99, (c).
116. Cf. canon 2254, 3; De Smet, *De Absolutione,* n. 132; Moriarty, *Extraordinary Absolution,* pp. 241-244.
117. 25 dec. 1925, pars de facultatibus, vii — *AAS,* XVII (1925), 616.

In the absolution allowed in virtue of these jubilee faculties there was no question of danger of death or of the emergency cases considered in canon 2254, §§ 1, 3, and yet confessors were entitled to absolve from the sin specified in canon 894, and the excommunication enacted in canon 2363, on the promise by the penitent that he would comply with the conditions of canon 2363. The interpretation given by Pius XI in his Constitution "*Servatoris Iesu Christi*" is no direct proof that a promise of retractation and of the reparation of harm is sufficient for the use of the emergency faculties granted in canon 2254. It serves, however, as an indication that the opinion defended by a few of the canonists is not radically incompatible with the practice of the Church.[118]

In view of the liberality of the legislator in arranging for the application of the provisions of canon 2254 it is respectfully maintained here that the clause, "*a qua nequit ullo in casu absolvi, nisi falsam denuntiationem formaliter retractaverit, et damna, pro viribus reparaverit*" is to be given a broad interpretation which favors the calumniator when he is in great need of an indulgent attitude. Through the use of the faculty granted in canon 2254 there is no evasion of the requirements as demanded by canon 2363. The law itself in canon 2254, § 3, threatens reincidence if the satisfaction and reparation of harm are not made within a month, and in using the powers delineated in canon 2254, § 1, when it issues its mandates the *Sacra Poenitentiaria* can always do so with the proviso that any culpable failure to observe the imposed mandates within the specified time would imply also a reincurring of the earlier disability and censure.

b. Reparation Of The Harm.

The second condition to be fulfilled before absolution from the censure can be given is the reparation of the harm that has come to the innocent priest. The penitent must use all the means at his disposal to repair the damage that has ensued (*et damna, si qua inde secuta sint, pro viribus reparaverit*). It is not so difficult to measure in material value the loss of income (*lucrum cessans*) and the ensuing damage (*damnum emergens*) which result

118. Moriarty, *op. cit.*, p. 272.

from loss of benefice, office, and incarceration in a penitential house. Such harm can as a rule be adequately compensated by monetary returns. No material compensation, however, can equalize the humiliation that was suffered by the maligned priest as occasioned by his suspension.

Authors who were hesitant in permitting absolution after a promise exacted from the penitent to make formal retractation were more liberal in allowing absolution on the condition of a serious promise to repair the harm that has come to the calumniated priest. In their estimation the phrase *"pro viribus reparaverit"* can be extended to the degree in which a serious promise can still come within its ambit. In addition to Cerato, De Smet, Cipollini, Moriarty, Cocchi, Vermeersch-Creusen and Jone,[119] many more commentators acknowledge the serious promise to repair the ensuing harm as sufficient for meeting the requisite condition set for the obtaining of absolution.[120] The same reasons that were presented in the foregoing discussion as warranting the benefit of absolution after a serious promise to make a formal retractation are applicable also when the promise deals with the reparation of the harm.

It may here be advisable with reference to the conclusion submitted by the writer to caution the reader that the promise of retractation and of the reparation of harm is considered as warranting the use of the faculties granted in canon 2254 only when the retractation cannot be obtained in any other manner. The conditions of canon 2363 are to be strictly adhered to whenever a privileged confessor absolves from the excommunication. They are likewise to be followed when a confessor in all ordinary cases applies for the needed faculties to absolve from this specially reserved censure. The less formal retractation made to the confessor in writing, or made orally before two witnesses, can however be considered sufficient whenever circumstances allow one to resort to the use of the faculties granted in canons 882 and 2254. The

119. Cf. *supra,* footnotes 109-114.

120. Cf. Augustine, *Commentary,* VIII, 425; Coronata, *Institutiones,* IV, 505; Regatillo, *Institutiones,* II, n. 1111; Cavigioli, *De Censuris,* p. 92; Sipos, *Enchiridion,* pp. 1012, 1013; De Meester, *Compendium,* III, Pars, II, 268, f.

promise of a formal retractation and | or the reparation of the harm is adequate only when the retractation and reparation cannot be obtained in any other form. The latter contingency will be relatively rare. When physical impossibility precludes the full or partially formal retractation, then the above indicated intrinsic reasons conjoined with the available extrinsic authority seem sufficiently strong to constitute a probable opinion that a serious promise of a formal retractation and of the reparation of the harm will justify the granting of the absolution. This is applicable in danger of death and in the emergency cases considered in canon 2254, §§ 1, 3.

c. The Grave And Protracted Penance.

The *poenitentia gravis et diuturna* mentioned in canon 2363 is not a sacramental penance for the crime, but a distinct juridical penance for the censure.[121] The penance for the censure ordinarily should be the same kind of grave penance that would be prescribed if no censure were attached. Chelodi recommends that the quantity and the quality of the penance for the false denunciation of an innocent confessor of the crime of solicitation be equal to that imposed for a *peccatum gravissimum.*[122] The accumulation of two grave penances however constitutes an unduly grave hardship. Accordingly, then, one or the other can be mitigated to some extent.[123]

Canon 2363 demands that the penance be both of an exacting and of a protracted character. Since the Code itself has enumerated the principal penances in canon 2313, § 1, most of the authors have restricted their recommendations for grave penances to one or the other of the penances indicated in that canon. They consist chiefly in the recitation of determined prayers, in the making of pilgrimages, in the keeping of special fasts, in the giving of alms, and in the performance of spiritual exercises in a religious house. The proposed penance must be commensurate with the gravity of the crime, and

121. De Smet, *De Absolutione,* n. 128, 4; Moriarty, *Extraordinary Absolution,* pp. 246, 273; Coronata, *Institutiones,* IV, 184; Cappello, *De Censuris,* nn. 101, 132, 4; Cerato, *Censurae Vigentes,* pp. 265, 296, 297; Kelly, *The Jurisdiction of the Simple Confessor,* p. 176.

122. *Ius Poenale,* n. 88.

123. Moriarty, *op. cit.,* p. 246.

proportionate to the physical, mental and spiritual disposition of the penitent.[124]

The confessor is to be aware of his position as judge and healer, and is therefore to provide for the honor that is due to God and for the means whereby he can promote the salvation of souls.[125] If these considerations are ignored through an unwise choice of the imposed penance, the medicinal purpose of the penance will be defeated. The objective norm of what constitutes a grave penance has been crystallized by the practice and usage current in the Church.[126]

That penance is generally considered grave which corresponds to a good work prescribed *sub gravi* by the Church.[127] In addition to the classification given under canon 2313, § 1, attendance at mass, and the observance of fasts are the classic examples. Other good works that are morally equivalent to these are also acceptable. The recitation of the small office, of five decades of the rosary, the making of the Way of the Cross, are recommended. In some cases the saying of prayers on bended knees is suggested.

The notion of *diuturnitas* depends on the type of penance imposed. It stands to reason that the hardship incident to the making of an arduous pilgrimage cannot rank simply with the recitation of a rosary. The number of rosaries and the length of time these are to be said must vary greatly when compared with the

124. *Cf.* canon 887.

125. Canon 888, § 1.

126. ". . .Potestne iniungi poenitentia per tres tantum menses, verum pluribus per hebdomadam vicibus adimplenda, quando praescripta est *gravis et diuturna,* ac per unum solum mensem cum statuta fuit *gravis poenitentia* salutaris. . .?

R.' In praefinienda poenitentiae qualitate, gravitate, duratione, etc., quae dispensantis aut delegati arbitrio iuri conformi remittuntur, neque severitatis, neque humanitatis fines esse excedendos, rationemque habendam conditionis, aetatis, informitatis, officii, sexus, etc., eorum quibus poena irrogari iniungitur." — S. Poenitentiaria Ap. (*Nicotrien. et Tropien.*), 8 apr. 1890 — *Collectanea,* n. 1725.

127. Cf. Beste, *Introductio in Codicem,* p. 914; Ayrinhac-Lydon, *Penal Legislation,* p. 262; Coronata, *Institutiones,* IV, 184; Cappello, *De Poenitentia,* n. 608.

number of pilgrimages that involve an expenditure of time and money. The great divergence between grave penances will be a determining factor in any consideration of the length of time for which a specified penance is to be performed. The lighter the penance the longer it is to endure. The hardship accompanying the performance of the penance is to be in inverse ratio to the *diuturnitas*. Cappello considers the daily performance of a grave penance for two or three weeks, the weekly performance for two months, and the monthly performance for a half year, as satisfying the requirements of the two elements that combine to constitute a grave and protracted penance.[128]

Without specifying the number of times the grave penance is to be performed Cocchi,[129] Ayrinhac-Lydon[130] and Chelodi,[131] recommend that the *diuturnitas* reflect a duration of about six months. Vermeersch-Creusen[132] and Coronata[133] vary these recommendations slightly. In the main, however, they keep the same ratio. They suggest a weekly recitation of the rosary on bended knees, a weekly fast, a Way of the Cross two or three times a week, two or three extended visits to the Blessed Sacrament each week. Each of these penances is to last for a period of three months. Vermeersch-Creusen also recommend the alternative of a pilgrimage. This is to be made several times if it does not involve great hardship.[134]

Sipos extends the *diuturnitas* from three to six months for the weekly performance of a grave penance.[135] When the grave penance is to be performed monthly, Beste wants it to last one year,[136] and Coronata from one to two years.[137]

Cerato is the strictest of all. A grave penance is to consist

128. *De Poenitentia,* n. 608; *De Censuris,* nn. 101, 290.
129. *De Delictis et Poenis,* n. 224, c).
130. *Penal Legislation,* p. 262.
131. *Ius Poenale,* n. 88.
132. *Epitome,* III, n. 565, 2.
133. *Institutiones,* IV, 506.
134. *Loc. cit.*
135. *Enchiridion,* p. 1013.
136. *Introductio in Codicem,* p. 914.
137. *Op. cit.,* IV, 184.

of the recitation of the rosary three times a week, or of a weekly fast, or of a monthly confession; a *poenitentia longa* is a grave penance performed at least once a week for one year; a *poenitentia diuturna* under like conditions is one that continues for a period of three years.[138]

Though there is a divergence of opinions among the authors as to what length of time constitutes a *diuturnitas,* and as to the number of times each week a grave penance is to be performed, a prudent confessor will find a happy medium in selecting the type of penance suited to his particular penitent.

138. *Censurae Vigentes,* pp. 260-263, 296.

CHAPTER VIII

FALSE DENUNCIATIONS AND ORIENTALS

There has never been any dispute since 1710 that Orientals are subjected to the papal legislation concerning the crime of solicitation. On June 13, 1710, the Holy Office gave an interpretation regarding the universality of the pontifical constitutions against solicitation that had been issued up to that date. Every nation, the Greeks as well as the Armenians, were included.[1] In his Constitution *"Etsi pastoralis"* of May 26, 1742, Pope Benedict XIV stated that the Latins and Greeks alike were comprised under the law.[2]

In so far as the Constitution *"Sacramentum Poenitentiae"* contained the penalties for false denunciations, and the Constitution *"Etsi pastoralis"* extended the application of that Constitution to the Orientals, it did seem that they were subjected to the penalty for false denunciations. No commentators have been discovered by the writer who between the years of 1742 and 1866 gave this matter attention. The Instruction of the Holy Office on February 20, 1866, definitely stated that there was no doubt that all nations were under the prescriptions, prohibitions, and reservations of the Constitution *"Sacramentum Poenitentiae,"* June 1, 1741, of Pope Benedict XIV, and of the Constitution *"Universi,"* August 30, 1622, of Pope Gregory XV.[3]

1. S. C. S. Off., 13 iun. 1710. "Le constituzioni pontificie emanate *contra sollicitantes* comprendono tutte le nazioni, ed in coseguenza cosi obbligano i greci come gli armeni." — *Fontes,* n. 775; *Collectanea,* n. 279.
2. § IX, n. V. "Tum subiectis omnibus et singulis Romanorum Pontificum Constitutionibus, contra sollicitantes praesertim in confessione editis, quae in singulas nationes universim vires suas extendunt, ac Latinos aeque, ac Graecos sua amplitudine comprehendunt." — *Fontes,* n. 328.
3. "Nullum sane dubium est, quin hae praescriptiones, prohibitiones, reservationes omnes et singulae in cunctas nationes universim vires suas extendant, et ubique terrarum *inconcusse ac inviolabiliter observandae sint.* Quod quidem vel legenti Gregorii XV et Benedicti XVI Constitutiones evidentissime patet; et idipsum consequentium Pontificum suffragio, prout se dedit occasio, ad hanc usque diem confirmatum est." — *Fontes,* n. 990. (Italics in original). The phrase

Since the Constitution *"Sacramentum Poenitentiae"* in its third paragraph mentioned the penalty for false denunciations, and the Instruction of February 20, 1866, held Orientals to its prescriptions, there can be no doubt that Orientals were subject to the papally reserved sin. In the very same Instruction there is mention of the closely subsequent decree of the same Office issued on June 26, 1866, which denied faculties to all Ordinaries to absolve from the papally reserved sin. This decree was to be intimated to all Ordinaries without exception who previously had enjoyed special faculties in this matter.[4]

An encyclical letter of the Sacred Congregation for the Propagation of the Faith of August 6, 1885, answered a doubt whether Orientals were affected by the censures and reservations of the Constitution *"Apostolicae Sedis"* of Pius IX, issued on October 12, 1869. In its answer the Congregation replied that the Constitution *"Apostolicae Sedis"* did not introduce any changes affecting the Orientals. The same Congregation manifested that they were subjected to those censures that dealt with matters of dogma, and to the

hae praescriptiones etc. has their antecedent in the previous two paragraphs of the Instruction wherein are synopsized four paragraphs of the Constitution *"Sacramentum Poenitentiae."* The pertinent passage concerning the crime of false denunciations to which all nations are bound reads: "Praeterea tertio loco Apostolicae Sedi reservatur, excepto mortis articulo, eorum casus qui innoxios sacerdotes apud ecclesiasticos iudices falso sollicitationis insimulant, vel sceleste procurant ut id ab aliis fiat. . ."

4. "Et proxime SSmus D. N. Pius Papa IX decreto huius supremae Inquisitionis sub feria IV die 27 iun. anno 1866 edixit, *in facultatibus quibus Episcopi aliique locorum Ordinarii ex concessione Apostolica pollent absolvendi ab omnibus casibus Apostolicae Sedi reservatis, excipiendos semper in posterum et exceptos habendos esse casus reservatos in Bulla Benedicti XIV quae incipit* "SACRAMENTUM POENITENTIAE." . . .Hoc decretum vero omnibus ubique terrarum Ordinariis praedicta absolvendi facultate donatis absque ulla exceptione significandum mandavit." — *Fontes,* n. 990. All pre-Code authors and *ASS* (III, [1867], 499) cite the Instruction as dated February 20, 1867 instead of 1866. The year 1867 seems to be the proper date, for the Preamble to the Instruction just cited refers to the decree issued on June 27, 1866, four months later than the indicated date of the Instruction itself.

papally reserved sin and censures that were specified in the Constitution *"Sacramentum Poenitentiae"* of Benedict XIV.[5]

Since the promulgation of the Code no papal document has appeared in which the Orientals are clearly said to be under the reservation and the penalty enacted in canons 894 and 2363 respectively. The particular law for the Ruthenians quotes a portion of the Constitution *"Sacramentum Poenitentiae,"* but not the paragraph which treats of the penalty for false denunciations,[6] and the particular law for the Syrian Maronites refers to the crime of solicitation, but not to false denunciations.[7]

Since the Orientals were *nominatim* mentioned in various decrees of the Holy See before the Code, they are definitely subject to the penalty as it is enacted in the Constitution *"Sacramentum Poenitentiae."* Despite the norms of canon 1, which excludes Orientals from subjection to the disciplinary law of the Code, that canon does not abrogate the laws of the Latin discipline which obligated Orientals before the Code. The conclusion then stands that when-

5. S. C. de Prop. Fide, litt. encycl. 6 aug. 1885, "Essendo stato promosso, il dubbio se gli orientali siano soggetti alla Constituzione *Apostolicae Sedis* pubblicata dalla f. m. di Pio IX, in data dei 12 Ottobre 1869, la Suprema Congregazione de S. Offizio con successiva approvazione della Santita di N. S. ha dichiarato quanto segue nella feria IV, 15 Iuglio corrente anno:

   1. Per Constitutionem *Apostolicae Sedis* nihil esse innovatum circa censuras eorumque reservationes pro fidelibus rituum orientalium.

   2. Eosdem fideles subiici omnibus censuris ab Apostolica Sede latis in materia dogmatum et in Constitutionibus in quibus implicite de iis disponitur, nempe ubi materia ipsa demonstrat eos comprehendi, quatenus non de lege mere ecclesiastica agitur, sed ius naturale et divinum declaratur.

   Vuole poi la sudd. Supr. Congregazione che per mezzo dei Rmi Delegati Apostolici siano notificate queste disposizioni a tutti i Patriarchi, Arcivescovi e Vescovi di rito orientale compresi nella rispettiva loro Delegazione, e che si ricordi loro: "illos fideles subiici nominatim nedum censuris, sed etiam Apostolicis reservationibus latis in Const. Benedicti XIV, *Sacramentum Poenitentiae. . ."* — *Fontes,* n. 4910; *Collectanea,* n. 1640.

6. *Codificazione Canonica Orientale "pro Ecclesia Orientali," Fonti* (XV Fasciculi, Romae: Tipographia Poliglotta Vaticana, 1931-1933, Fasciculus XI, *"Ius Particulare Ruthenorum,"* nn. 704, 705.

7. *Fonti, Fasciculus XII, Disciplina Antiochena Maroniti,* nn. 1335, 1414.

ever an Oriental falsely accuses an innocent priest (*sacerdos*) of the crime of solicitation the sin is reserved to the Holy See. Whenever he denounces an innocent confessor (*confessarius*) he does not, like the Latin, incur the excommunication enacted in canon 2363, but again the sin is reserved *ratione sui* in the manner in which that reservation was in force before the Code.[8]

8. John Aloysius Duskie (*The Canonical Status of the Orientals in the United States,* The Catholic University of America Canon Law Studies, n. 48, [Washington, D.C.: The Catholic University of America, 1928], pp. 133, 134) considers them subject also to the excommunication in view of the change in the law through the addition of a new penalty. Cappello (*Summa Iuris Canonici in Usum Scholarum Concinnata* [3 vols., Vol. I, 3. ed., Romae: Apud Aedes Gregorianae, 1938], I, n. 62, 3°) subjects them to the reserved sin of canon 894. It does appear however that he does not hold them to the excommunication enacted in canon 2363, for he excludes that canon from the list in which he enumerates the canons which affect Orientals. Cf. *op. cit.,* I, n. 62, 5°. Cerato (*De Delicto,* n. 5, Adn.) not only excludes the Orientals from subjection to the reservation and the penalty mentioned in canons 894 and 2363 respectively, but he also states that, since the crime of solicitation is an ecclesiastical law, the Orientals are in view of the norm of canon 1 not subject to the law on the crime of solicitation. That doctrine is an untenable one, for the Code did not abrogate the law that affected Orientals prior to its promulgation. Moreover, the June 8-9, 1922 *Pagella* of the Holy Office on its flyleaf states in bold type that the Instruction is also to be sent to Orientals (*ad omnes. . . Ordinarios* **"Etiam Ritus Orientalis").** Cf. also *Fonti,* Fasciculus II, 609. Iorio (*Compendium,* II, n. 582 bis, *Quaer.* 30°) does not hold the Orientals either to the reservation stated in canon 894 or to the excommunication determined in canon 2363. For his reason he points to the statement made in canon 1, and cites Cerato to support him in his view.

CONCLUSIONS

1. Contrary to popular belief, legislation against the crime of solicitation originated, not in Spain, but in Germany, at the Council of Trier held on March 1, 1227.

2. The elements that constitute the crime of solicitation became crystallized in the Constitution *"Sacramentum Poenitentiae"* of Pope Benedict XIV, issued on June 1, 1741. No changes have been introduced since.

3. The law which demands that solicited penitents report their confessors who committed the crime of solicitation had its origin in the edicts of the inquisitors. Pope Gregory XV made this a universal law in his Constitution *"Universi"* on August 30, 1622.

4. The first legislation imposing a penalty for the false denunciation of innocent priests and confessors was enacted by Pope Benedict XIV in his Constitution *"Sacramentum Poenitentiae,"* § 3. Besides the sanction which reserved the sin *ratione sui* to the Holy See as mentioned in this Constitution, the Code has also added the penalty of excommunication reserved *speciali modo* to the Holy See.

5. The false denunciation can take place in three forms:

   1. by falsifying the attempted seduction to sins of impurity;
   2. by falsifying the circumstances in which the sins of impurity were committed; and
   3. by falsify both elements, the attempted seduction to sins of impurity and the circumstances in which these sins allegedly were committed.

6. It can be seriously questioned whether the more common opinion that the sin specified in canon 894 is identical with the crime mentioned in canon 2363 merits such a rating. The intrinsic arguments favoring a duality of transgressions as found in the contrast that exists between the words *sacerdos* and *confessarius* used in the respective canons is strong enough to constitute a solidly probable opinion.

7. The basis for a distinction between canons 894 and 2363 in the contrasted phrases *apud iudices ecclesiasticos* and *apud Su-*

periores is not sound; the distinction which derives from the supposition that canon 894 speaks of judicial denunciations and canon 2363 of simple denunciations cannot be supported with strong arguments.

8. The sin referred to in canon 894 is similar to the crime considered in canon 2363 in all respects except:

1. the former treats of the false denunciation of an innocent priest (*sacerdos, confessarius improprie dictus*), that is, of a priest who not only did not hear the calumniator's confession but also did not solicit him, but who is reported to have heard his confession and to have solicited him in that alleged confession; the latter canon treats of the false denunciation of an innocent confessor (*confessarius propriae dictus*), that is, of a confessor who *de facto* did hear the penitent's confession;
2. Canon 894 reserves the absolution of the transgression to the Holy See; canon 2363 excommunicates the false delator and reserves the censure *speciali modo* to the Holy See. The two penalties do not coalesce.

9. The false denunciation of an innocent bishop who *de facto* heard his accuser's confession brings the denunciator under the penalty of canon 2363. The false accusation of an innocent bishop who did not hear the alleged confession does not entail for the denunciator either the excommunication or the reservation of his sin.

10. In all cases (in the transgression mentioned in canon 894 as well as in the crime considered in canon 2363) the denunciation is postulated as being necessarily judicial in character, that is, made in the form specified in the Instruction of the Holy Office issued on June 8-9, 1922: the competent recipients of such judicial denunciations are the officials of the Holy Office, the local Ordinary (exclusive of the vicar general), or their delegates.

11. No local Ordinary can lawfully punish a denounced confessor or priest unless a judicial denunciation has been received and the norms of the 1922 Instruction have been followed to the very finger tips (*ad unguem*). The purpose of the strictness of these

formalities is to prevent the punishment of innocent confessors. It is certain doctrine today that the extraordinary mode of punishing priests by means of the *suspensio ex informata conscientia* cannot be lawfully resorted to; the imposed suspension would probably also be invalid in its intended effect.

12. No penalty is visited upon the calumniator who brings a simple denunciation to the officials designated by the Instruction of the Holy Office; nor if the denunciation is brought to the proper officials, but is defective because of negligence in keeping the prescribed form outlined by that same Instruction. *A fortiori* no penalty can be inflicted if the denunciation of a non-existing crime of solicitation is brought to ecclesiastical persons, or even to lay persons, who are not recognized as competent by the Holy Office to review denunciations that treat of the crime of solicitation.

13. The false denunciation of an innocent confessor or priest can also be made by a mandatary. He will incur or escape the enacted sanction or penalty according as his co-operation with the *mandans* to perpetrate the denunciation was of a formal or of a purely material character.

14. It is a practically incontestable doctrine that ignorance of the reservation of sins reserved *ratione sui* will not excuse the sinner from having his sin subjected to the reservation. When there is question however, of the ignorance concerning the papally reserved sin there is a degree of extrinsic probability that ignorance of the reservation will excuse the calumniator because of the element of penalty that is attached to the reservation. Though the opposite theory is the more probable one, the suppletory principle of canon 209 can be invoked and the more liberal view may be followed.

15. The serious promise to retract the false accusation and to repair the ensuing harm suffices for the penitent to receive the benefit of absolution from the reserved sin mentioned in canon 894. It is a probable opinion that in danger of death, and also in the urgent cases contemplated in canon 2254, absolution from the excommunication can be imparted to the calumniator before he has made a fully formal retractation of his false charge and repaired

the harm that had ensued, provided however that he has made a less formal retractation. In all cases of physical impossibility of making even the less formal retractation, the serious promise to make a formal retractation as soon as possible will entitle the denunciator to the benefit of absolution.

16. While Orientals are now as formerly subject to the legislation contained in the Constitution "*Sacramentum Poenitentiae,*" they are not subject to the law enacted in canon 2363. Consequently, with reference to the crime of false denunciation as considered in canons 894 and 2363, the transgression eventuates as a reserved sin for all Orientals, but it does not give rise to the penalty of excommunication.

BIBLIOGRAPHY

Sources

Acta Apostolicae Sedis, Commentarium Officiale, Romae, 1909-1929; Civitate Vaticana, 1929-.

Acta Sanctae Sedis, 41 vols., Romae, 1865-1908.

Bullarum Diplomatum et Privilegiorum Sanctorum Romanorum Pontificum Tauriensis Editio, 24 vols. et 2 Appendices, Augustae Taurinorum — Neapoli, 1857-1885.

Canones et Decreta Concilii Tridentini, Editio Stereotypa, Ratisbonae, 1884.

Codex Iuris Canonici Pii X Pontificis Maximi iussu digestus Benedicti Papae XV auctoritate promulgatus, Westminster, Maryland: The Newman Bookshop, 1942.

Codicis Iuris Canonici Fontes cura Emi Petri Card. Gasparri editi, 9 vols., Romae (postea Civitate Vaticana): Typis Polyglottis Vaticanis, 1923-1939. (Vols. VII-IX ed. cura et studio Emi Iustiniani Card. Seredi.)

Codificazione Canonici Orientale "pro Ecclesia Orientali" Fonti, XV Fasciculi, Romae: Tipographia Poliglotta Vaticana, 1931-1933.

Collectio Resolutorum Responsorumque S. Officii — Sollicitantes — Analecta Ecclesiastica, IV (1896), nn. 1551-1597, pp. 361-364.

Collectanea S. Congregationis de Propaganda Fide, 2 vols., Romae: ex Typographia Polyglotta Vaticana, 1907.

Decretum Gratiani emendatum et notationibus illustratum una cum glossis, Romae, 1582.

Denzinger, Henr., Bannwart, Clem., Umberg, Ioan., *Enchiridion Symbolorum, Definitionum et Declarationum de Rebus Fidei et Morum,* 21-23. ed., Friburgi Brisgoviae: Herder, 1937.

Hardouin, Jean, Acta Conciliorum et Epistolae Decretales ac Constitutiones Summorum Pontificum, 12 vols., Parisiis, 1714-1715.

Jaffe, Phillipus, *Regesta Pontificum Romanorum ab condita Ecclesia ad annum post Christum natum MCXXVIII,* 2. ed., cura G. Wattenbach, F. Kaltenbrunner, P. Ewald, S. Loewenfeld, 2 vols., Lipsiae: Veit et Com., 1885-1888.

Liber Sextus Decretalium una cum Clementinis et Extravagantibus Earumque Glossis Restitutis, Romae, 1582.

Mansi, Ioannes, *Sacrorum Conciliorum Nova et Amplissima Collectio,* 53 vols, in 60, Parisiis, 1901-1927.

Thesaurus Resolutionum S. Congregationis Concilii, 167 vols., Romae, 1718-1908.

REFERENCE WORKS

Aertnys, Josephus, *Theologia Moralis iuxta Doctrinam S. Alphonsi Mariae de Liguorio,* 11. ed., nunc tertio ex integro recognovit, C. A. Damen, 2 vols., Taurinorum Augustae: Marietti, 1928.

Albitius (Albizzi), Franciscus Card., *De Inconstantia in Iure Admittenda vel Non,* Pars Prima, De Inconstantia in Fide, Amstelodami, 1683.

Alphonsus Liguori, St., *Theologia Moralis,* Editio Stereotypa, 9 vols., Taurini, 1872.

Arregui, Antonius, *Summarium Theologiae Moralis ad Recentem Codicem Iuris Canonici Accommodatum,* 11. ed., Bilbao: El Mensajero Del Corazon de Jesus, 1930.

Augustine, Charles, *A Commentary on the New Code of Canon Law,* 8 vols., Vol. IV, *On the Sacraments (except Matrimony) and Sacramentals,* 3 ed., 1925; Vol. VIII, *Penal Code,* 3. ed., 1931, St. Louis: Herder.

Ayrinhac, H. A., and Lydon, P.J., *Penal Legislation in the New Code of Canon Law,* revised edition, New York: Benziger, 1936.

Badii, Caesar, *Institutiones Iuris Canonici,* 3. ed., 2 vols., Vol. II, *De Rebus,* 1922, Florentiae: Libreria Editrice, 1921-1922.

Ballerini, Antonius-Palmieri, Dominicus, *Opus Theologicum Morale,* 7 vols., Prati, 1889-1893.

Benger, Michael, *Compendium der Pastoraltheologie,* 2. ed., Regensburg, 1872.

——————— Pastoraltheologie, 3 vols., Regensburg, 1863.

Berardi, Aemilius, *De Sollicitatione,* Faventiae, 1886; 2. ed., 1897. The first edition is used. Whenever the second edition is consulted reference to it will be made each time.

——————— *Theologia Moralis,* 5 vols., Faventiae, 1905.

Beste, Udalricus, *Introductio in Codicem,* 2. ed., Collegeville, Minn.: St. John's Abbey Press, 1944.

Blat, Albertus, *Commentarium Textus Codicis Iuris Canonici,* 5 vols. in 6, lib III Pars I, *De Sacramentis,* 2. ed., Romae: ex Typographia Pontificia in Instituto Pius IX, 1924; lib. V, *De Delictis et Poenis,* Romae: Collegio Angelico, 1924.

Bouix, D., *De Judiciis Ecclesiasticis,* 2 vols. in 1, Parisiis, 1855.

Bucceroni, Januarius, *Institutiones Theologiae Moralis secundum Doctrinam S. Thomae et S. Alphonsi,* 3. ed., 2 vols., Romae, 1898.

——————— *Commentaria De Casibus reservatis, De Censuris, De C. Pii IX "Apostolicae Sedis", De C. Benedicti XIV "Sacramentum Poenitentiae", De Absolutione danda, differenda, deneganda,* 5. ed., Romae, 1899.

Cappello, Felix, *Tractatus Canonico-Moralis de Sacramentis,* 3 vols., in 6, Romae: Marietti, 1932-1939. Vol. II, *De Poenitentia,* 3. ed., 1938.

——————— *Tractatus Canonico-Moralis de Censuris iuxta Codicem Iuris Canonici,* 3. ed., Taurinorum Augustae: Marietti, 1933.

——————— *Summa Iuris Canonici in Usum Scholarum Concinnata,* 3 vols., Vol. I, 3. ed., Romae: Apud Aedes Universitatis Gregorianae, 1938.

Cavigioli, Joannes, *De Censuris Latae Sententiae Quae in Codice Iuris Canonici Continentur Commentariolum,* Torino: Libreria Editrice Internazionale, 1919.

Cerato, Prosdocimus, *Censurae Vigentes Ipso Facto a Codice Iuris Canonici Excerptae,* 2. ed., Patavii: Typis Seminarii, 1921.

——————— *De Delicto Sollicitationis,* Patavii: Typis Seminarii, 1922.

Chelodi, Joannes, *Ius Poenale et Ordo Procedendi in Iudiciis Criminalibus iuxta Codicem Iuris Canonici,* Tridenti: Libr. Edit., 1925 [1920?].

Cipollini, Albertus, *De Censuris Latae Sententiae iuxta Codicem Iuris Canonici,* Taurini: Marietti, 1925.

Claeys Bouuaert, F.,-Simenon, G., *Manuale Juris Canonici,* 3 vols., Vols. I, III, 3. ed., 1931; Vol. II, 2. ed., 1935, Liege: Dessain.

Cocchi, Guidus, *Commentarium in Codicem Iuris Canonici,* 8 vols. in 5, Taurinorum Augustae: Marietti, 1922-1930; Vol. VIII, *De Delictis et Poenis,* 3. ed., 1938.

Colli-Lanzi, Camillus, *Theologia Moralis Universa,* 3 vols., Taurini-Romae: Marietti, 1926-1928.

Coronata, Matthaeus Conte a, *Institutiones Iuris Canonici ad Usum Utriusque Cleri et Scholarum,* 5 vols., Vols. I-II, 2. ed., 1939, Vols. III-V, 1933-1936, Taurini: Marietti.

——————— *Institutiones Iuris Canonici Ad Usum Utriusque Cleri et Scholarum, De Sacramentis Tractatus Canonicus,* 2 vols., Taurini: Marietti, 1943.

Craisson, D., *Manuale Totius Iuris Canonici,* 5. ed., 4 vols., Pictavii, 1877.

D'Annibale, Josephus, *Summula Theologiae Moralis,* 5. ed., 3 vols., Romae, 1908.

Dargin, Edward V., *Reserved Cases According to the Code of Canon Law,* The Catholic University of America Canon Law Studies, n. 20, Washington, D.C.: The Catholic University of America, 1924.

Davis, H. J., *Moral and Pastoral Theology,* 4 vols., London: Sheed and Ward, 1935.

Del Bene, Thomas, *De Officio Sanctae Inquisitionis circa Haeresim,* 2 vols., Lugduni, 1666.

De Meester, Alphonsus, *Iuris Canonici et Iuris Canonico-Civilis Compendium,* nova ed., 3 vols., in 4, Brugis: Desclee, 1921-1928.

De Smet, Aloysius, *De Absolutione Complicis et Sollicitatione,* 2 ed., Brugis: Beyaert, 1921.

DuCange, Dom. Carolus Dufresne, *Glossarium ad Scriptores Mediae et Infimae Latinitatis,* 10 vols., Paris, 1733. *Glossarium Novum ad Scriptores Medii Aevi cum Latinos tum Gallicos, seu Supplementum ad auctiorem Glossarii Cangiani Editionem collegit et digessit* D. P. Carpientier, 10 vols., Paris, 1766.

Duskie, *John Aloysius, The Canonical Status of the Orientals in the United States,* The Catholic University of America Canon Law Studies, n. 48, Washington, D.C.: The Catholic University of America, 1928.

Eichmann, Eduard, *Das Strafrecht des Codex Iuris Canonici,* Paderborn, 1920.

Eltz, Louis Anthony, *Cooperation in Crime,* The Catholic University of America Canon Law Studies, n. 156, Washington, D.C.: The Catholic University of America Press, 1942.

Facciolati, Jacob, *Totius Latinitatis Lexicon,* consilio et cura Jacobi Facciolati, Opera et Studio, Aegidii Forcellini, edidit Jacobus Bailey, 2 vols., London, 1828.

Fagnani, Prosperus, *Commentaria in Quinque Libros Decretalium,* 4 vols., Romae, 1661.

Farrugia, Nicholaus, *De Casuum Conscientiae Reservatione iuxta Codicem Iuris Canonici,* 2. ed., Augustae Taurinorum-Romae: Marietti, 1922.

Ferraris, Lucius, *Prompta Bibliotheca Canonica Iuridica Moralis Theologica necnon Ascetica Polemica Rubricistica Historica,* 9 vols., Editio a Bucceroni curata, Romae, 1885-1899.

Ferreres, Ioannes, *Casus Conscientiae,* 2 vols., Barcinone: Eugenius Subirana, 1926.

——————— *Compendium Theologiae Moralis,* 14. ed., 2 vols., Barcinone: Eugenius Subirana, 1928.

Genicot, Eduardus, *Institutiones Theologiae Moralis,* 14. ed., Quam recognovit I. Salsmans, 2 vols., Buenos Aires-Dedebec: Edicione Desclee, De Brouwer, 1939.

Giraldi, Ubaldus, *Expositio Iuris Pontificii,* 2 vols., Romae, 1829.

Goepfert, Franz Adam, *Moraltheologie,* Dritter Band, Paderborn: Ferdinand Schoeningh, 1902.

Gury, Ioannes, et Ballerini, Antonius, *Compendium Theologiae Moralis,* 7. ed., 2 vols., Romae, 1882.

Haring, Johann B., *Grundzuge des katholischen Kirchenrechts,* 2 vols., Graz: Ulrich Mosers Buchhandlung, 1924.

Hefele, Carl, *Conciliengeschichte,* 5. ed., 9 vols., Freiburg im Breisgau, 1886.

Heiner, F., *De Processu Criminali Ecclesiastico,* Latine vertit ac denuo edidit Dr. Arthurus Wynen, Romae: Fridericus Pustet, 1912.

Hollweck, Joseph, *Die kirchlichen Strafgesetzte,* Mainz, 1899.

Iorio, Thomas, A., *Compendium Theologiae Moralis, iuxta methodum Ioannis Petri Gury ad normam Codicis Iuris Canonici redactum a Raphaele Tummolo,* 5. ed., quam recognovit emendavit et auxit, Thomas A. Iorio, 2 vols., Neapoli: M. D'Auria, 1934-1935; 6. ed., 3 vols., 1938-1939. The fifth edition was used throughout.

Jone, Heribert, *Gesetzbuch des kanonischen Rechtes,* 3 vols., Paderborn: Ferdinand Schoeningh, 1939-1940. Vol. II *Sachenrecht;* Vol. III, *Prozess und Strafrecht.*

——————— *Moral Theology,* Englished and Adapted to the Code and Customs of the United States of America by Urban Adelman, Westminster, Maryland: The Newman Bookshop, 1945.

Kelly, James Patrick, *The Jurisdiction of the Simple Confessor,* The Catholic University of America Canon Law Studies, n. 43, Washington, D.C.: The Catholic University of America, 1927.

Kostler, Rudolf, *Worterbuch zum Codex Iuris Canonici,* Muenchen: Friedrich Pustet, 1927-1929.

Konings, A., *Theologia Moralis,* 7. ed., 3 vols., New York, Cincinnati, Chicago: Benziger Bros., 1889.

Lega, Michael Card., *Praelectiones in Textum Iuris Canonici, De Iudiciis Ecclesiasticis,* 4 vols., Romae: Typis Vaticanis, 1896-1901. Vol. I, 1896, Vol. II, 1898, Vol. III, 1899, Vol. IV, 1901.

Lehmkuhl, Augustinus, *Theologia Moralis,* 11. ed., 2 vols., Freiburg im Breisgau: Herder, 1910.

Leitner, Martin, *Handbuch des katholischen Kirchenrechts,* 4 vols., Regensburg: Jos. Kosel and Friedrich Pustet, 1921.

Linahen, Leo James, *De Absolutione Complicis in Peccato Turpi,* The Catholic University of America Canon Law Studies, n. 164, Washington, D.C.: The Catholic University of America Press, 1942.

Marc, Cl., Gestermann, Fr. X., et Raus, J.B., *Institutiones Morales Alphonsianae,* 18. ed., 2 vols., Lugduni: Vitte, 1927.

Merkelbach, Benedictus Henricus, *Summa Theologiae Moralis ad Mentem D. Thomae et ad Normam Iuris Nove,* 3. ed., 3 vols., Parisiis: Typis Desclee, De Brouwer, 1938-1939.

Michel, P., *Nouveau Code Canonique,* 6. ed., Alger: Mission d'Afrique des Peres Blancs, Maison Carree, 1930.

Moersdorf, Klaus, *Die Rechtssprache des Codex Iuris Canonici, — Goerres-Gesellschaft*: Veroffentlichungen der Sektion fur Rechts-und Staatswissenschaft, Koln: 1908-1910; Paderborn, 1910-, Verlag Ferdinand Schoningh, Heft 74, 1937.

Moriarty, Francis E., *The Extraordinary Absolution from Censures,* The Catholic University of America Canon Law Studies, n. 113, Washington, D.C.: The Catholic University of America, 1938.

Mothon, Pie Joseph, *Institutions canoniques a l'Usage des Curies Episcopales, du Clerge Paroissial, et des Familles Religieuses,* 3 vols., Lille-Bruges: Desclee, 1922-1924.

Motry, Hubert Louis, *Diocesan Faculties According to the Code of Canon Law,* The Catholic University of America Canon Law Studies, n. 16, Washington, D.C.: The Catholic University of America, 1922.

Muniz, T., *Procedimientos Ecclesiasticos,* 2. ed., 3 vols., Sevilla: Imp. y Lib. de Sabrino de Izquierdo, 1925.

Noldin, H., *Summa Theologiae Moralis,* 5. ed., 3 vols., Vol. III, *De Sacramentis,* Oeniponte: Fel, Rauch-Pustet, 1904.

Noldin, H., et Schmitt, A., *Summa Theologiae Moralis iuxta Codicem Iuris Canonici,* 20. ed., 3 vols., Vol. III, *De Sacramentis,* Oeniponte: Fel. Rauch-Pustet, 1930.

Noldin, H., et Schmitt, A., *De Sexto Praecepto et De Usu Matrimonii,* 24. ed., Oeniponte: Fel. Rauch-Pustet, 1931.

Noldin, H., et Schonegger, A., *De Censuris,* 24. ed., Oeniponte: Fel. Rauch-Pustet, 1931.

Noval, Iosephus, *Commentarium Codicis Iuris Canonici Libri IV De Processibus,* Pars I, *De Iudiciis,* Augustae Taurinorum-Romae: Marietti, 1920.

Ojetti, Benedictus, *Synopsis Rerum Moralium et Iuris Pontificii,* 2. ed., 2 vols. in 1, Romae, 1904.

Pennacchi, Josephus, *Commentaria in Constitutionem "Apostolicae Sedis,"* 2 vols., Romae, 1883.

Pighi, J. B., *Cursus Tehologiae Moralis,* 4. ed., 4 vols., Veronae: in Via Croce Verde, 1926.

Pignatelli, G., *Consultationes Canonicae,* 4 vols., Venetiis, 1716-1721.

Pistocchi, Mario, *I Canoni Penali del Codice Ecclesiastico Esposti e Commentati,* Torino-Romae: Marietti, 1925.

Potestas, *Examen Ecclesiasticum,* 2 vols., Venetiis, 1722.

Pruemmer, Dominicus, *Manuale Iuris Canonici in Usum Clericorum Praesertim Eorum Qui ad Instituta Religiosa Pertinent,* 3. ed., Friburgi Brisgoviae: Herder, 1922.

——————— *Manuale Theologiae Moralis secundum Principia S. Thomae Aquinatis,* 2. et 3. ed., 3 vols., Friburgi Brisgoviae-St. Louis: Herder, 1923.

Raus, J. B., *Institutiones Canonicae iuxta Novum Codicem Iuris pro Scholis vel ad Usus Privatum synthetice Redactae,* 2. ed., Lugduni-Parisiis; Typis Emanuelis Vitte, 1931.

Regatillo, Eduardus, F., *Institutiones Iuris Canonici,* 2 vols., Vol. II, *De Rebus, De Processibus, De Delictis et Poenis,* Sal Terrae: Santander, 1942.

Reiffenstuel, Anacletus, *Ius Canonicum Universum,* 7 vols., Parisiis, 1864-1870.

Rota, P., *Enchiridion Confessarii et Iudicis Ecclesiastici,* Augustae Taurinorum, 1884.

Salmanticenses, *Cursus Theologiae Moralis,* 6 vols. in 4, Venetiis, 1714-1728.

Salucci, Raffaele, *Il Diritto Penale secondo il Codice di Diritto Canonico,* 2 vols. in 1, Subiaco: Tipographia dei Monasteri, 1926-1930.

Santi, Franciscus, *Praelectiones Iuris Canonici iuxta ordinem Decretalium Gregorii IX,* 4. ed., 5 vols. in 3, Emendata et Recentissimis Decretis Accommodata cura Martini Leitner, Ratisbonae: Pustet, 1903-1905.

Scaccia, Sigismund, *Tractatus de Iudiciis,* 3. ed., 2 vols., Coloniae Agrippinae, 1738.

Schmalzgrueber, Franciscus, *Ius Ecclesiasticum Universum,* 5 vols. in 12, Romae, 1843-1845.

Schuech, Ignatz, *Handbuch der Pastoraltheologie,* 5. ed. Linz, 1880.

Sipos, Stephanus, *Enchiridion Iuris Canonici ad Usum Scholarum et Privatum,* 3. ed., Pecs: ex Typographia "Haladas R. T.", 1936.

Sole, Iacobus, *Praelectiones in Lib. V Codicis Iuris Canonici, De Delictis et Poenis,* Romae: Pustet, 1920.

Stadalnikas, Casimir Joseph, *Reservation of Censures,* The Catholic University of America Canon Law Studies, n. 208, Washington, D.C.: The Catholic University of America Press, 1944.

Swoboda, Innocent R., *Ignorance in Relation to the Imputability of Delicts,* The Catholic University of America Canon Law Studies, n. 143, Washington, D.C.: The Catholic University of America Press, 1941.

Tanquerey, Ad., *Synopsis Theologiae Moralis et Pastoralis,* 11. ed. 3 vols., Vol. I, *De Paenitentia, De Matrimonio et Ordine,* Parisiis-Tornaci-Romae: Desclee, et Socii, 1930.

Vermeersch, Arthurus-Creusen, Josephus, *Epitome Iuris Canonici cum Commentariis ad Scholas et ad Usum Privatum,* 3. ed., 3 vols., Mechliniae-Romae: Dessain, 1927-1928.

Vindiciae Alphonsianae, 2. ed., 2 vols., Tornaci, 1874.

Voit, Edmundus, *Theologia Moralis,* 2 vols., Augustae Taurinorum, 1833.

Wernz, Franciscus, *Ius Decretalium ad Usum Praelectionum in Scholis Textus Canonici sive Iuris Decretalium,* 2. ed., 6 vols., Romae-Prati, 1906-1913.

Wernz, Franciscus-Vidal, Petrus, *Ius Canonicum ad Codicis Normam Exactum,* 7 toms. in 8 vols., Vol VII, *Ius Poenale Ecclesiasticum,* 1937, Romae: Apud Aedes Universitatis Gregorianae, 1923-1938.

Wouters, Ludovicus, *Manuale Theologiae Moralis,* 2 vols., Brugis: Beyaert, 1932-1933.

Woywod, Stanislaus, *A Practical Commentary on the Code of Canon Law,* 2 vols., New York: Joseph F. Wagner, 1925.

Articles

Checchi, Petrus, "De casuum reservatione et de conditionibus ad eam incurrendam requisitis," — *Analecta Ecclesiastica,* VI (1898), 312-314.

Connolly, Joseph F., "The Emergency Powers of Canons 1043, 1044 and 1045, and Some War Time Considerations," — *The Jurist,* V (1945), 20-53.

Darmanin, A., "De Reservatione Peccatorum Iure Codicis Piano-Benedictini," — *Angelicum,* V (1928), 55-70; 213-241; 539-554.

Dalpiaz, Vig., "De abusu matrimonii et crimine sollicitationis," — *Apollinaris,* VI (1933), 244-249.

Gearin, M. A., "The Crime of False Accusation - Again," — *American Ecclesiastical Review*, LX (1919), 61-69.

Kaiser, Maurus. "De obligatione denunciandi confessarios sollicitantes," — *Analecta Ecclesiastica*, VI (1898), 502-505.

———————— "De absolutione a reservatis Romano Pontifici," — *Analecta Ecclesiastica*, VI (1898), 374-376.

Many, S., "De Peccato Sollicitationis," — *Le Canoniste Contemporain*, XVIII (1895), 513-530; 705-723.

Maroto, P., "De ignorantia quoad falsam delationem, qua sacerdos innocens accusatur de crimine sollicitationis," — *Apollinaris*, V (1932), 96-105.

Planchard, I., "Procedure contre les Sollicitants," — *Nouvelle Revue Theologique*, XXIII (1891), 414-433; 538-552; 614-633.

Rieder, Ign., "Zur Absolutio a censuris Papae reservatis," — *Theologisch praktische Quartalschrift*, LI (1898), 907-911.

Roberti, F., "De Iure Denuntiandi Nullitatem Matrimonii - Animadversiones," — *Apollinaris*, III, (1930), 248-250.

Slater, T., "False Accusation of Solicitation and the New Code," — *American Ecclesiastical Review*, LIX (1918). 458-463.

Woywod, Stanislaus, "False Accusation of Solicitation," — *Homiletic and Pastoral Review*, XXXVIII (1938), 718-722.

Anonymous, "Commentaire sur la Constitution '*Apostolicae Sedis*' de Pie IX: EXCOMMUNICATIONS NON RESERVEES," — *Nouvelle Revue Theologique*, XII (1880), 10-47.

———————— "Il Codice di Diritto Canonico: Riassunto e Delucidazioni," — *Il Monitore Ecclesiastico*, XXXI (4. Series, Vol. I) (1919), 36-47; 80-88; 112-117; 145-149; 177-187; 347-363.

———————— "Instruction de la S. Congregation de l'Inquisition Touchant la Denonciation des Confesseurs," — *Nouvelle Revue Theologique*, VIII (1876), 345-361.

———————— "Collectio Resolutionum Responsorumque S. Officii - Sollicitantes," — *Analecta Ecclesiastica*, IV (1896), 361-364.

PERIODICALS

Analecta Ecclesiastica, Romae, 1893-1911.

Angelicum, Romae, 1924-.

Apollinaris, Romae, 1928-.

Canoniste Contemporain, Le, 1878-1922; *Canoniste, Le*, 1924-1926.

Ecclesiastical Review, The (Originally, *The American Ecclesiastical Review*), Philadelphia, 1889-1943; Washington, 1944-

Homiletic and Pastoral Review, The, New York, 1900-.

Jurist, The, Washington, 1941-.

Monitore Ecclesiastico, Il, Romae, 1876-.

Nouvelle Revue Theologique, Tournai, 1869-.

Theologisch-praktische Quartalschrift, Linz, 1832-.

Abbreviations

AAS — Acta Apostolicae Sedis

ASS — Acta Sanctae Sedis

ER — Ecclesiastical Review

Fontes — Codicis Iuris Canonici Fontes

HPR — Homiletic and Pastoral Review

Le Canoniste — Le Canoniste Contemporain

NRT — Nouvelle Revue Theologique

PCI — Pontificis Commissio Interpretationis

ALPHABETICAL INDEX

Biographical Note

Herbert Linenberger was born March 9, 1909, at Victoria, Kansas where he attended St. Fidelis grade and high schools. On September 9, 1924, he began his studies for the priesthood under the supervision of the Fathers of the Most Precious Blood at St. Mary' Preparatory Seminary, Burkettsville, Ohio, St. Joseph's of Indiana, Collegeville, Indiana, and St. Charles Seminary, Carthagena, Ohio. He was professed on December 4, 1927 and was ordained by Bishop Joseph Albers, D.D., J.C.D. on May 12, 1935. From June 16, 1935 until September 23, 1943, he was assistant at St. Anthony's Parish, Detroit, Michigan. In September 1943, he enrolled in the School of Canon Law at the Catholic University of America where he received the Baccalaureate in Canon Law in May 1944, and the Licentiate in Canon Law in May 1945.

CANON LAW STUDIES*

1. FRERIKS, REV. CELESTINE A., C.PP.S., J.C.D., Religious Congregations in Their External Relations, 121 pp., 1916.
2. GALLIHER, REV. DANIEL M., O.P., J.C.D., Canonical Elections, 117 pp., 1917.
3. BORKOWSKI, REV. AURELIUS L., O.F.M., J.C.D., De Confraternitatibus Ecclesiasticis, 136 pp., 1918.
4. CASTILLO, REV. CAYO, J.C.D., Disertacion Historico-Canonica sobre la Potestad del Cabildo en Sede Vacante o Impedida del Vicario Capitular, 99 pp., 1919 (1918).
5. KUBELBECK, REV. WILLIAM J., S.T.B., J.C.D., The Sacred Penitentiaria and Its Relation to Faculties of Ordinaries and Priests, 129 pp., 1918.
6. PETROVITS, REV. JOSEPH, J.C., S.T.D., J.C.D., The New Church Law on Matrimony, X-461 pp., 1919.
7. HICKEY, REV. JOHN J., S.T.B., J.C.D., Irregularities and Simple Impediments in the New Code of Canon Law, 100 pp., 1920.
8. KLEKOTKA, REV. PETER J., S.T.B., J.C.D., Diocesan Consultors, 179 pp., 1920.
9. WANENMACHER, REV. FRANCIS, J.C.D., The Evidence in Eccelsiastical Procedure Affecting the Marriage Bond, 1920 (Printed 1935).
10. GOLDEN, REV. HENRY FRANCIS, J.C.D., Parochial Benefices in the New Code, IV-119 pp., 1921 (Printed 1925).
11. KOUDELKA, REV. CHARLES J., J.C.D., Pastors, Their Rights and Duties According to the New Code of Canon Law, 211 pp., 1921.
12. MELO, REV. ANTONIUS, O.F.M., J.C.D., De Exemptione Regularium, X-188 pp., 1921.
13. SCHAAF, REV. VALENTINE THEODORE, O.F.M., S.T.B., J.C.D., The Cloister, X-180 pp., 1921.
14. BURKE, REV. THOMAS JOSEPH, S.T.D., J.C.D., Competence in Ecclesiastical Tribunals, IV-117 pp., 1922.
15. LEECH, REV. GEORGE LEO, J.C.D., A Comparative Study of the Constitution "Apostolicae Sedis" and the "Codex Juris Canonici," 179 pp., 1922.
16. MOTRY, REV. HUBERT LOUIS, S.T.D., J.C.D., Diocesan Faculties According to the Code of Canon Law, II-167 pp., 1922.
17. MURPHY, REV. GEORGE LAWRENCE, J.C.D., Delinquencies and Penalties in the Administration and the Reception of the Sacraments, IV-121 pp., 1923.
18. O'REILLY, REV. JOHN ANTHONY, S.T.B., J.C.D., Ecclesiastical Sepulture in the New Code of Canon Law, II-129 pp., 1923.

---

* From nn. 1-100 inclusive only nn. 25 and 57 are still obtainable. From n. 101 onward all numbers are available except the following: nn. 101-118 inclusive, and also n. 122.

19. MICHALICKA, REV. WENCESLAS CYRIL, O.S.B., J.C.D., Judicial Procedure in Dismissal of Clerical Exempt Religious, 107 pp., 1923.
20. DARGIN, REV. EDWARD VINCENT, S.T.B., J.C.D., Reserved Cases According to the Code of Canon Law, IV-103 pp., 1924.
21. GODFREY, REV. JOHN A., S.T.B., J.C.D., The Right of Patronage According to the Code of Canon Law, 153 pp., 1924.
22. HAGEDORN, REV. FRANCIS EDWARD, J.C.D., General Legislation on Indulgences, II-154 pp., 1924.
23. KING, REV. JAMES IGNATIUS, J.C.D., The Administration of the Sacraments to Dying Non-Catholics, V-141 pp., 1924.
24. WINSLOW, REV. FRANCIS JOSEPH, M.M., J.C.D., Vicars and Prefects Apostolic, IV-149 pp., 1924.
25. CORREA, REV. JOSE SERVELION, S.T.L., J.C.D., La Potestad Legislativa de la Iglesia Catolica, IV-127 pp., 1925.
26. DUGAN, REV. HENRY FRANCIS, A.M., J.C.D., The Judiciary Department of the Diocesan Curia, 87 pp., 1925.
27. KELLER, REV. CHARLES FREDERICK, S.T.B., J.C.D., Mass Stipends, 167 pp., 1925.
28. PASCHANG, REV. JOHN LINUS, J.C.D., The Sacramentals According to the Code of Canon Law, 129 pp., 1925.
29. PIONTEK, REV. CYRILLUS, O.F.M., S.T.B., J.C.D., De Indulto Exclaustrationis necon Saecularizationis, XIII-289 pp., 1925.
30. KEARNEY, REV. RICHARD JOSEPH, S.T.B., J.C.D., Sponsors at Baptism According to the Code of Canon Law, IV-127 pp., 1925.
31. BARTLETT, REV. CHESTER JOSEPH, A.M., LL.B., J.C.D., The Tenure of Parochial Property in the United States of America, V-108 pp., 1926.
32. KILKER, REV. ADRIAN JEROME, J.C.D., Extreme Unction, V-425 pp., 1926.
33. MCCORMICK, REV. ROBERT EMMET, J.C.D., Confessors of Religious, VII-266 pp., 1926.
34. MILLER, REV. NEWTON THOMAS, J.C.D., Founded Masses According to the Code of Canon Law, VII-93 pp., 1926.
35. ROELKER, REV. EDWARD G., S.T.D., J.C.D., Principles of Privilege According to the Code of Canon Law, XI-166 pp., 1926.
36. BAKALARCZYK, REV. RICHARDUS, M.I.C., J.U.D., De Novitiatu, VIII-208 pp., 1927.
37. PIZZUTI, REV. LAWRENCE, O.F.M., J.U.L., De Parochis Religiosis, 1927. (Not Printed).
38. BLILEY, REV NICHOLAS MARTIN, O.S.B., J.C.D., Altars According to the Code of Canon Law, XIX-132 pp., 1927.
39. BROWN, MR. BRENDAN FRANCIS, A.B., LL.M., J.U.D., The Canonical Juristic Personality with Special Reference to its Status in the United States of America, V-212 pp., 1927.

40. CAVANAUGH, REV. WILLIAM THOMAS, C.P., J.U.D., The Reservation of the Blessed Sacrament, VIII-101 pp., 1927.
41. DOHENY, REV. WILLIAM J., C.S.C., A.B., J.U.D., Church Property — Modes of Acquisition, X-118 pp., 1927.
42. FELDHAUS, REV. ALOYSIUS H., C.PP.S., J.C.D., Oratories, IX-141 pp., 1927.
43. KELLY, REV. JAMES PATRICK, A.B., J.C.D., The Jurisdiction of the Simple Confessor, X-208 pp., 1927.
44. NEUBERGER, REV. NICHOLAS J., J.C.D., Canon 6 or the Relation of the Codex Juris Canonici to the Preceding Legislation, V-95 pp., 1927.
45. O'KEEFE, REV. GERALD MICHAEL, J.C.D., Matrimonial Dispensations, Powers of Bishops, Priests and Confessors, VIII-232 pp., 1927.
46. QUIGLEY, REV. JOSEPH A. M., A.B., J.C.D., Condemned Societies, 139 pp., 1927.
47. ZAPLOTNIK, REV. JOHANNES LEO, J.C.D., De Vicariis Foraneis, X-142 pp., 1927.
48. DUSKIE, REV. JOHN ALOYSIUS, A.B., J.C.D., The Canonical Status of the Orientals in the United States, VIII-196 pp., 1928.
49. HYLAND, REV. FRANCIS EDWARD, J.C.D., Excommunication, Its Nature, Historical Development and Effects, VIII-181 pp., 1928.
50. REINMANN, REV. GERALD JOSEPH, O.M.C., J.C.D., The Third Order Secular of Saint Francis, 201 pp., 1928.
51. SCHENK, REV. FRANCIS J., J.C.D., The Matrimonial Impediments of Mixed Religion and Disparity of Cult, XVI-318 pp., 1929.
52. COADY, REV. JOHN JOSEPH, S.T.D., J.U.D., A.M., The Appointment of Pastors, VIII-150 pp., 1929.
53. KAY, REV. THOMAS HENRY, J.C.D., Competence in Matrimonial Procedure, VIII-164 pp., 1929.
54. TURNER, REV. SIDNEY JOSEPH, C.P., J.U.D., The Vow of Poverty, XLIX-217 pp., 1929.
55. KEARNEY, REV. RAYMOND A., A.B., S.T.D., J.C.D., The Principles of Delegation, VII-149 pp., 1929.
56. CONRAN, REV. EDWARD JAMES, A.B., J.C.D., The Interdict, V-163 pp., 1930.
57. O'NEIL, REV. WILLIAM H. J.C.D., Papal Rescripts of Favor, VII-218 pp., 1930.
58. BASTNAGEL, REV. CLEMENT VINCENT, J.U.D., The Appointment of Parochial Adjutants and Assistants, XV-257 pp., 1930.
59. FERRY, REV. WILLIAM A., A.B., J.C.D., Stole Fees, V-136 pp., 1930.
60. COSTELLO, REV. JOHN MICHAEL, A.B., J.C.D., Domicile and Quasi-Domicile, VII-201 pp., 1930.
61. KRÈMER, REV. MICHAEL NICHOLAS, A.B., S.T.B., J.C.D., Church Support in the United States, VI-136 pp., 1930.
62. ANGULA, REV. LUIS, C.M., J.C.D., Legislation de la Iglesia sobre la intencion en la application de la Santa Misa, VII-104 pp., 1931.

63. Frey, Rev. Wolfgang Norbert, O.S.B., A.B., J.C.D., The Act of Religious Profession, VIII-174 pp., 1931.

64. Roberts, Rev. James Brendan, A.B., J.C.D., The Banns of Marriage, XIV-140 pp., 1931.

65. Ryder, Rev. Raymond Aloysius, A.B., J.C.D., Simony, IX-151 pp., 1931.

66. Campagna, Rev. Angelo, Ph.D., J.U.D., Il Vicario Generale del Vescovo, VII-205 pp., 1931.

67. Cox, Rev. Joseph Godfrey, A.B., J.C.D., The Administration of Seminaries, VI-124 pp., 1931.

68. Gregory, Rev. Donald J., J.U.D., The Pauline Privilege, XV-165 pp., 1931.

69. Donohue, Rev. John F., J.C.D., The Impediment of Crime, VII-110 pp., 1931.

70. Dooley, Rev. Eugene A., O.M.I., J.C.D., Church Law on Sacred Relics, IX-143 pp., 1931.

71. Orth, Rev. Clement Raymond, O.M.C., J.C.D., The Approbation of Religious Institutes, 171 pp., 1931.

72. Pernicone, Rev. Joseph M., A.B., J.C.D., The Ecclesiastical Prohibition of Books, XII-267 pp., 1932.

73. Clinton, Rev. Connell, A.B., J.C.D., The Paschal Precept, IX-108 pp., 1932.

74. Donnelly, Rev. Francis B., A.M., S.T.L., J.C.D., The Diocesan Synod, VIII-125 pp., 1932.

75. Torrente, Rev. Camilo, C.M.F., J.C.D., Las Processiones Sagradas, V-145 pp., 1932.

76. Murphy, Rev. Edwin J., C.PP.S., J.C.D., Suspension Ex Informata Conscientia, XI-122 pp., 1932.

77. MacKenzie, Rev. Eric F., A.M., S.T.L., J.C.D., The Delict of Heresy in its Commission, Penalization, Absolution, VII-124 pp., 1932.

78. Lyons, Rev. Avitus E., S.T.B., J.C.D., The Collegiate Tribunal of First Instance, XI-147 pp., 1932.

79. Connolly, Rev. Thomas A., J.C.D., Appeals, XI-195 pp., 1932.

80. Sangmeister, Rev. Joseph V., A.B., J.C.D., Force and Fear as Precluding Matrimonial Consent, V-211 pp., 1932.

81. Jaeger, Rev. Leo A., A.B., J.C.D., The Administration of Vacant and Quasi-Vacant Episcopal Sees in the United States, IX-229 pp., 1932.

82. Rimlinger, Rev. Herbert T., J.C.D., Error Invalidating Matrimonial Consent, VIII-79 pp., 1932.

83. Barrett, Rev John D. M., S.S., J.C.D., A Comparative Study of the Third Plenary Council of Baltimore and the Code, IX-221 pp., 1932.

84. Carberry, Rev. John J., Ph.D., S.T.D., J.C.D., The Juridical Form of Marriage, X-177 pp., 1934.

85. Dolan, Rev. John L., A.B., J.C.D., The Defensor Vinculi, XII-157 pp., 1934.
86. Hannan, Rev. Jerome D., A.M., S.T.D., LL.B., J.C.D., The Canon Law of Wills, IX-517 pp., 1934.
87. Lemieux, Rev. Delise A., A.M., J.C.D., The Sentence in Ecclesiastical Procedure, IX-131 pp., 1934.
88. O'Rourke, Rev. James J., A.B., J.C.D., Parish Registers, VII-109 pp., 1934.
89. Timlin, Rev Bartholomew, O.F.M., A.M., J.C.D., Conditional Matrimonial Consent, X-381 pp., 1934.
90. Wahl, Rev. Francis X., A.B., J.C.D., The Matrimonial Impediments of Consanguinity and Affinity, VI-125 pp., 1934.
91. White, Rev. Robert J., A.B., LL.B., S.T.B., J.C.D., Canonical Ante-Nuptial Promises and the Civil Law, VI-152 pp., 1934.
92. Herrera, Rev. Antonio Parra, O.C.D., J.C.D., Legislacion Ecclesiastica sobra el Ayuno y la Abstinencia, XI-191 pp., 1935.
95. Kennedy, Rev. Edwin J., J.C.D., The Special Matrimonial Process in Cases of Evident Nullity, X-165 pp., 1935.
94. Manning, Rev. John J., A.B., J.C.D., Presumption of Law in Matrimonial Procedure, XI-111 pp., 1935.
95. Moeder, Rev. John M., J.C.D., The Proper Bishop for Ordination and Dimissorial Letters, VII-135 pp., 1935.
96. O'Mara, Rev. William A., A.B., J.C.D., Canonical Causes for Matrimonial Dispensations, IX-155 pp., 1935.
97. Reilly, Rev. Peter, J.C.D., Residence of Pastors, IX-81 pp., 1935.
98. Smith, Rev. Mariner T., O.P., S.T.Lr., J.C.D., The Penal Law for Religious, VII-169 pp., 1935.
99. Whalen, Rev. Donald W., A.M., J.C.D., The Value of Testimonial Evidence in Matrimonial Procedure, XIII-297 pp., 1935.
100. Cleary, Rev. Joseph F., J.C.D., Canonical Limitations on the Alienation of Church Property, VIII-141 pp., 1936.
101. Glynn, Rev. John C., J.C.D., The Promoter of Justice, XX-337 pp., 1936.
102. Brennan, Rev. James H., S.S., M.A., S.T.B., J.C.D., The Simple Convalidation of Marriage, VI-135 pp., 1937.
103. Brunini, Rev. Joseph Bernard, J.C.D., The Clecical Obligations of Canons 139 and 142, X-121 pp., 1937.
104. Connor, Rev. Maurice, A.B., J.C.D., The Administrative Removal of Pastors, VIII-159 pp., 1937.
105. Guilfoyle, Rev. Merlin Joseph, J.C.D., Custom, XI-144 pp., 1937.
106. Hughes, Rev. James Austin, A.B., A.M., J.C.D., Witnesses in Criminal Trials of Clerics, IX-140 pp., 1937.
107. Jansen, Rev. Raymond J., A.B., S.T.L., J.C.D., Canonical Provisions for Catechetical Instructions, VII-153 pp., 1937.

108. Kealy, Rev. John James, A.B., J.C.D., The Introductory Libellus in Church Court Procedure, XI-121 pp., 1937.
109. McManus, Rev. James Edward, C.SS.R., J.C.D., The Administration of Temporal Goods in Religious Institutes, XVI-196 pp., 1937.
110. Moriarity, Rev. Eugene James, J.C.D., Oaths in Ecclesiastical Courts, X-115 pp., 1937.
111. Rainier, Rev. Eligius George, C.SS.R., J.C.D., Suspension of Clerics, XVII-249 pp., 1937.
112. Reilly, Rev. Thomas F., C.SS.R., J.C.D., Visitation of Religious, VI-195 pp., 1938.
113. Moriarity, Rev. Francis E., C.SS.R., J.C.D., The Extraordinary Absolution from Censures, XV-334 pp., 1938.
114. Connolly, Rev. Nicholas P., J.C.D., The Canonical Erection of Parishes, X-132 pp., 1938.
115. Donovan, Rev. James Joseph, J.C.D., The Pastor's Obligation in Prenuptial Investigation, XII-322 pp., 1938.
116. Harrigan, Rev. Robert J., M.A., S.T.B., J.C.D., The Radical Sanation of Invalid Marriages, VIII-208 pp., 1938.
117. Boffa, Rev. Conrad Humbert, J.C.D., Canonical Provisions for Catholic Schools, VII-211 pp., 1939.
118. Parsons, Rev. Anscar John, O.M.Cap., J.C.D., Canonical Elections XII-236 pp., 1939.
119. Reilly, Rev. Edward Michael, A.B., J.C.D., The General Norms of Dispensation, XII-156 pp., 1939.
120. Ryan, Rev. Gerald Aloysius, A.B., J.C.D., Principles of Episcopal Jurisdiction, XII-172 pp., 1939.
121. Burton, Rev. Francis James, C.S.C., A.B., J.C.D., A Commentary on Canon 1125, X-222 pp., 1940.
122. Miaskiewicz, Rev. Francis Sigismund, J.C.D., Supplied Jurisdiction According to Canon 209, XII-340 pp., 1940.
123. Rice, Rev. Patrick William, A.B., J.C.D., Proof of Death in Prenuptial Investigation, VIII-156 pp., 1940.
124. Anglin, Rev. Thomas Francis, M.S., J.C.D., The Eucharistic Fast, VII-183 pp., 1941.
125. Coleman, Rev John Jerome, J.C.D., The Minister of Confirmation, VI-153 pp., 1941.
126. Downs, Rev. John Emmanuel, A.B., J.C.D., The Concept of Clerical Immunity, XI-163 pp., 1941.
127 Esswein, Rev. Anthony Albert, J.C.D., Extrajudicial Penal Powers of Ecclesiastical Superiors, X-144 pp., 1941.
128. Farrel, Rev. Benjamin Francis, M.A., S.T.L., J.C.D., The Rights and Duties of the Local Ordinary Regarding Congregations of Women Religious of Pontifical Approval, V-195 pp., 1941.
129. Feeney, Rev. Thomas John, A.B., S.T.L., J.C.D., Restitutio in Integrum, VI-169 pp., 1941.

130. FINDLAY, REV. STEPHEN WILLIAM, O.S.B., A.B., J.C.D., Canonical Norms Governing the Deposition and Degradation of Clerics, XVII- 279 pp., 1941.
131. GOODWINE, REV. JOHN, A.B., S.T.L., J.C.D., The Right of the Church to Acquire Property, VIII-119 pp., 1941.
132. HESTON, REV. EDWARD LOUIS, C.S.C., PH.D.. S.T.D., J.C.D., The Alienation of Church Property in the United States, XII-222 pp, 1941.
133. HOGAN, REV. JAMES JOHN, A.B., S.T.L., J.C.D., Judicial Advocates and Procurators, XIII-200 pp., 1941.
134. KEALY, REV. THOMAS M., A.B., Litt.B., J.C.D., Dowry of Women Religious, IX-152 pp., 1941.
135. KEENE, REV. MICHAEL JAMES, O.S.B., J.C.D., Religious Ordinaries and Canon 198, V-164 pp., 1942.
136. KERIN, REV CHARLES A., S.S., M.A., S.T.B., J.C.D., The Privation of Christian Burial, XVI-279 pp, 1941.
137. LOUIS, REV. WILLIAM FRANCIS, M.A., J.C.D., Diocesan Archives, X-101 pp., 1941.
138. MCDEVITT, REV. GILBERT JOSEPH, A.B., J.C.D., Legitimacy and Legitimation, X-247 pp., 1941.
139. MCDONOUGH, REV. THOMAS JOSEPH, A.B., J.C.D., Apostolic Administrators, X-217 pp., 1941.
140. MEIER, REV. CARL ANTHONY, A.B., J.C.D., Penal Administrative Procedure Against Negligent Pastors, XI-240 pp., 1941.
141. SCHMIDT, REV. JOHN ROGG, A.B., J.C.D., The Principles of Authentic Interpretation in Canon 17 of the Code of Canon Law, X-331 pp., 1941.
142. SLAFKOSKY, REV. ANDREW LEONARD, A.B., J.C.D., The Canonical Episcopal Visitation of the Diocese, X-197 pp., 1941.
143. SWOBODA, REV. INNOCENT ROBERT, O.F.M., J.C.D., Ignorance in Relation to the Imputability of Delicts, IX-271 pp., 1941.
144. DUBE, REV. ARTHUR JOSEPH, A.B., J.C.D., The General Principles for the Reckoning of Time in Canon Law, VIII-299 pp., 1941.
145. MCBRIDE, REV. JAMES T., A.B., J.C.D., Incardination and Excardination of Seculars, XX-585 pp., 1941.
146. KROL, REV. JOHN T., J.C.D., The Defendant in Ecclesiastical Trials, XII-207 pp., 1942.
147. COMYNS, REV. JOSEPH J., C.SS.R., A.B., J.C.D., Papal and Episcopal Administration of Church Property, XIV-155 pp., 1942.
148. BARRY, REV. GARRETT FRANCIS, O.M.I., J.C.D., Violation of the Cloister, XII-260 pp., 1942.
149. BOLDUC, REV. GATIEN, C.S.V., A.B., S.T.L., J.C.D., Les Etudes dans les Religions Clericales, VIII-155 pp., 1942.
150. BOYLE, REV. DAVID JOHN, M.A., J.C.D., The Juridic Effects of Moral Certitude on Pre-Nuptial Guarantees, XII-188 pp., 1942.

151. CANAVAN, REV. WALTER JOSEPH, M.A., Litt.D., J.C.D., The Profession of Faith, XII-143 pp., 1942.
152. DESROCHERS, REV. BRUNO, A.B., PH.L., S.T.B., J.C.D., Le Premier Concile Plenier de Quebec et le Code de Droit Canonique, XIV-186 pp., 1942.
153. DILLON, REV. ROBERT EDWARD, A.B., J.C.D., Common Law Marriage, X-148 pp., 1942.
154. DODWELL, REV. EDWARD JOHN, PH.D., S.T.B., J.C.D., The Time and Place for the Celebration of Marriage, X-156 pp., 1942.
155. DONNELLAN, REV. THOMAS ANDREW, A.B., J.C.D., The Obligation of the Missa pro Populo, VII-131 pp., 1942.
156. ELTZ, REV. LOUIS ANTHONY, A.B., J.C.D., Cooperation in Crime, XII-208 pp., 1942.
157. GASS, REV. SYLVESTER FRANCIS, M.A., J.C.D., Ecclesiastical Pensions XI-206 pp., 1942.
158. GUINIVEN, REV. JOHN JOSEPH, C.SS.R., J.C.D., The Precept of Hearing Mass, XIV-188 pp., 1942.
159. GULCZYNSKI, REV. JOHN THEOPHILUS, J.C.D., The Desecration and Violation of Churches, X-126 pp., 1942.
160. HAMMIL, REV. JOHN LEO, M.A., J.C.D., The Obligations of the Traveler According to Canon 14, VIII-204 pp., 1942.
161. HAYDT, REV. JOHN JOSEPH, A.B., J.C.D., Reserved Benefices, XI-148 pp., 1942.
162. HUSER, REV. ROGER JOHN, O.F.M., A.B., J.C.D., The Crime of Abortion in Canon Law, XII-187 pp., 1942.
163. KEARNEY, REV. FRANCIS PATRICK, A.B., S.T.L., J.C.D., The Principles of Canon 1127, X-162 pp., 1942.
164. LINAHEN, REV. LEO JAMES, S.T.L., J.C.D., De Absolutione Complicis In Peccato Turpi, 114 pp., 1942.
165. McCLOSKEY, REV. JOSEPH ALOYSIUS, A.B., J.C.D., The Subject of Ecclesiastical Law According to Canon 12, XVII-246 pp., 1942.
166. O'NEIL, REV. FRANCIS JOSEPH, C.SS.R., J.C.D., The Dismissal of Religious in Temporary Vows, XIII-220 pp., 1942.
167. PRINCE, REV. JOHN EDWARD, A.B., S.T.B., J.C.D., The Diocesan Chancellor, X-136 pp., 1942.
168. RIESNER, REV. ALBERT JOSEPH, C.SS.R., J.C.D., Apostates and Fugitives from Religious Institutes, IX-168 pp., 1942.
169. STENGER, REV. JOSEPH BERNARD, J.C.D., The Mortgaging of Church Property, 186 pp., 1942.
170. WALDRON, REV. JOSEPH FRANCIS, A.B., J.C.D., The Minister of Baptism, XII-197 pp., 1942.
171. WILLETT, REV. ROBERT ALBERT, J.C.D., The Probative Value of Documents in Ecclesiastical Trials, X-124 pp., 1942.
172. WOEBER, REV. EDWARD MARTIN, M.A., J.C.D., The Interpollations, XII-161 pp., 1942.

173. Benko, Rev Matthew Aloysius, O.S.B., M.A., J.C.D., The Abbott *Nullius*, XV-147 pp., 1943.
174. Christ, Rev. Joseph James, M.A., S.T.L., J.C.D., Dispensation from Vindicative Penalties, XIII-285 pp., 1943.
175. Clancy, Rev. Patrick M. J., O.P., A.B., S.T.Lr., J.C.D., The Local Religious Superior, X-229 pp., 1943.
176. Clarke, Rev. Thomas James, J.C.D., Parish Societies, XII-147 pp., 1943.
177. Connolly, Rev. John Patrick, S.T.L., J.C.D., Synodal Examiners and Parish Priest Consultors, X-223 pp., 1943.
178. Drumm, Rev. William Martin, A.B. J.C.D., Hospital Chaplains, XII-175 pp., 1943.
179. Flanagan, Rev. Bernard Joseph, A.B., S.T.L., J.C.D., The Canonical Erection of Religious Houses, X-147 pp., 1943.
180. Kelleher, Rev. Stephen Joseph, A.B., S.T.B., J.C.D., Discussions with non-Catholics: Canonical Legislation, X-93 pp., 1943.
181. Lewis, Rev. Gordian, C.P., J.C.D., Chapters in Religious Institutes, XII-169 pp., 1943.
182. Marx, Rev. Adolph, J.C.D., The Declaration of Nullity of Marriages Contracted Outside the Church, X-151 pp., 1943.
183. Matulenas, Rev. Raymond Anthony, O.S.B., A.B., J.C.D., Communication, a Source of Privileges, XII-225 pp., 1943.
184. O'Leary, Rev. Charles Gerard, C.SS.R., J.C.D., Religious Dismissed After Perpetual Profession, X-213 pp., 1943.
185. Power, Rev. Cornelius Michael, J.C.D., The Blessing of Cemeteries, XII-231 pp., 1943.
186. Shuhler, Rev. Ralph Vincent, O.S.A., J.C.D., Privileges of Religious to Absolve and Dispense, XII-195 pp., 1943.
187. Ziolkowski, Rev. Thaddeus Stanislaus, A.B., J.C.D., The Consecration and Blessing of Churches, XII-151 pp., 1943.
188. Heneghan, Rev. John Joseph, S.T.D., J.C.D., The Marriages of Unworthy Catholics: Canons 1065 and 1066, XVI-213 pp., 1944.
189. Carroll, Rev. Coleman Francis, M.A., S.T.L., J.C.L., Charitable Institutions.
190. Ciesluk, Rev. Joseph Edward, Ph.B., S.T.L., J.C.L., National Parishes in the United States.
191. Coburn, Rev. Vincent Paul, A.B., J.C.D., Marriages of Conscience, XII-172 pp., 1944.
192. Connors, Rev. Charles Paul, C.S.Sp., A.B., J.C.D., Extra-Judicial Procurators in the Code of Canon Law, X-94 pp., 1944.
193. Coyle, Rev. Paul Raymond, A.B., J.C.D., Judicial Exceptions, X-142 pp., 1944.
194. Fair, Rev. Bartholomew Francis, A.B., S.T.L., J.C.D., The Impediment of Abduction, XII-122 pp., 1944.

195. Gallagher, Rev. Thomas Raphael, O.P., A.B., S.T.Lr., J.C.D., The Examination of the Qualities of the Ordinand, X-166 pp., 1944.
196. Gannon, Rev. John Mark, S.T.L., J.C.D., The Interstices Required for the Promotion to Orders, XII-100 pp., 1944.
197. Goldsmith, Rev. J. William, B.C.S., S.T.L., J.C.D., The Competence of Church and State Over Marriages — Disputed Points, X-128 pp., 1944.
198. Goodwine, Rev. Joseph Gerard, A.B., S.T.B., J.C.D., The Reception of Converts, XIV-326 pp., 1944.
199. Kowalski, Rev. Romuald Eugene, O.F.M., A.B., J.C.D., Sustenance of Religious Houses of Regulars, X-174 pp., 1944.
200. McCoy, Rev. Alan Edward, O.F.M., J.C.D., Force and Fear in Relation to Delictual Imputability and Penal Responsibility, XII-160 pp., 1944.
210. McDevitt, Rev. Vincent John, Ph.B., S.T.L., J.C.L., Perjury.
202. Martin, Rev. Thomas Owen, Ph.D., S.T.D., J.C.D., Adverse Possession, Prescription and Limitation of Actions: The Canonical "Praescriptio," XX-208 pp., 1944.
203. Miklosovic, Rev. Paul John, A.B., J.C.L., Attempted Marriages and Their Consequent Juridic Effects.
204. Mundy, Rev. Thomas Maurice, A.B., S.T.L., J.C.D., The Union of Parishes, X-164 pp., 1944.
205. O'Dea, Rev. John Coyle, A.B., J.C.D., The Matrimonial Impediment of Nonage, VIII-126 pp., 1944.
206. Olalia, Rev. Alexander Ayson, S.T.L., J.C.D., A Comparative Study of the Christian Constitution of States and the Constitution of the Philippine Commonwealth, XII-136 pp., 1944.
207. Poisson, Rev. Pierre-Marie, C.S.C., A.B., Ph.L., Th.L., J.C.D., Droits Patrimoniaux des Maisons et des Eglises Religieuses.
208. Stadalnikas, Rev. Casimir Joseph, M.I.C., J.C.D., Reservation of Censures, X-141 pp., 1944.
209. Sullivan, Rev Eugene Henry, S.T.L., J.C.D., Proof of the Reception of the Sacraments, X-165 pp., 1944.
210. Vaughan, Rev. William Edward, J.C.D., Constitutions for Diocesan Courts, X-210 pp., 1944.
211. Paro, Rev. Gino, S.T.D., J.C.L., The Right of Apostolic Legation.
212. Balzer, Rev. Ralph Francis, C.P., J.C.D., The Computation of Time in a Canonical Novitiate, X-227 pp., 1945.
213. Dougherty, Rev. John Whelan, A.B., S.T.L., J.C.D., De Inquisitione Speciali, XII-195 pp., 1945.
214. Dziob, Rev. Michael Walter, J.C.D., The Sacred Congregation for the Oriental Church, XII-181 pp., 1945.

215. EIDENSCHINK, REV. JOHN ALBERT, O.S.B., B.A., J.C.D., The Election of Bishops in the Letters of Pope Gregory the Great, VIII-200 pp., 1945.

216. GILL, REV. NICHOLAS, C.P., J.C.D., The Spiritual Prefect in Clerical Religious Houses of Study, X-140 pp., 1945.

217. HYNES, REV. HARRY GERARD, S.T.L., J.C.D., The Privileges of Cardinals, XII-183 pp., 1945.

218. McDEVITT, REV. GERALD VINCENT, S.T.L., J.C.D., The Renunciation of an Ecclesiastical Office, XIV-179 pp., 1945.

219. MANNING, REV. JOSEPH LEROY, J.C.D., The Free Conferral of Offices, VII-116 pp., 1945.

220. MEYER, REV. LOUIS G., O.S.B., A.B., S.T.B., J.C.D., Alms-gathering by Religious, XII-163 pp., 1945.

221. O'DONNELL, REV. CLETUS FRANCIS, M.A., J.C.D., The Marriage of Minors, XII-268 pp., 1945.

222. PRUNSKIS, REV. JOSEPH, J.C.D., Comparative Law, Ecclesiastical and Civil, in Lithuanian Concordat, X-161 pp., 1945.

223. SWEENEY, REV. FRANCIS PATRICK, C.SS.R., J.C.D., The Reduction of Clerics to the Lay State, X-199 pp., 1945.

224. VOGELPOHL, REV. HENRY JOHN, J.C.D., The Simple Impediments to Holy Orders, XVI-190 pp., 1945.

225. BROCKHAUS, REV. THOMAS AQUINAS, O.S.B., J.C.D., Religious who are known as *Conversi,* X-127 pp., 1945.

226. GRIESE, REV. ORVILLE NICHOLAS, S.T.D., J.C.D., The Marriage Contract and the Procreation of Offspring, XVI-224 pp., 1946.

227. BOUDREAUX, REV. WARREN LOUIS, J.C.L., The *"ab acatholicis nati"* of Canon 1099, § 2.

228. BOWE, REV. THOMAS JOSEPH, A.B., J.C.L., Religious Superioresses.

229. DIEDERICHS, REV. MICHAEL FERDINAND, S.C.J., J.C.D., The Jurisdiction of the Latin Ordinaries over their Oriental Subjects, XIV-153 pp., 1946.

230. DINGMAN, REV. MAURICE JOHN, A.B., S.T.L., J.C.L., The Plaintiff in Contentious Trials.

231. FRISON, REV. BASIL, C.M.F., M.MUS., J.C.D., The Retroactivity of Law, X-221, pp., 1946.

232. GALVIN, REV. WILLIAM ANTHONY, M.A., J.C.D., The Administrative Transfer of Pastors, XII-288 pp., 1946.

233. GORACY, REV. JOSEPH C., J.C.L., The Diriment Matrimonial Impediment of Major Orders.

234. HALE, REV. JOSEPH FRANCIS, M.A., S.T.L., J.C.L., The Pastor of Burial.

235. HENRY, REV. JOSEPH ARTHUR, A.B., J.C.D., The Mass and Holy Communion: Interritual Law, XII-138 pp., 1946.

236. LINENBERGER, REV. HERBERT, C.PP.S., J.C.L., The False Denunciation of an Innocent Confessor.

237. Lowry, Rev. James Martin, A.B., J.C.D., Dispensation from Private Vows, XII-216 pp., 1946.
238. Lynch, Rev. George Edward, A.B., S.T.L., J.C.D., Coadjutors and Auxiliaries of Bishops, X-107 pp., 1947.
239. Lynch, Rev. Timothy, M.S.SS.T., J.C.D., Contracts between Bishops and Religious Congregations, XIII-232 pp., 1946.
240. McClunn, Rev. Justin David, A.B., S.T.L., J.C.D., Administrative Recourse, VII-142 pp., 1946.
241. Lohmuller, Rev. Martin Nicholas, A.B., J.C.D., The Promulgation of Law, XII-140 pp., 1947.
242. McGrath, Rev. James, A.B., J.C.D., The Privilege of the Canon, XII-156 pp., 1946.
243. Marbach, Rev. Joseph Francis, A.B., J.C.D., Marriage Legislation for the Catholics of the Oriental Rites in the United States and Canada, XIV-314 pp., 1946.
244. Shimkus, Rev. Bernard Aloysius, A.B., J.C.L., The Determination and Transfer of Rite.
245. Smith, Rev. Vincent Michael, A.B., S.T.L., J.C.L., Ignorance Affecting Matrimonial Consent.
246. Wachtrle, Rev. Paul Anthony, A.B., J.C.L., The Baptism of the Children of Non-Catholics.

www.ingramcontent.com/pod-product-compliance
Lightning Source LLC
LaVergne TN
LVHW050240080826
844660LV00012B/567

* 9 7 8 0 8 1 3 2 2 4 1 6 9 *